MANDEL, Morris. *Advice to the Lonely, Frustrated and Confused.* 288p. index. Jonathan David. 1972. $6.95. ISBN 0-8246-0146-7. LC 72-77125.

PSYCH

Don't be put off by the title or the prose: under the awful figures of speech ("To be successful you must drink at the fountain of knowledge, not merely gargle") lurks a good deal of sound advice; Mandel has borrowed liberally from Albert Ellis' rational therapy. The book consists of a series of questions and answers selected from Mandel's weekly column "Problems in Human Emotions." The main topics are: the search for individual identity and for love, marriage, children, in-laws, and growing older. This self-help book will appeal to many religious, older, or more conservative library patrons.—*Martha Maring, formerly at Haddonfield Public Library, N.J.*

This is an uncorrected proof of a review scheduled for Library Journal, Oct. 15, 1972

ADVICE
to the
LONELY
FRUSTRATED
and
CONFUSED

Books by the Same Author

AS THE TWIG IS BENT

THIRTEEN: A TEEN-AGE GUIDE TO JUDAISM

HEAVEN, MAN AND A CARROT

A CONCISE GUIDE TO EVERYDAY LIVING

PATTERNS FOR LIVING

STORIES FOR SPEAKERS

TAKE TIME TO LIVE

STORY ANTHOLOGY FOR PUBLIC SPEAKERS

HOW TO BE MARRIED AND HAPPY

ISRAEL THROUGH 8 EYES (co-author)

ISRAEL: STORY OF A MIRACLE (co-author)

SIDRA BY SIDRA (co-author)

ADVICE

TO THE

LONELY

FRUSTRATED

AND

CONFUSED

by
MORRIS MANDEL

 JONATHAN DAVID PUBLISHERS
MIDDLE VILLAGE, N.Y. 11379

ADVICE TO THE LONELY
FRUSTRATED AND CONFUSED

Library of Congress Catalogue Card No. 72-77125

ISBN 0-8246-0146-7

TO MY ESTEEMED FRIEND

SHALOM KLASS

AND HIS WIFE, IRENE

WHO HAVE UNDERTAKEN THE TASK OF SPREADING
THE LIGHT OF UNDERSTANDING, STIRRING ALL MEN
TO EXERT THEIR INFLUENCE FOR A BETTER TOMORROW

THIS BOOK IS

AFFECTIONATELY DEDICATED

PREFACE

If there is one feature that distinguishes man from the rest of the animal world, it is the ability of the human brain to think freely. It is this inherent ability that has translated man's ancient dream of a journey into space into reality. Today, man rules rivers and oceans, has reached the peaks of mountains, has mastered the air waves, has conquered the earth's gravitational pull; in fact, he controls just about everything, except himself.

It has been said that "knowledge is power." If this is so, then man surely should be happier than he is today. He does live in a world of elaborate luxury. Labor saving devices cut down to a minimum the list of chores he must perform. Music is piped into every room of his home. An AM-FM radio adds to the enjoyment of his car. The television set offers him a variety of endless entertainment.

Yet, he is beset with harassing problems. Though he is aware of the manifold challenges that confront his imperfect life, he is often unable to cope with them. He searches for acceptance, yearns for understanding, hungers for love. Desperately, he tries to forge ahead toward a deeper appreciation of his commitment, toward maintaining and bettering his own potentialities. At the same time, he is greatly disturbed at the loss of his once secure, predictable little world. In his efforts concentrated on earning a living, he has lost the art of making a life.

Through my weekly column, "Problems in Human Emotions," I receive several hundred letters each week which serve as constant reminders that problems today have become more acute. Fortunately, people are endeavoring to seek understanding. They have come to realize how interwoven are these questions that vex their hearts. Fortunately, too, these individuals are conscious of the impact of their problems on daily life. Perplexing to them are the problems of ego fulfillment, of faith, of love, marriage, child rearing, growing into the golden years, the dissatisfaction of the young, problems that are challenges to the old way of life.

Man is constantly in search of fulfillment. Beset with the problems of modern life, he seeks solutions by reading, by attending lectures and open forums, and by consulting with professionals who have made a more profound study of man's emotional and spiritual needs. The letters received by me week after week are evidence enough that many have not fully come to terms with the problems of life; that demands are made which hinder the enjoyment of life; that people involved in deep relationships grope for better understanding. These letters take in every facet of existence; and though no two cultures are alike, and no two people make identical adaptations, or approach life the same way, or rear children by the same book, nevertheless, some basic rules of positive living can be put down.

Though it has been estimated that there are some three thousand "known" languages throughout the world, man lives without understanding, even in terms of his own language. What is spoken is not heard! What is heard was not spoken! Man hears, but does not listen. The result: doubt, insecurity, frustration, disappointment and anger.

How does one person speak with another? Must words always be so vague and so confusing? One of the great problems with which man contends today is lack of communication.

How wonderful it would be if we could develop a language that really communicated, that could be understood by men and women, old and young, lover and loved, husband and wife, parents and children. The time has come for us to make an effort to understand and be understood.

My column, "Problems in Human Emotions," began about thirteen years ago. Writing this column has been an awesome responsibility, but has returned compensations in many ways. While my answers to those who have written to me have incorporated the "real" and "practical," it has been my aim at all times to guide the correspondent toward the responsibility of fulfilling his own needs. My aim has been directed towards helping people establish a feeling of self-worth. If I have been able to alleviate some suffering, to dispel some fears, to help some achieve happiness, I am gratified.

And so, this book was really born many years ago, and has been developed for more than a decade. It is a book for everybody, because behind the front that people put on for the public, most are perturbed, others are worried to the point of confusion, some are openly frustrated. These men and women do not feel up to par; they feel the nabbing pain of apprehension. They have muddled through their lives, trying to avoid—but always managing to stumble over—new, nagging troubles, never quite reaching a healthy day-to-day living. They have failed to learn a most important lesson in life: how to conduct themselves so that they might live.

This book is not to be considered as a substitute for psychoanalysis or psychiatric care. It is for individuals who are discouraged, troubled, concerned about themselves, and who are able to effect changes in their own behavior. It is the determination of each individual that will help him change situations that are troubling. It is my belief, bolstered by experience, that a reading and studying of the problems and answers in this volume, will help many to work intelligently toward a more meaningful life.

I am grateful to my publisher, Alfred J. Kolatch for his encouragement and enthusiasm, and for his usual practical down-to-earth advice.

I am indebted to my brother, Ben, who undertook the task of giving the manuscript a careful and critical reading. He gave me invaluable suggestions which helped make the book stimulating and valuable.

Shirley Horowitz deserves a special expression of thanks for her great support and continuous encouragement, and for her motivation to embark upon such an enterprise.

To the men and women, both young and old who have either written to me or came for discussion and help, I owe the most. They helped clarify and sharpen the old, but ever new and challenging problems that beset us all in a world that is changing at a dizzying rate.

MORRIS MANDEL

Brooklyn, N. Y.

Table of Contents

Book IV—PARENTS AND CHILDREN

Book V—THE QUESTION OF IN-LAWS

Book VI—GROW OLD ALONG WITH ME

BOOK ONE

THE SEARCH FOR
LIGHT

THE SEARCH FOR LIGHT

Introduction

Fantasy certainly is not new in the world. Science fiction is not a modern invention. Ever since the earliest days of history, man has dreamed about placing the world at his service. He wrote about places where the forces of nature were harnessed by man.

There is a story told about an island where all the winds of the world were imprisoned. As in all myths, there was a king on that island. He was a benevolent king, and released the winds from time to time. When a wind was needed to bring rain, that wind was sent on its mission. When a wind was needed to help a ship sail across the ocean, that wind was dispatched. This was a rather convenient arrangement.

One day, a famous warrior landed on the very island where the winds were kept. Of course, he was greeted by the king and was wined and dined. Days later, when the warrior announced his intention of returning home, the king gave him a queer present. It was an immense bag tied with a heavy cord, and it contained all the winds but one. That one, the east wind, was free to blow the ship home.

"Do not open the bag while you are on the ship," the king cautioned. "If you do, the winds will rush out and drive you far

2

across the seas, and it will be a long time before you will reach your destination."

The warrior, in turn, warned his men not to touch the bag. "It is dangerous," he ordered, "and I don't want any of you to touch it." Curiosity and doubt soon assailed the crew. The men kept looking at the bag, and they wondered what was in it. "What valuable treasure is our leader taking home for himself?" they asked each other. "Why does he keep telling us not to open the bag?"

For nine days and nights the east wind blew, and the ship sailed through the waves on its way home. During this time the warrior hardly slept for fear something might happen to the ship. Finally, exhausted, he fell asleep.

"Now is our time," said one of the men. "Let us just peep into the bag and see what it contains. The captain will never know we even looked." All the men agreed and they quickly untied the heavy cord.

W H I Z !

Out rushed the winds with a tremendous roar. They lashed up towering waves which tossed the ship around as if it were a matchstick. Several men were thrown overboard by the heavy gusts. Once released, the winds could not be contained. The storm raged, and it was a long time before the peace and safety of a port were sighted.

There is an analogy between this story and life, because in life, too, we have a bag of winds and forces which must be controlled—anger, prejudice, intolerance. As long as these are bottled up tight, we can go on living. As long as our emotions are under control, and not permitted to run rampant, life can be lived. However, if we loosen the strings they can blow our lives to pieces, destroying love, friendship and happiness.

It is difficult for us to realize what we do to ourselves when we lose our self-control. Emotional discord produces discord in the body. If we can keep our minds in harmony, our bodies will not fall apart. When we are unable to control our emotions, whatever they are, we are permitting a deep-seated ulcer to eat away at our peace of mind. It is like a deadly malignancy which destroys a vital organ of life, a poison which contaminates the pools of compassion in a man's heart. It prevents clear thinking and improves nothing, except, that is, the curiosity of neighbors.

Sociologists and psychologists have named the seventeenth century the Age of Enlightenment. The eighteenth century is known as the Age of Reason. The nineteenth century goes down in history as the Age of Progress. And for whatever it is worth, the twentieth century will be known as the Age of Anxiety. True enough, physical ills have been conquered to a great extent. No longer is civilized man fearful of the black plague, of famines and epidemics. But replacements have come. Instead of the physical plagues which once slaughtered mankind, man is now beset with other subtler, psychological plagues—worry, insecurity, disillusionment, to mention but a few. He doubts whether or not he can weave a successful and happy course through the darkness and despair that makes up modern existence.

There is a constant search for happiness and meaning, but the path is not an easy one. There is a constant search for light for the road, but personal and social problems block the way. Wars have disrupted personal life. Depressions have drained human energy and happiness. Racial discrimination has hurt both the individual and the community. Homes broken by divorce have left emotional scars upon parents and children alike. Excessive personal competition has aggravated modern man's insecurities. With all his anxieties, he has unfortunately few moral beliefs to guide him or to make him feel that life is meaningful and worthwhile.

Is it any wonder that on every side we see anxious, unhappy, bewildered people who are missing the fulfillment of their best potential because they cannot achieve a satisfactory adjustment to problems that seem just too great? Is it any wonder that the psychiatrist's couch never gets a chance to cool off? Is it any wonder that hundreds of millions of dollars of tranquilizers, and many tons of aspirins are sold each year? Is it any wonder that 40,000,000 sleeping pills are gulped down each night? Man has permitted all the winds to escape from the bag and seems unable to gain control once again.

If life is worthwhile, then life's problems can be solved. If life is meaningful then life's disappointments can be overcome. How often have I received letters which read, "Dr. Mandel, how can I go on living?" Invariably, I tell them "before you know how you can go on living, find a reason *why* you should go on living." Once anyone learns the "why," he will find the "how."

This is for certain, we must build with what we have. We cannot wish away the events that have taken place, rather we must learn to use them for growth. A friend once showed John Ruskin a costly handkerchief on which a blot of ink had been made. "Nothing can be done with it now," said the owner, "it is absolutely worthless."

Ruskin made no reply, but carried it away with him. After a time he sent it back, to the great surprise of his friend, who could scarcely recognize it. In a most skillful and artistic way Ruskin had made a design in India ink, using the blot as a basis, and making the handkerchief more valuable than ever. A blotted life is not necessarily a useless life.

To obtain the good things in life you must get out and accept challenges, face dangers, seek opportunities, set up goals. A great deal of the joy in life consists in doing as perfectly as you can, everything which you attempt to do. There is a sense of satisfaction, a pride in surveying a finished piece of work. True success lies in aiming at what you ought to achieve and pressing forward until that result is reached. It is amazing what a human being can accomplish in a life when he has a goal—and when he strives to reach it. For then there is a purpose to his every working act.

How true was the sage who counseled, "you better live your best and act your best and think your best today; for today is the sure preparation for tomorrow and all the other tomorrows that follow." Time is a fixed income and, as with any income, the problem facing you is how to live successfully within your daily allotment.

You are searching for light? Who isn't? You have a problem? Who doesn't? You are faced by a challenge? Which person is happy who has no challenges in life? The net makes tennis an interesting sport, just as the sand trap puts suspense into golf. The thing to do is to look at life with joy and expectation. The man who looks sourly upon the world will only have the world frown back at him.

There was a man who lived some years ago who always put on his glasses when he was about to eat strawberries. He wanted the fruit to look larger and more tempting.

Perhaps this is the way life ought to be lived. I recall the title of a song that was popular decades ago: "I'm Looking at the World Through Rose Colored Glasses and Everything Is Rosy Now." A person should face his problems with positive optimistic feelings. He should consider it a glorious privilege to live, to know, to act, to listen, to see, to learn, to love. The longer I live, the more deeply I am convinced that that which makes the difference between one man and another—between the happy and the sad, the great and the insignificant, is the outlook a person has toward life.

An ancient wise man once counseled that "there are three marks of a superior man: being virtuous, he is free from anxiety; being wise, he is free from perplexity; being brave, he is free from fear." I'd like to add a fourth mark and that is the ability of knowing when to say "yes" and when to say "no." I came across a poem some years back which could have been entitled, "A Matter of Choice." I quote some of the verses:

> To succeed in living, you really should know
> When to say "yes" and when to say "no."
> It's rather dangerous to venture a guess
> At when to say "no" and when to say "yes."
> Men who are single and their live's in a mess
> Bemoan the day when they might have said "yes."
> Others are cursing at night apropos
> The time it was "yes" but should have been "no."
> Women regret the times they said "No"
> To Richard, to Morris, to Leo, to Joe.
> If they'd only had wisdom to whisper a "yes,"
> Children and grandchildren today they could bless.
> Psychologists are mum; they don't have the rules
> Little help is offered in most of our schools.
> Experience is useful but it's hard to remember
> Your summer mistakes by the first of December.
> You're never consistent; you discover a reason
> For changing your mind with each change in season.
> It was wise saying "yes" when your birthday was eight
> The same "yes" at eighteen alters your fate.
> Please consider these tentative hints
> "No" to the broker who promises mints,
> "No" to the man who says color the truth.
> "Yes" to the group that works for our youth.
> "No" to the gossip who dirties your ear
> "Yes" to the act which brings you good cheer.
> "Yes" to the wish to help men of all races.
> "No" to the impulse to be in wrong places.
> "Yes" to a smile and "no" to a frown.
> "No" to the man who is always the clown.
> Always good friends, use your discretion
> Say "no" when you're offered three drinks in succession.

Remember dear reader, careers and successes
Depend on your choice of "noes" and of "yesses."

And so we turn our attention to the problems of men and women who are our friends, neighbors, family, and business associates. All seek advice. Some said, "Yes" when the answer should have been "no," and now they are confronted with situations that make them feel unhappy and uncomfortable. They seek help and advice, light for the road. They search and search for answers, as we all do.

*How does one make life
worth living for himself
and his family?*

–1–

Purpose of Life

A mighty king condemned one of his subjects to die. The poor wretch offered to teach the king's horse to fly if the king would only postpone the execution for one year.

"Why delay the inevitable?" a friend asked the condemned man.

"It's not inevitable," he replied, "The odds are 4 to 1 in my favor:

1. The king might die; 2. I might die; 3. The horse might die; 4. I might teach the horse to fly."

A wise man once stated all things are possible to him who believes. If you aim at nothing, you have a target you can hardly miss. But neither do you carry away any awards for marksmanship. It is important to have a goal in life; something to strive for, something to work for. John Ruskin wrote, "We are not sent into the world to do anything into which we cannot put our hearts. We have certain work to do for bread, and that is to be done strenuously; other work to do for our delight, and that is done heartily—neither is to be done by halves, but with a will, and what is not worth the effort, is not to be done at all."

An old sage once said: "One whose wisdom is greater than his deeds, what is he like? A tree whose branches are many and whose roots few, and the wind comes and uproots it. But one whose deeds exceed his wisdom is like a tree whose branches are few and roots many. Even if all the winds that are in the world come and blow upon it, they will not move it from its place."

A sense of purpose is needed in daily life. Without real purpose, the daily grind becomes monotonous. Remember, God never places anyone in a spot too small to grow. Wherever you are— in a factory, behind a counter, at the kitchen sink, in an office— a sense of purpose enables you to do a better job. Make up your mind what you think you want, set your course, and keep headed in that direction. Too many people today merely drift with the tide. Life demands drivers, not hitch-hikers.

Set attainable goals and when these goals are reached, set other goals which are higher. "Weeds spring up of themselves and thrive," wrote Hanina B. Pazzi, "but to produce wheat, how much toil and trouble must be endured." A man achieves according to what he believes.

Do not flounder on the ship of life because you failed to chart a course. To be successful you must drink at the fountain of knowledge, not merely gargle. A man who is contented with what he has done will never become famous for what he will do. Length of life, in reality, has very little significance. What's really important is the quality, because the measure of your life is not its duration but its donation. A useless life is short even if it lasts a century. If you are determined to milk all possible pleasure out of life, buy your own cow, don't milk somebody else's through the gap in the fence. The most unhappy in the world are those who face the days without knowing what to do with their time.

An old man bought some applies of a new variety and found them so delicious that he requested his son to plant a tree for him. The son objected on the grounds that it would take too long for the tree to start bearing fruit. The grandson objected for a similar reason. The grandfather, bent on having a tree of the apples, planted it himself and lived to eat the fruit for some time. Such is life. It's impossible to enjoy fruit from trees that are never planted. If you have a secret desire, no matter what, begin now to work on it. Who knows; the horse may learn to fly!

*Can a person overcome
the feeling that life is
not worthwhile?*

-2-

You Can't Turn Back the Clock!

THE PROBLEM

"Two years have passed since I had my terrible troubles, and I'm no better off today than I was at that time. I can't sleep well. My past mistakes keep buzzing in my mind all the time. I think of what my life could have been and how I ruined it by permitting my parents to make all my decisions for me.

"What a miserable home life I had. There was no joy, no warmth, no love. No matter what I did, my father would jump at me and call me all sorts of names. He had nothing but contempt for me, and yet I know he didn't hate me. I heard only foul words directed at me, my mother, and the entire world. When I wanted to answer back, my mother would caution me with, "He's a father, show some respect." But I was never given any respect. I was made to feel stupid, inept, immature.

"All my years were spent in a cold water flat on the lower east side. My parents didn't seem to care. They were accustomed to living that way, and when I complained, my mother would reply, 'Get married and get out of this house.' How could I get married after seeing the type of married life my parents led?

"I worked hard all my life, saved every penny I made. I deprived myself of all luxuries, hoping some day to be in business for myself. This I failed to accomplish. I was always advised to stick to my steady civil service job, that I was not cut out for the business world. Now, at 45, all I have is a nagging, aggravating, frustrating feeling of failure, a bitterness about my wasted years.

"I blame my mother for all this. Had she not discouraged me from going into business I would never have become involved in the market and never would have lost my life's savings. To many, a civil service job is only a stepping stone to other opportunities. For me, it marked the end of the road, and a dead end road at that. There is an old expression which is very true and keeps on echoing in my mind: 'It is better to have tried and failed at something, than to have never tried and always be left in doubt.'

"God gives every person only one life, and it is up to each one of us to make what we want of it. Life can be beautiful and precious, if only we take advantage of it while on earth. For me, with my life more than half over, I feel there is little to live for. I just don't know how to pick up the broken pieces and start life anew. How does one turn the clock back?"

THE REPLY

He doesn't. When an archer misses the mark, he looks for the fault within himself. He knows that failure to hit the bulls-eye is never the fault of the target. He rather seeks to improve his aim. Thousands of well-educated individuals, like you, seek the privacy of the analyst's office to have their fragmentized personalities glued together. They are overcome by complexes, fears, inhibitions, and desires, and they seek redemption from their enslavement. They all cry, "Give my life meaning and purpose," as they blame someone else for their misery.

You and countless men and women would never need to turn to the psychiatrist's couch if you had achieved a little healthy-minded objectivity about living. No life is so difficult that you can't make it easier by the way you meet it. You need not remain in despondency longer than you choose. You need not be a slave to your surroundings. If you wish to go to bed at night with satisfaction, you must arise each morning with determination. Seldom can you find life worth living; you must make it worth living.

You blame your mother, your father, your environment, and your circumstances. All are responsible for your unmarried state, for your unhappy job, for your "wasted" years. Yet you seem so totally blind to the passive part you have played. You are so busy feeling sorry for yourself that you don't see how you permitted yourself to settle deeper and deeper into the quicksand of discontent. If you're not better off now than you were ten years ago, surely you can't blame this on your departed parents. You hated your job, your home, your environment. Good! Discontent should lead to change. However, in your case it led only to the beating of your breast and the wringing of your hands.

If you were not so busy bemoaning your fate, perhaps you would have used your spare time to engage in some business venture. You permitted your father to talk you out of business ventures because you feared tackling business. Isn't that the reason you plunged into the stock market? "I'll get rich quick," was going to be your reply to your parents.

Your chief foe and adversary is your own self. You've had more trouble with yourself than with any other person. Blame whomever you want but you must realize that you have been the main architect of your destiny. If you wanted to get ahead, nothing should have stopped you.

Nothing can ever stop a determined man. Cripple him, and you have a Sir Walter Scott; put him in prison, and you have a John Bunyan; bury him in snow in Valley Forge, and you have a George Washington; have him born in great poverty and you have an Abraham Lincoln; afflict him with asthma as a boy, and you have a Theodore Roosevelt; stab him with rheumatic pains until he cannot sleep without opiate, and you have a Charles Steinmetz; paralyze his legs, and you have a Franklin Roosevelt. In short, it's character that determines destiny.

A young boy was leading his sister up a mountain path. "Why," she complained, "it's not a path at all. It's all rocky and bumpy." "Sure," replied the brother, "the bumps are what you use to climb on." "I was the son of an immigrant," said Bernard Baruch. "I experienced every type of discomfort but I never allowed them to embitter me."

At 45 you feel your life is over, and you desperately wish for some miracle to turn the clock back and give you an unblemished start in life. You want a life unmarred by difficulties, defeats, and detours. It can't be done! Get up, look in the mirror, and see just who you are. Understand that yesterday's misfortunes are over; that yesterday is dead; the check is cancelled. Disappointments should strengthen you, not break you. Trouble may demolish a bank account, but it could build up character. Crises refine life. A diamond cannot be polished without friction. Stop thinking that life is a crib which offers food and protection at all times.

Get on Daylight Savings Time! Don't turn the clock back, turn it ahead, and get more sunlight in each day.

He lives on a daily diet
of worries, frustrations,
and disappointments.
Can anything be done?

-3-

"Pity Me, I'm a Sad Sack"

THE PROBLEM

It is a pity that I go through the motions of everyday living and can't or won't permit myself, or just don't know how, to enjoy it. There are always good things intermingled with the daily bad, but, try as I may, I cannot even seem to enjoy the good. I remember that the good won't last long, and that it is really foolish to enjoy something that is so temporary. The result is that I despise myself for being a "sad sack."

It was worse at one time when everything bothered me. Then I lived on a daily diet of worries, frustrations, and disappointments, as well as tears and tedium. Now, I must admit that I have triumphed over some adversities. I've changed a hateful job, moved to a new apartment, dropped old friends and made new ones.

Why then am I not singing a triumphal tune instead of a mournful dirge? I neither enjoy this kind of music nor do I like being this type of musician. I would much rather be the star singing a happy aria than the one singing a long, drawn-out, dying solo.

Perhaps the answer is "impatience." Perhaps I cannot wait for better times, and the immediate cessation of whatever troubles me. Perhaps I want next year to be now, though only God knows why. It might very well be that next year I may be wishing for something equally as impossible—for the past year to return again.

I have worked patiently for many years, and many unhappy situations have indeed gone away with time. But my patience is worn thin, my nerves are strained, my tolerance is at the breaking point. From day to day, I find things more and more difficult to tolerate, not necessarily because things are worse, but because I am fraying at the edges. I played a game once, and I lost. I accept this. But how long can I keep on losing? How long can I be prevented from seeing the rays of a bright sun? When do I get a break out of life?

THE REPLY

You are guaranteeing your own unhappiness by making excuses for yourself, bewailing your fate and indulging in self pity. You are a defeatist at heart and you spend the hours of the day feeling sorry for yourself. You are so swayed by your own emotions that you fail to get an accurate picture of the world you live in. You are guided by your fears rather than by faith. You run the gamut of emotions—over-optimistic when things are good, and over-pessimistic when you are in a melancholy frame of mind. You have failed to discount emotional attitudes which do not reflect reality. In short, you suffer from neurotic pessimism.

You are not ready to face the truth. You refuse to adjust yourself to the world as it is. Instead, you want to adjust to a world as you would like it to be. You must realize that in life there are shocks to be withstood, disappointments to be endured, frustrations to be tolerated. There are many causes of tension and distress in daily life: quarrels, misunderstandings, loneliness, defeat, failure, boredom, bereavement, unpaid bills, broken promises—every human being has to face such hardships. The mature person understands this and develops a frustration tolerance. Evidently, you cannot face up to "the slings and arrows of outrageous fortune." This pessimistic philosophy of life fails to fortify you against all kinds of "emotional weather."

It would seem that your life lacks love. Where there is a real spirit of deep love, there is genuine optimism. When you love, you are able to see both the dark and the bright side of things, and yet enjoy the bright. Love permits you to face the facts of life, with its triumphs and tragedies, sunshine and shadows, and yet convince yourself that God has arranged the universe for truth, righteousness, and happiness.

Every day of our lives, to some degree, we are affected by either faith or frustration. Frustrations disrupts our world; faith sets things right in an orderly manner. It's the stabilizing force which everyone needs sooner or later for consolation and refuge.

You have driven faith from your life. Why not take off your

dark sun glasses and permit the rays of the sun to reach you? Happy is the person who knows that a life has many difficulties. He has taken to heart the lines in Ecclesiastes: "In the day of prosperity be joyful, and in the day of adversity consider: God made the one as well as the other."

Get your happiness out of your work or you will never know what happiness is. Life to the person who has developed the ability to overcome difficulties becomes easier as it progresses; the rough places appear smoother, and are quickly passed over; on the other hand, life to the one who habitually fails becomes more and more burdensome and the effort to advance loses vigor. Life can be described as a kind of grindstone. Whether it grinds a man down or polishes him depends upon the kind of stuff he is made of.

Stop being dissatisfied. Stop permitting your mind to wander to what you think you lack. Stop contrasting your life with someone else's. Just think how happy you'd be if you lost everything now—and then got it back again. Stop thinking misfortune and turn your thoughts along more positive roads.

Stop for a moment and re-read your own letter! You clearly indicate that you are not even permitting yourself to enjoy the blessings in your life. You claim you have won victories—changed to a new and better position, made new friends. Good, take stock of these positive elements. And might I advise that

> Who puts his faltering feet
> And gropes through darkness to the light of day
> Will find that for each step in faith, though dim,
> God will advance a shining mile to him.

A married woman, the mother of four children is worried about her quick temper, her angry reactions, and her alternating between love and hate.

–4–

Am I Neurotic?

THE PROBLEM

My problem is a serious one and is causing me tremendous unhappiness. I can state it quite simply: I love and hate to an excess, and I can go from one extreme to another in quick time. In other words, I cannot control my temper.

I am a married woman, the mother of four children. All attend school. My husband is a quiet man who runs from any argument. When I am good and angry, he remains silent though I secretly hope that he will tell me to shut my mouth.

My children can upset me with trivial acts. Friends can make me so angry that a fearful headache is the result. All this makes life a struggle with happy days at a bare minimum.

I could go on and on and tell you how sensitive I am, how the slightest incident can upset my day. A traffic snarl and I believe it is meant to delay me. Noise upstairs and I am tempted to hit the ceiling with a broom.

However, when I am at peace with myself, the world is wonderful, my husband a darling, and my children the most precious in the universe. I love them all and would do almost anything for them. With all this love I sense that my children and husband fear my temper, fear my tantrums, fear my silence. All this makes me quite miserable.

My mother tells me I'm neurotic. My brother calls me a nut. My sister refers to me as a slave of moods. I don't even want to think of the names and titles given to me by my husband and children.

What can I do? How do I solve this problem? I need your help. Whatever you do, do not include my name nor my initials in your column. We are all regular readers of the column and I would not like my family to know how weak and insecure I feel.

THE REPLY

To get ahead in life and earn the happiness you want and deserve, you must learn to control your emotions. This you know, and this is why you took the time to write to me.

Let me offer four simple suggestions that might just work wonders for you. Of course, the suggestions are not miracles and will certainly require your patience.

First, study yourself and determine your weak spots. What are the things that irritate you, upset you? I suggest that in most instances they are simply not worth bothering about at all. So study to strengthen yourself where you are emotionally weak.

Second, study people. This will be interesting. You will feel like a detective. When a person upsets you, instead of getting angry, try to understand what is bothering the individual. Was he tense? Is a member of his family ill? Does he owe money? In other words, instead of their upsetting you, get interested in them and maintain your own self-control.

Third, study the price you pay for getting upset. This you know. It involves headaches, pills, medical bills. In addition, your lack of control is destroying the peace of your home. Nothing in life is more precious than the love of mate and children. But if you keep on "flying off the handle," saying things you do not mean, pouting, nagging, and acting like a spoiled child, even that love can be killed. To lose the peace and joy of your home is a mighty high price to pay.

Finally, study the wisdom of our prophets and sages. The prophet Isaiah said, "In quietness and in confidence shall be your strength." To become strong, learn to control your emotions.

The writer, the mother of four children has no feelings toward her own father and is worried that she will experience guilt should he die.

-5-

I Feel Guilty

THE PROBLEM

For some time I have felt like writing to you and only now do I take the courage to do so.

I am a mother of four children, and come from a family of two brothers and two sisters. I lost my mother when I was a very young child and so was brought up quite alone. I must say that my grandmother and my father did their best to raise all of us.

I recall now that all during my growing years my father became more and more nervous and always spoke to us quite coarsely. He yelled, shouted, threatened, but we realized that this was due to the great pressure on him.

When my sister married she took my father in to live with her. The reason for that was to help out with her own expenses. My father became very close to her children, but to my children he remained cold, and very cold to me as well. From time to time I asked him to eat at my home or be an overnight guest but he always said, "NO!"

Now that he can no longer work, my sister feels that he is on her back, that he watches over her children too closely and acts like some kind of policeman. This does not make for a peaceful situation.

Again I must point out that he is cold to my children and when I question his attitude he states that my children are too wild. Believe me, I try in all ways to be warm but I get nowhere.

Now, I feel no feelings that I can have for him, feel that I cannot respond to him—he feels exactly the same way to me and my children. My problem is that I know I will have guilt feelings if anything should go wrong with him. I am very frightened of what will happen to my father and how this will affect me. Please answer my letter.

THE REPLY

I am very tempted to begin my answer with the popular response of most women by telling you "to weep some more, my lady." I say this because you are worried now about a universal experience that most of us experience in life. The person who lives the longest goes to the funerals of the people he loves. This might be called one of the penalties of living to a ripe old age.

You are now becoming grief-stricken about something that God has indicated must occur to all of us at different times. You are frightened and seek some sort of safety valve so that you will not condemn yourself in the future. There are no magic tablets, no tranquilizers that I can offer you to free you from the emotional distress except to tell you to keep on trying to get close to your father.

There are many ways that you might use. Why not demand of your sister that you pay part of his upkeep? You indicated that he no longer helps with her expenses, so why don't you! He is your father. By the way, he need never know what you are doing. It is enough that you know that you are doing your job.

If you know his favorite dishes, why not prepare them and actually bring them to your sister's house? Don't be jealous of her relationship with your father. It is natural for him to feel close to her and her children; he lived with them for a good part of his life.

Your children must be taught to respect their grandfather even if he does not display too much love for them. Tell them, he loves them nevertheless in his own way. Instead of being concerned of how you will feel in the future, do something in the present while he is still with you and the family. Let him talk to you, motivate him to do so. Tell him about your problems, ask his advice, get your children to visit with him. Make him part of your own family. If you wish to have good memories in the future, do good things in the present.

*An unmarried girl of 24
thinks she is just "run
of the mill" and wants
to know how she can
make herself more inter-
esting.*

– 6 –

I'm Not Much!

THE PROBLEM

Of this I am certain, I am unhappy, and at the same time seem powerless to do anything about it. I pushed my way through high school, and am doing the same now at college. I've never failed any subjects, but then again, never really hit the top in any class.

At 24 years of age, I am one of four in a family—the only girl. My three brothers all seem to get a great deal out of life, I get nothing. You see, I am the "run of the mill" type of girl, neither ugly nor beautiful. Since I come from a middle income family, my clothes are adequate but not particularly attractive. In reality, I have nothing to offer except a willingness to plod away. I see no great future for myself in this world. If I am successful in any area, it is making myself and all others around me, miserable.

I envy most of my friends who seem to be able to get around with ease, who mix in groups with freedom, and who date more often than I do. My phone rings every once in a while and I get a date, but few of the dates I get seem to care enough to call a second time. Somewhere, somehow, I turn them off.

At 24, I feel old and decrepit. In fact, I almost think I ought to go around with a sign on my back saying, "For Sale—young woman who could make a devoted wife and loving mother."

My folks aren't any help either. Their reminding me "why don't you go out on dates" makes me want to commit murder —theirs and mine. Don't they understand that if I am not going out, it is not of my own choosing?

What can I do to make my life more interesting? Am I a hopeless case? Will I grow up to be another one of the bachelor girls who runs from weekend to weekend, trying to dress like a young chick when they look like old hens? Do I blow my brains out now or later?

THE REPLY

There is one item that could guarantee you the best of everything, no matter who you are, what you do, or where you live. No, it isn't brains, beauty, or billions. There are men and women who are rich in all three categories and yet find their existence unhappy and miserable. What really can tune you into a full and happy existence is self-esteem. With self-esteem, even the humblest person can find a kind of joy that cannot be purchased by all the gold in Fort Knox.

Self-esteem is the feeling that you are an adequate person, that you function, are productive and likeable. It is thinking of yourself as someone whose company is desirable and enjoyable. It is accepting yourself with your share of shortcomings, which by the way are no worse than other people's. It is being solidly on your own side; confident that you can achieve your goals by your own efforts. It is delight with yourself for being you.

True, you do not feel perfect and are working to strengthen your weaknesses, to enlighten your ignorance, to improve your performances. But this is because you love to accept a challenge, to succeed at even more complicated undertakings, and to become even better at whatever you are and do. Self-esteem, in other words, is total deep-down, spontaneous, and genuine self-approval.

You are pleased with your face, your body, your personality, your abilities, your dreams, your today, and your prospects for even a happier tomorrow. Because you like yourself, you never give up striving for new and better ways to give yourself more of what you need for happiness. But you never despise yourself because your desires are not being gratified. The person with self-esteem generally knows what he wants, and also knows how to go about getting it. The person with self-esteem takes it for granted that "I am worthy. And I am entitled to have what will make me happy."

The one without self-esteem feels: "I am nothing. And I deserve nothing." Blowing your brains out will surely prove the accuracy of the latter—and nothing more. Professional counseling will help you understand yourself much better.

A 31 - year - old postal clerk feels hopeless because he cannot attract friends — male or female.

–7–

I'm Just a Hopeless Case

THE PROBLEM

There is so much that is the matter with me that I just don't know where to begin. Nothing that I do ever turns out right. In fact, the statement that "if I became a hat maker, children would be born without heads" must have been made about me. I am full of despair; my life is just one hopeless mess.

I wish I could point out one area of difficulty but I can't. I am 31 years of age and unmarried. I work for the Postal Department as an executive, but somehow when I say post office to a girl, it just turns her off. But this is the least of my worries. I can accept bachelorhood, so many others have. What bothers me more is that I don't seem to attract any friends, male or female.

The sense of "giving up" has been with me for years. I am the "simpleton," the one who is made fun of. Socially, I seem to do the wrong thing at the right time, and the right thing at the wrong time. Again, I repeat I am hopeless.

There is so much in life that I want and so little that I have been able to get for myself. I've even tried to live up to all the TV commercials with little results. I use the right hair dabs, the right toothpaste, the right after-shave lotion, cologne, the right soap—all with negative results.

What makes things worse now is that I feel hopeless, know it is hopeless, and so look hopeless. The best thing for me to do is to move to Israel and perhaps get killed by an Arab bomb. Then at least I'd be dying for a good cause.

As I re-read this letter, I see that even my writing is hopeless.

THE REPLY

To begin with, if you wish to move to Israel and I am all for it, go there to live, to strengthen the country, to help in its effort, and not to get in the way of an Arab bomb. Israel needs courageous men and women who possess the greatest desire to live and produce.

As long as a person breathes, he should be hopeful. Hopelessness? There's no such thing! On the contrary there should exist in the human soul a deep-seated hopefulness. Generally, man expects and tends to get what he wants and what he creates effort for. According to Freud, the infant not only wants satisfaction of his basic needs, he demands it instantly. But the time comes when he has to give up this expectation. He is asked to accept with grace the idea that he gets some of the things he wants some of the time. As an adult, he must go all the way and accommodate himself to the fact that only by working for it can he hope to obtain the adequacy of existence.

Whoever cannot acknowledge this truth will never fit into any productive relationship. Such an individual may suffer the distressing feelings of meaninglessness and emptiness, which he explains and defines as "hopelessness."

The adult, who feels hopeless, is actually experiencing frustration and depression that started very early in childhood. Somehow in his early years he did not receive the parental love he needed, which for many years he tried to win by pleasing others, especially his elders.

Hopelessness is not unique to such adults only. On the contrary, it is a mood most of us experience at times. Human existence is so full of mortifications of our pride, it is average to wonder now and then: "What's the use?" The healthy minded individual snaps out of it before long, and focuses his energies on another try for a more realistic goal.

What can you do when you feel mired with hopelessness? To begin with, realize that this is just a feeling, not a reality. Things aren't hopeless! You just feel that way. Regardless of how despondent you may be, look at the facts. How could you alter the situation, even in a small way? A small step in any constructive undertaking is an excellent start.

You feel that the post office is not giving you status, so, take a course in a subject you've never learned before. It will broaden your mind and at the same time open opportunities for you to meet members of both sexes. Join a club whose purposes intrigue you. Here, too, you will be given opportunities to meet new people with new points of view.

Make your leisure time pay dividends by engaging in worthwhile activities. Practice the art of conversational give-and-take in informal discussion groups. Hundreds of opportunities exist and are open to everyone seriously interested in transforming his gloominess into lighter spirits.

But start now; don't wait until tomorrow! When you do something in your own behalf you help renew your inborn hope that whatever you desire eventually will be granted to you if you don't give up your quest. Perhaps this time, with this try, that hope will be fulfilled.

This does not mean that you should completely repress your despair; not at all. Don't be afraid or ashamed of it. Let it come out of your depths when you're alone; cry if you must. Let your tears flow. Soon, they may be followed by anger; the anger that can provide you with the extra push you need to initiate a new enterprise. Just don't cry in your own coffee. Stop feeling sorry for yourself, lest you drown in the quicksand of your own despair. The most potent antidote to hopelessness is trying. Never give up on yourself. With professional help if need be, alone if you can manage it, keep trying to change those negative thoughts and actions that are making you so miserable. Even if you have no confidence in the outcome, force yourself.

If you do, one day you are sure to know again the hope you expressed when you entered this world with your first cry of "wanting attention." You will also have learned this optimistic truth about yourself: *you have it within you* to achieve that something. Best of all, you will have discovered that attaining your desires by your own efforts is a guaranteed way of overcoming hopelessness.

Many years ago, Philo counseled "Hope is the source of all

happiness. . . . None is to be considered a man who does not hope in God." The thing to do is to keep on saying, "while I live I hope." No person should deprive himself of hope that the future can be improved. Where there is no hope, there can be no real attempt to improve the situation.

Of course, hope by itself will do very little. With hope comes genuine effort. Franklin wisely warned, "He that lives on hopes will die fasting." Hoping alone leads to hopelessness.

Hopelessness leads to despair. Despair is the offspring of fear, of laziness, and impatience—all negative terms. So, get going. Enough of "Why was I born" routine. You were born, were given life—now make the most of it. You cannot remake the past, but you can control the present and so make the future a better place for you.

Edgar A. Guest, summed it up with

'Tis vain to whimper or call to mind
What might have been had the fates proved kind.
Had I turned to the left, 'twere a different case,
But I turned to the right, so this I face.

I'm a beaten man now. Oh, that fact is true,
I've been given a beaten man's task to do,
And a beaten man's duty is very plain,
He must gather his hopes and begin again.

*What can be done for
the person who bemoans
the fact that he cannot
stand up for his own
rights?*

-8-

Why Am I So Timid?

THE PROBLEM

What bothers me is my absolute timidity in standing up for my rights. When I get involved, I quickly withdraw to a back seat before I have to defend my position. Everyone gets the better of me—my brother, my married sister, my mother and father. They seem to be making all my decisions. They make up my mind for me, so much so, that at the present time I never, or seldom ever make my own decisions. Was I born this way? My brother is a straight-talking person who demands what he wants, who fights for what he thinks is his share of living. Why am I such a piece of milk-toast? How do you explain it?

THE REPLY

It is doubtful that you were born this way. Timidity about standing up for one's rights may be based on a deep reluctance to assume the burdens of adult responsibility. As long as I cannot make decisions, mother and father will make them for me, and then I will be in good hands.

To such men and women, you included; to contemplate making your own choices: marrying a person of your choice, embarking on a career that suits your needs rather than your parents, just throws you and the others into a turmoil. In addition to which, you are so worried about the affection of your parents that you feel, should you have a different opinion from the one they have, love and affection will be withdrawn.

You are an adult; act like one. Don't always try to do what you think will please others. Don't always say the things you feel others want to hear. With belief in yourself, give your own opinions. Regain your bearing. Don't only look like an adult, act like one.

It might be wise to take stock of yourself. Realize that your self-esteem is in danger. A realistic evaluation of yourself might be of great help to you. Begin with small items. Do your own shopping. If you like a certain suit, buy it without worrying whether or not it will please your parents. If you have a certain opinion about who should be elected as our president, give it, even though you are certain it is not your father's choice. Gradually your behavior will change and you will welcome opportunities to be yourself, instead of a carbon copy of your mother and father.

When this will be done, you will then be able to accept your limitations and errors, and you will realize that it isn't always imperative that you be in first place on all matters.

You sound indignant in your letter; now let this indignation change your way of meeting problems. You don't have to act like Mama's favorite. She will love you even more when you act your age.

A 38-year-old married man feels inept, inadequate, and unnecessary, and thinks he has failed both himself and his family.

– 9 –

I'm a Born Loser!

THE PROBLEM

So finally I have decided to write to you seeking advice. I should have written years ago, but this is the way I am. Discouragement has so taken hold of me that I just keep postponing things that should be done. You see, I am a born 100% loser.

To begin with I am a married man of 38 years of age. I must say I have a wonderful family. My four children are devoted, respectful, help around the house and understand that parents are given but once in a lifetime. Each of them has certain chores and they do them. They demand very little in the way of financial help and feel that we are working too hard.

The truth is that I have failed them. I have a simple mechanical job in a small manufacturing concern that puts out an inexpensive line of ties. I earn a living, if you can call it that. I cannot give my wife nor my children the luxuries to which they are entitled. Vacations and summer camps are out, all because I am a loser.

I never finished high school; again a loser. I never became a proficient operator to merit promotion; again a loser. I attempted business and failed; again a loser. I'm not much of a reader, less of a scholar; always a loser, a loser.

All this has given me a feeling of despair and despondency. I feel guilty in front of my children and my wife. Other families have so much; I give too little. This feeling of being a complete failure, a 100% loser has almost deadened any initiative I might have once had.

My wife loves me as do my children. And for this I am eternally grateful to the Almighty. How do I rid myself of this feeling of being inept, inadequate, and unnecessary?

THE REPLY

There is no such thing as being a 100% loser. Being a devoted husband, a reliable employee, a moral person, a dedicated father, a good citizen are but a few examples of the hundreds of life-enhancing aptitudes and attitudes in which you are a winner. You are a successful husband and father. Your wife loves you; your children respect you; all make for a good home. I wonder how many fathers and mothers can say about their children what you said about yours. So the fact of being a 100% loser does not exist. What does exist is a "partial loser" and this makes you feel you are a complete loser.

Your self-portrait needs some touching up because you have developed the self-image of being a loser. I dare say that your early childhood experiences contributed to this feeling of yours.

Now, how do you go about changing your self-image? To begin with, talk about your accomplishments. Indicate your joy at the way your family has turned out, the way your children have developed. Talk about their meaningful and perceptive attitudes of life. Convince yourself and others of the successes you have achieved. Believe me, no one expects that you are a loser, unless you tell them that this is what YOU expect of YOURSELF.

Their confidence in you, their respect and admiration, will help reinforce your trust in yourself as an individual who CAN, who MUST, and who WILL realize an adequate way of life.

The thing to do is to rid yourself of all your fears and anxieties. Remind yourself: It's all right. I'm a father, a husband, and an adult and I will be guided by reason rather than by irrational fear.

The real question for you to answer at this time is: how many more areas can I succeed in from now on? It would be interesting to try, that is, to try without the feeling of being a 100% loser. God must have had confidence in you—He gave you life. Now learn to live!

A chronic liar, who cannot keep his friends, asks for help in breaking this destructive habit.

– 10 –

I Am a Chronic Liar!

THE PROBLEM

It isn't everyone who is ready to admit a terrible flaw in his personality and character. I am. My failing has made me lose business opportunities, friends, and I think the love and trust of husband and children. To put it tersely and simply—I AM A LIAR.

What makes things even worse is that I lie when there is nothing to be gained from lying. It doesn't matter whether it is a purchase, a description of a weekend, a meeting with a friend, a date, before I realize what I am doing, I have lied. To cover up, I add a few additional lies, until when the story is completed, it is built on a fabrication of lies. Invariably, I am discovered.

I have lied to defend actions of mine, when I feared the discovery of the truth. I have lied to gain prestige. Generally I lie because I feel the truth will hurt my image. What a price I have paid for my habit of toying with the truth. I might add that I am a poor liar. I change my story as I am being questioned so that I contradict my lies with new lies.

How true the words: A person's lies are first taken as the truth; later, the truth he speaks is taken as lies. Most of the time my statements go unbelieved. I can take any oath, but even the oath I take is not believed. I have paid a price for this defect in my character and I am continuing to pay a price. Though I have promised myself that I will not lie, the coming of the next day brings with it incidents which I want to cover up, and I do this with a lining of lies—and stupid ones at that.

I am miserable, unhappy, hate myself. First I am befriended and then I am abandoned. The years are going by and I cannot say that I have a single good friend. I can't go on this way. The walls of my home are closing in. I am in a self-imposed, lonely prison. What do I do?

THE REPLY

There is nothing to be gained in entering into discussions on the psychological motivation for lying. You are a liar, know you are a liar, have suffered because of your chronic lying—lost opportunities, friends, prestige, mate and marriage. If you have the strength enough, the emotional courage to fight the delicious aromas of delicacies because of a keen desire to fit into a certain size dress, then you better muster up all that strength and fight your habit of lying.

A simple beginning might be to live each day so that you need not apologize for it. If your day is one spent rightly, morally, ethically, civilly, you won't have to lie. Actions that don't require defending do not need to be lied about. It is when you feel that you wish to hide what you have done that you resort to lies. I am referring to the "juicy" lies, not the ones about costs of dresses, suits, and fancy hair-dos. You understand, don't you!

You know that "He who tells a lie is not sensible how great a task he undertakes; for he must be forced to invent twenty more to maintain that one." And you don't even have a good memory, something that is a necessity for those who tamper with the truth. After all, as Mark Twain said, "If you tell the truth you don't have to remember anything."

Right now you are living a life of lies. It might be that you lie so much of the time that you yourself are beginning to believe your own fabrications. I don't know how old you are, but whatever your age (you are a wife and mother) *change*. If you can't do it on your own, consult someone trained in helping people with problems such as yours.

Be sensible! Use your head! Have brains! The price is too high! Why continue a practice that is bringing you only misery! To lie, is to sigh, cry, and then die. You'll find the truth much less painful and in the end much more rewarding. You doubt me? Join Liars Anonymous.

The writer cannot forget hurts suffered at the hands of others, and so, bearing grudges, is very unhappy.

–11–

I Bear a Grudge

THE PROBLEM

I am a sincere, loyal, serious-minded person, who really goes all out for friendship. I don't believe any one of my friends can point a finger at me and complain that I was anything but loyal. To me, loyalty holds high priority.

Unfortunately, I cannot say the same for some of the people I have met. They misuse confidences, trade in gossip, and really make friends compete against one another. When I come across such an incident with the people I know, I just can't forgive them. It is a great, terrible hurt to be betrayed by friends, and to me lack of loyalty, is betrayal.

There were people I loved and now I just can't be with them. At one time I felt they enriched me by their presence. Now I just can't look them in the eyes. The incident which caused this, in itself, is not important, but I just can't forget that they were not loyal to a friendship.

My husband has repeatedly told me to forgive and forget, and has admonished me that both must go hand in hand. I can't do this. I remember and nurse the hurts that have been inflicted on me. Sometimes I feel I am torturing myself with all the memories of people who have disappointed me and incidents which have hurt me. Yet, as I indicated before, I am honest, sincere, and loyal and expect nothing less from my friends and relatives.

I guess I should admit that my husband and I do not have too many friends, but what we lack in quantity, we make up for in quality. Frankly, now that I reread my letter I wonder why I am writing to you in the first place. I am a "rememberer," and not a "forgetter." If this is a sin, then I am guilty, guilty but with the above explanation.

THE REPLY

The conclusion to your letter is rather interesting. You write, "now that I re-read my letter I wonder why I am writing to you in the first place." If you really thought that way, why did you invest a six cent stamp to send it along to me? Why boast of your virtues to me? Why plead your cause to me?

I'll tell you why you wrote to me. You wrote because you are unhappy with your trained psychological memory that dredges up old grudges, ancient humiliations, aged insults, threats to your ego and prestige. You have become a collector of hurts, and you treasure your collection with the same feeling that a miser treasures his savings. Unfortunately, your collection clouds your mind, mars the warmth of the day, colors your judgment, and encourages fear and suspicion in your day to day living.

Did you ever ask yourself why you cherish prior insults as if they were antique works of art? Could it be that you think so little of yourself and your position in the world that you must seek ways of distracting your thoughts of yourself? Do you need a scapegoat or a punching bag on which to let out your own disappointments in yourself?

It seems to me as if you have made a necklace of all your previous grudges and you count the beads on this necklace daily. You not only count the beads, you attempt to recall every particular insult it represents. This makes you feel so virtuous and so much the martyred saint. You are walking a straight road to paranoia. Is this what you want?

You feed your grudges daily, recite them to your husband at the dinner table, take them with you to bed at night. In the morning, no sooner are you awake, that you begin to mentally attack and destroy those who hurt you. All this feeds a murderous rage that builds up within you.

Why don't you ask yourself a simple question: "Why can't I forget the real and imagined insults I have suffered?" Who knows, it might be that blaming others is an easy way to build up your own feeling of importance. If you are not as important as you would like to be, it is simple to blame the outside world. It isn't too difficult for you to feel that you are a big shot though the world judges you to be only a dud. Blaming others makes you rise in your own estimation and gives you an opportunity to look down on others.

It must be tough for your husband to hear your voice blaming, belittling, and condemning others. It must be even tougher for him to listen to your self-praise and your holier-than-thou attitude. I am certain, though you have not stated this in your letter, that you have your own list of grievances against him, and that he has to atone for them daily.

A former writer once said: "He that cannot forgive others, breaks the bridge over which he himself must pass if he would ever reach heaven; for every one has need to be forgiven." Chesterfield advised: "Little, vicious minds abound with anger and revenge, and are incapable of feeling the pleasure of forgiving their enemies."

Your husband rightly advised you to forgive and forget. To say, "I can forgive, but I cannot forget," is only another way of saying, "I will not forgive." Forgiveness ought to be like a cancelled note—torn in half, and burned up, so that it never can be seen again.

The writer suffers from the habit of worrying and thus makes life miserable for himself and his family.

-12-

I Worry!

THE PROBLEM

I can state my problem in just four words: "I am a worrier." My constant worrying has caused me to develop an ulcer. Now, every time I take a bite I worry how it will affect me. Bottles of Maalox are always in my medicine case. I just can't seem to do anything right. The harder I try the more goals I miss. If things are going right, I worry that this situation will soon end. If things are not going right, I certainly have cause to worry. When my children are ill, I am almost consumed with worry. Every symptom of every illness filters into my mind. By the time the doctor comes, I have convinced myself that the worst will happen. If they are well, I worry that they remain in good health. I constantly caution them: "Stay out of hallways, keep away from people who cough, cover your neck, don't sit near open windows, wear your gloves, eat slowly, don't get over-heated." When my husband's business hits a slow season, I worry that he may be worried. When business is good, I worry that the weather remains good so that he can continue doing good business. There is hardly a morning that I arise with a clear mind and an easy heart. If I have nothing on hand to worry about, I begin to feel that I have grown calloused to the happenings of my family, and this causes me great concern. This constant state of worrying worries me. What can I do?

THE REPLY

There is one sure way to get you to worry even more, and that is to say, "Don't worry!" In fact, "Don't worry" is foolish advice some people offer on almost all occasions. Unless a person is completely wrapped up in himself, he cannot help but worry during times of serious trouble. Any person who claims he never worries, either has no character, or lacks the mentality necessary to project himself into the future.

Worry is a clue that motivates men and women to act. Worrying about passing an examination has induced many a student to burn the midnight oil studying, instead of watching one T.V. thriller after another. Worry about a serious illness causes people to seek regular medical examinations. Proper food habits result from concern about health. The weight-watchers are concerned about excess weight. Major medical insurance is taken out to relieve worrying about lengthy illness. Liability insurance takes some worry out of driving. Burglary insurance, as well as fire insurance, offers peace of mind to the homeowner.

These, however, pertain to selective worry. Life presents many problems that must be solved and thinking people spend time trying to solve them. Concentration about a matter of importance should not be confused with worry.

However, you are different! You worry about everything, essentials and non-essentials alike. You constantly predict dire consequences. You see only disaster. This indulging in futile emotional exercises consumes time, energy, and health. After all, your ulcer was caused by your mountain climbing over molehills. Worry bows the head and turns the spirit to dust. Worry a little every day and in a lifetime, you will lose a few years.

Your trouble is that you see a cloud and worry about rain; you see rain and worry about your children catching cold; you hear a prediction of snow and you worry about its effect on your husband's business. You don't act, you worry! You don't seem to realize that worry, like an infant, grows larger by nursing.

Worry is an immature way of dealing with your difficulties. All worry does is to compel you to think about your predicament over and over again, causing you to repeat useless, non-productive responses. You react emotionally and stew over the past. You seldom reach any decision. You are not constructive. A practical man once advised, "If you don't intend to do anything about it, worry is silly. If you do intend to do something, worry isn't necessary. The trouble with worrying so much about your security in the future is that you feel so insecure in the present.

The mature person proceeds in a more intelligent manner. He sets a definite time during which he devotes full attention to the problem. He states his problem clearly and definitely because he is aware that fears will only lead him to magnify his difficulties. "I am going to call the doctor," he thinks to himself, "and the doctor will prescribe the proper medication." Or, "I must engage a tutor for my son if he is to pass in his college examinations." Both are far more effective than merely groaning, moaning, and bewailing your fate. Elsie, Borden's Contented Cow, need not ponder about challenges and solutions. But who wants to be a cow?

The mature person considers possible solutions and weighs each one in terms of its results. He is alert to the possibility that his concern with non-essentials may be an effort to conceal fears about matters much more serious. He realizes that if people are going to be concerned with his worry, they make themselves unable to deal with the problem on hand. The mature person understands that carrying out a decision about a problem involves some distress.

You write that, "This constant state of worrying worries me, what shall I do?"

To begin with, realize that your problems are not by any means unique. Others have had to meet the same problems. Bear in mind that worry, because it is fear, actually keeps you from succeeding with your problem. Work, don't worry. Plan ahead with optimism, instead of projecting into the future with pessimism.

And at the end of each day, empty your mind of resentments, disappointments, doubts, and frustrations. Try to imagine these destructive thoughts flowing out of your mind just as water flows out of a bath-tub. However, don't permit your mind to become a vacuum, because that will cause you worry. Therefore, negative thoughts should be replaced by positive, pleasant ones. There are many pleasing memories you can dwell on. Do this and it won't be long before your thoughts will follow a more meaningful path, your days will improve, your head will clear. You will be less tense, more relaxed.

A worried father cannot control his temper and is quickly upset by wife, children and neighbors.

– 13 –

What Do I Do About My Temper?

THE PROBLEM

My temper will surely ruin my marriage and my life as well. All through my teenage years, I could not discuss any question. Any remark that seemed to be slighting was enough to make me angry. On the face of it, all this seems tame, but my anger cut my heart into ribbons. I neither could eat nor sleep. I lost friends, could not make new ones.

At college, I fared no better: Teachers upset me easily. I took offense and talked back. Need I tell you what the results were? How I ever earned a degree I'll never know.

Don't tell me to repress my indignation when I am or think I have been insulted. I tried that several times and almost developed an ulcer. The anger that I was attempting to control was seething inside me and I felt as if I would have a stroke.

At the present time I am married and the father of four children. They upset me; my wife upsets me; the neighbors upset me. It doesn't take more than an extra word to make me fly off the handle and yell, curse, and slap. Of course, later I'm sorry but the damage has been done. My children will grow up with warped personalities if I keep up this uncontrolled conduct. My wife is not the same girl I married, and I am the cause of her trouble. She can't discuss anything with me because I take criticism as a form of insult.

I know I need help, and I realize that your answer to my letter must be limited in space. Yet, I appeal to you for some brief message that I can take with me and that will help me when I reach the brink of uncontrolled anger.

THE REPLY

Anger, like other emotions, can be a curse or a blessing; it can enhance or deform life, depending upon how it is used. In your case, it is destroying your home and your own peace of mind.

Anger can be a blessing when you use the energies evoked in you by rage, to fight off an aggressor who threatens your life, or the lives of your loved ones. But your anger is the kind that plagues you because it is the result of someone's remark, a question, a suggestion, a criticism, or some imagined facial expression. You become infuriated because you believe that you are being belittled.

In cooler moments, you recognize your wrath as an over-reaction to a trivial provocation, and you realize that your anger is a curse because it cannot be controlled and causes you to say the word or do the deed that will harm your marriage, your job, your friendships, or your own self-esteem.

You ought to try to understand your anger. The next time you are angered, try to pinpoint the essence of the problem. Take the time to consider a variety of responses. Why slap your child? Why not select behavior that promises to lead to a solution which will gratify your true needs? In other words, carry out the decision that is a result of intelligence rather than be compelled to "act out" the ruinous impulse prompted by your rage.

The next time your temper is in danger of flaring up, call a "cooling-off period" before you react. Instead of berating your wife, belittling your friend, telling your boss off, moving out of the house, take the time to ask yourself a question or two. Why am I angry? Was the remark really aimed at me? And if it were, am I over-reacting?

What I suggest sounds difficult but it will work. Develop in yourself a higher self, a calmer self, a thinking self. This higher self will help you become more aware of your own personal problems and the reasons for your fury. Freud called this the "observing self."

This higher self will not permit rage to sweep away your own reason. Instead, it will help you use your judgment to better understand the facts of whatever is causing this emotional upheaval.

Your anger is caused by your super-sensitivity. You may feel that you have not made much of your life, have not progressed enough, have not provided enough for your family. These feelings will cause you to fight any remark which you think is a threat to your personality. It's a question of interpretation and of self-appreciation. Do you think of yourself as a "top-banana," or an "underdog?"

When you overact with fury to someone's behavior, it may be because the incident is evoking in you feelings of fear, resentment, insecurity, in fact, the same feelings you experienced when you were much younger and incapable of protecting yourself.

When people are hurt and become angry, they can travel along certain avenues. They can become sullen, sour, and non-cooperative. This response causes them to retreat behind a newspaper or book, or sends the angry person into the next room for an evening of television. Some people take an opposite course. They placate the other person while repressing their own desires. Still others rebel; they become abusive, spiteful and negative. They turn back food, refuse to be social, act rudely, hurt other innocent members of the family. None of these really leads to a successful resolution of the conflict that is causing the tension.

This you realize: your method of reaction can be spelled with a capital "S" which stands for Self-destruction. You are now the father of children, and should not react the way tots and teenagers react. Drop the behavior pattern of your younger days. It did not help you then; it surely will not help you now. After all, a mature person is expected to use his intelligence, his judgment and his experience to solve problems, rather than to create them.

With serious, consistent effort to evoke a higher self, the time will surely come when you will be characteristically reasonable, moderate, even-tempered and wise in the emotional crises of your life. In addition, there will be an even greater reward. People around you who observe your responses to your own stress, may come to trust you when they are in conflict. They may ask you to help them handle difficult situations which require tact, delicacy, common sense, good will, self-control. They may call upon you to bring peace to warring parties; in other words you may become an effective mediator and peacemaker. This you might do immediately in your own home.

Coping with anger constructively will not only make your private life more beautiful, it will make it more productive. You will be able to make a small personal contribution towards cop-

ing creatively with some of the raging aggressions which are
scarring and marring human relationships everywhere on this
frightened, tortured, beloved planet.

Now that you have written this letter, follow it up with some
concrete action. Now that you are certain this fury of yours is
wrecking your life, your wife's life, and the lives of your children,
control it. Now that you say "my temper will surely ruin my
marriage and my life as well," apply the brakes. Yes, SLOW
DOWN THE ACTION. It may be difficult at the start but the
dividends are well worth the effort.

Remember to think well of yourself and your mate. Treat
her as an equal genuine partner, with full respect, and not as
an IT. If you will bear this in mind, if you will understand that
the people around you have a right to live and enjoy; if you
will understand that your purpose in life is to interact joyfully
with them, your temper will be in control.

Counting up to a thousand is not enough. You must think
as well.

Why lose your temper? Nobody wants it anyhow.

*She claims to be very
sensitive and is hurt
easily, nor can she for-
give or forget.*

– 14 –

I Can't Find Happiness!

THE PROBLEM

My husband claims I'm too sensitive; my children feel I'm
too revengeful; my friends say that I nurse a hurt. I don't know
who is right and who is wrong, but I do know that I am not
a happy person. Unfortunately, when I am given a dose of bad
for good, of ingratitude for generosity, of sham and falseness
for sincerity, I don't easily forget it.

You see, I am a sincere friend, a person who is willing to share. Only too well do I realize that no man lives alone, that lives can be made when rights of others are respected. However, when these feelings are not returned, I feel let down. The result is that I drop those who have failed me. The truth of the matter is that I am plagued with a good memory.

It would seem that I always have my inner-built radar up, ready to catch the slightest infraction of social and moral rules. This deprives me, I think, of sociability, of comradeship, of being invited to parties and gatherings, much to the unhappiness of my family.

Just what do I do?

THE REPLY

There is little to be gained in holding on to resentment, self-pity, or embarrassment. Keeping these feelings alive in our hearts serves to keep the fires of anger burning. If you say, "I can't forget what has been done to me," I will say to you, "What you mean to say is that you don't want to forget." After all the will can be trained to overcome memory.

Today, life demands that we "remember to forget." There are events in our lives that need not be remembered. Only by forgetting can we really live from day to day. "I want to forget, doctor," you say, "but I don't know how."

Just let me give you a few simple thoughts in the art of forgetting.

When you don't like a particular television program, you turn the dial, and lo, a different program appears on the screen. The same can be done with your mind. Don't revive an image that brings you unhappiness.

There are so many heart-warming themes that you can always keep in mind—your child's wedding, the cute things the grandchildren did the other day, the coming family Simcha, summer plans, the charity bazaar, to name but a few. Every one of us has such themes—our work, our hobbies, our current reading.

Remember those experiences that give you pleasure, and forget the ones that bring you pain. Dealt with in this way, what you want to forget loses its power. After all, inwardly you do want to forget. Finish off all this old business and get it over with. Remove hatred and guilt from your mind.

Of course, you might be unable to forget the hurts you have

inflicted on others. Again and again during the course of a day you mull over in your mind the things you said which should never have been said, the things you did which never should have been done. To forget these words and needs requires an additional factor. You see, no person can hope to forget the wrongs he has committed until he has righted them. If you have wronged another person, make amends. It is easier to say I am sorry than to be constantly plagued with guilt feelings. A gnawing conscience poisons the blood, weakens the heart, spoils the appetite, and mars the beauty of the day.

So, remember to forget! Forget words, forget incidents, forget insults—remember the beauty of summer, the art of forgiving, the power of faith, the healing balm of the Almighty. It pays to REMEMBER what gives you joy; it pays to FORGET what brings you pain.

Remembering makes life worthwhile.

Forgetting makes life possible.

A young girl feels she cannot be married because her husband would find her body repulsive!

– 15 –

I Can Never Get Married!

THE PROBLEM

I am almost 20 years old, very much in love, and yet the most unhappy person on earth. I just can't get married. I can't accept myself the way I look, and I am afraid of losing the man I love right after our wedding night.

You see, my entire body is covered with millions of hairs. There is just no bare spot on me. I am undergoing electrolysis but the process is very slow and the results almost nonexistent.

It might take years until I will look half way human, or like a woman.

At the beginning of the treatments I had hope, and was able to endure every pain of the needle. But now as time marches on, my hopes of being "clean" become smaller and my despondency greater.

I cry myself every night to sleep. My life is full of inner conflicts. I accuse myself of being vain, self-centered, and yet I cannot bring myself to the point of self-acceptance. I am a volcano, with no inner peace. Whenever a new vista opens up, the door seems to close on me, because of my freakish appearance.

I mentioned at the beginning that I am in love. But that wonderful feeling is choked completely by my awareness that the man I love will reject me and this again brings upon me torments beyond description. My parents suffer with me. I am impatient, difficult and hostile. Probably in my subconscious I blame them for my handicap. I know it's wrong, because they are wonderful and ready to do anything to help me. They pay very large bills for electrolysis, which at this point becomes to be symbolic with torture.

Believe me, my nerves are on edge. However, no psychiatrist can help me as long as my terrible problem is not solved.

Dear doctor, of all the letters you receive, this one must be unique. I turn to you like a father, and please, advise me like you would advise your own daughter.

I respect your wisdom.

I love you for your compassion for men.

Please answer me as soon as possible . . . I am desperate.

THE REPLY

"Tell me, my daughter, what is courage? Is courage the ability to stand up to an enemy and fight?"

No, not at all. Courage is more than a display of physical bravery, it is a much rarer quality of mind and spirit. Courage is that precious ingredient that enables a person to stand up and check his fears, to face reality, to chart a new course to be followed.

Different people must contend with different trials, but adversities, in some shape or other, come to everyone. There are those who are injured in war or accident, and those who are born with disabilities which prevent them from leading normal lives.

What a frightful thing it is to be born blind, or deaf, or dumb! What a terrifying experience it must be for individuals whose legs are crippled and whose arms are deformed! Yet, somehow they face their handicaps and find the courage to go on.

I don't suppose you ever heard of Betsy Barton, who at the age of sixteen had great beauty, high intelligence, and all the advantages which her parents could give her. The world was hers—beauty, charm, intelligence, femininity—all of these were part of her endowment.

Then came the automobile accident which broke her back and left her permanently paralyzed. She suffered great physical pain, and when the pain lessened and she found herself in a wheelchair, her will to live almost died.

But she fought to return to life, to find in her own words that "wisdom and vision are granted to few, and the few who gain these do so . . . in the degree that they suffer." She did succeed in making a life for herself. It wasn't the life she had planned, but in accepting reality, she continued to live, to see beauty, to function.

You ask me to advise you as though I were your father and you my daughter. How I wish you were now standing before me so that I could talk to you about the necessity of minimizing your despair. Together, father and daughter, we could discuss the challenges that await you. I would talk to you about love and explain to you that love is not the monopoly of the few chosen physically beautiful people—that it belongs to all human beings, the tall and the short, the rich and the poor, the brilliant and the dull, the beautiful and the ordinary.

Every autobiography and biography is the record of someone who succeeded in the face of disability, in the face of hardship, despite handicaps. You are the author, the director, the star in your life and you can make your life what you want it to be. There is little to be gained in dreaming about what you could be, what you could do were you different. It is what you do with what you have that makes for success or failure in life.

Were you my daughter I would talk to you about belief, about religion, about faith, about God. Surely, the Almighty has prepared a partner for you, one who will love you for your mind, your depth of feeling, your character, your courage, your strength and not for the shape of your face, the size of your nose, the color of your eyes, the beauty of your figure. Loving a person for physical beauty alone leads one to emotional bankruptcy.

Have faith, I would say to you. And again I would preach that in adversity a man is saved by hope. How important it is for you to release yourself from the terrors of fear and to tear yourself away from thoughts of disaster. "Just as I, your father, love you with all my heart and soul, so some day your chosen mate will whisper words of love to you."

And then, armed with hope, with faith, with belief in God and in His justice and wisdom, I would encourage you to locate a doctor somewhere who knows how to treat such a condition. I would never give up, nor would I permit you, my daughter, to give up. My constant thought would be to help you free yourself from fear, from constant preoccupation with what you consider a severe handicap.

I would point out that you have two eyes with which to see the beauty of the world, two legs to take you wherever you wish to go, two hands to help the less fortunate. And I would get you to enrich your mind and heart and to encourage you to go through life thinking not only about the outward beauty of a person, but rather of the interior decorations. Uppermost in my mind as a father would be to get you to realize your value as a daughter, as a human being, as one of God's children, and oh, yes, as a future wife and mother.

A husband and father seeks perfection in his home and is met with anger and hostility!

– 16 –
What Is Wrong With Perfection?

THE PROBLEM

When I was younger and a student at school, I was always taught that a mark of 100 on a test is excellent. As I grew older I was impressed with the fact that a person should seek perfection in his daily life. He should always be punctual in his appointments, that his speech should be perfect, and that he should not be satisfied with anything less than perfection.

Now, I am a married man, the father of three children. My eldest is a student at Brooklyn College; the other two attend a public high school. I would say that I am reasonably happy with my wife and my family. My wife is devoted to the home and takes care of my needs. Meals are served on time and I have no complaints about buttons being missing from my shirts, the usual complaint of most married men. She is a normal dresser, that is to say, she is not untidy but certainly she is completely unimaginative. Secretly, I always hoped she'd listen to my advice when it came to buying clothing.

My three children leave a great deal to be desired. They are not top students at school. In fact, they seem to have developed a knack of doing very little scholastic work, and have to work hard at the last minute to just get by. When I criticize them for this lack of effort, they retort with, "We passed, didn't we?" In addition, they are not too careful with their personal belongings and personal habits. All this is leading me to a mild nervous breakdown.

I have attempted to change the atmosphere in my home. I have tried to teach them perfection. I point out to my wife that her closets and drawers are not neat, that there is a waste of food in the refrigerator. I examine the clothing as it comes from the laundry and indicate to her the imperfections in shirts and pillow cases. She should be grateful for my attention, but on the contrary, when I do this, she goes into a tantrum and tells me to get out of the house.

I have noticed that both she and the children are irritated with my desire for perfection. They act as if I am a queer, an annoying queer who makes life miserable for them.

"Why aren't you like other men?" my wife asks. "Why don't you watch television, go bowling, or look for an evening job instead of hanging around finding fault with my laundry, my closets, with the food in the refrigerator?"

My children are no different. I guess they take after their mother. They often tell me that I am a psychological case with my great desire for perfection. It's getting so that I am afraid to open my mouth to tell them the mistakes I see in their behavior. I'd like to know what's wrong with perfection?

THE REPLY

There is a great deal wrong with perfectionism. The perfectionist is an insecure, frightened, competitive individual who desires to be on top of the ladder. It is perfectly all right to believe that "whatever is worth doing at all is worth doing well"—but to be obsessed with the idea of perfection to an excess is merely a sign of personality weakness. The demand for perfection is one of the most viscous mental outlooks contributing to human maladjustment. The person who goes to excess in trying to comply with the need for perfection loses his focus on life, and can lead to mental breakdown.

You want to be above criticism and therefore superior to those who are less perfect. You constantly keep comparing yourself with others and you feel exposed should an error be allowed to creep into your activity. You do not seem to be aware of your hostile attitude to those whom you regard as less perfect. You belittle their work and their personal value in order to exalt your own.

Truthfully, the perfectionist is a fault finder and nothing is ever good enough for him. You fall into this category. You keep on disrupting situations by your belittling of others and you interfere with the cooperation in a group by trying to impose your standards upon them. You certainly are not a delight at home if you spend your time checking on the neatness of the closets and cupboards.

The person who has to do everything just right, whether it is playing the piano, washing the dishes, or keeping the garage spotlessly clean, really is tormenting himself and makes those around him miserable as well. The man who wears himself all out chasing for perfection is so weary at the end of a day that he just cannot be a fit person to live with.

You are setting standards which are just too high. Your overexacting demands result in constant nagging of your wife and children. The truth is that you look for the flaws rather than the merits in any performance. It has been said that finding fault with others is activated, in part, by an unconscious attempt to alleviate the sense of *one's* own shortcomings.

It is evident that one of the joys in your life is to collect and tabulate evidence against others to prove their inferiority as human beings and thus put yourself in a clear light of superiority.

You are alert to seek and expose the imperfections of other people.

I am not going to discuss the psychological problems involved in making you the type of person you are. There must be something in you that urges you to seek perfection in others; there must be something in you that sets you off to examine the kitchen closets, and to comment on their lack of perfection. You might look into it. To do this, first remove the tight-fitting halo from your head because it is not only giving others a headache, but makes you a pain in the neck.

When you come from work this evening, try to find something in your wife to praise. The chops may be just a bit tastier, the house a bit cleaner, the atmosphere a bit better. Tell her how happy you are having her as your wife. Speak positively. Discuss the accomplishments both of you have achieved. You might even tell her you like the dress she is wearing, or the way she combed her hair.

When the children come around, don't ask about their marks. Instead, talk about college courses, college friendships, college activities. Become interested in the courses your sons are taking. Listen to them as they discuss a teacher, a principal, a piece of homework, the coming play or football game. Be human! Begin a sentence with, "I'm not so certain but I think. . . ." Pat one of them on the back and praise another. Let them feel you appreciate them, understand them, and love them. Do all this and remember, stay out of the closets!

At first you'll surprise and stun them. Later they'll be astonished and amazed! But ultimately they will love the new you. Strangely, you will be pleased with the results as well.

A college senior is confused and unhappy about his future in this country.

– 17 –

What Is Right?

THE PROBLEM

Frankly, I am confused. The daily newspaper, the television news reviews, conversations, and the actions of people in every part of the world—all have played a part in confusing me as well as tens of thousands of college girls and boys.

I am a senior at a private college. I've witnessed the college riots, lived through some harrowing experiences, have seen the American flag stepped upon and dishonored by American citizens, heard law and religion vilified, listened to college profs discussing the stupidity of parents. How much sicker and more confused can I become?

Often I've been tempted to cast aside study and college, to have a wild fling as others in my class are doing. I want to forget tradition, forget history, forget everything I've been taught, and with bottle and beau, make the most out of today. Who knows I might yet do just that!

My tremendous confusion is with the law-abiding adult, with the college dean and president, with the mayor and governor, with our great religious leaders who are doing absolutely nothing, except from time to time to agree with these very rebellious destructive leaders. Who is right? What is right? My confusion mounts from day to day.

You have a practical approach to problems. How can I distinguish between what is right and what is wrong? Tens of thousands of youngsters, as well as myself, need wise, practical immediate counseling. Tell us, won't you!

THE REPLY

What is right? and what is wrong? are questions over which all of us have struggled and on which few, if any, completely agree. I once wrote that a great preacher declared many years ago: "Behind a great deal of our modern immorality is not so much downright badness as a sincere confusion as to what is right and what is wrong."

There are those who say, "Let your conscience be your guide." It is good to listen to your conscience, yet a cannibal can kill and eat you with a perfectly clear conscience. Minority groups can burn and loot with pretty clear and untroubled conscience. The United States of America can commit its youth to death in an undeclared war in a foreign country. The world permitted 6,000,000 men and women, parents and children to be gassed and murdered like so much cattle. No conscience bothered them. The greatly over-rated United Nations sits in solemn assembly as countries whose hands are soaked with human blood decide the fate of other, less armed countries. Where is the collective conscience of the United Nations?

There is no doubt that if man followed the God-given Ten Commandments there would be little question as to what is right and what is wrong. There is no doubt that if man lived up to the word of God, he would not be troubled and confused and only one way, the right way, would be always ahead of him.

I can understand that along the pathway of life we come to those places where we are sincerely confused over what is right and what is wrong. We are confused because of the words and actions of those to whom we have looked for guidance, and who now seem to fail us. And we may suffer the remainder of our days if we make a mistake in what we are about to do.

You write that I am practical; so let me set up four simple guides that will help us decide when we are sincerely confused over what is right and what is wrong. You can modify or enlarge these rules if you will, but they make for a good start to lead you out of your present confusion.

1. To begin with, what you are about to do—must you keep it a secret? Generally, things that must be hidden are usually wrong. It is a good rule to keep clear of concealment and the need for concealment. When you must hide what you are doing, you fear its consequence. From then on the whole life is different. When you fear questions, when you fear the eyes of others, when you fear the light of detection, then the thing that is being planned or done is not right. You do understand this simple rule, don't you?

2. Where will it lead me? Look at the final result. Examine it.

Many seemingly harmless little things are wrong because they lead in the wrong direction.

Sam Reshevsky, a friend of mine, is one of the world's best chess experts, and has been one since the age of five. I remember asking him for some rules in chess so that my own game might be improved. I indicated that I had already studied the "book moves" and had played the game for some years. His reply might be used as a guide to life as well. "At the start of the game," he said, "you are free to move in any direction, but once you have moved, you are free no more. Every move demands a certain other move."

Life is pretty much like that. One action calls for another action. A little lie calls for a bigger lie. We can start wrong in a small, harmless way, but gradually we get in deeper and deeper. How often have you heard someone say: "How did I ever get into this mess?"

3. Which is your best self? No person is a single self. There is an educated self, an emotional self, a passionate self. It is a fact that we sometimes say and do things when we are angry or afraid, that we did not want to say and regret having said them.

There is a selfish self, a greedy self. Each one of us is an entire company of people. How many times have you heard a person say, "I was not myself when I did it." What is meant that it wasn't his real, composed self, but nevertheless, he did it.

Within each of us there is a "best self," which is much finer than our careless, emotion-packed, greedy self. Shakespeare rightly urges us, 'To thine own self be true, and it must follow as the night the day, thou canst not then be false to any man."

4. What would the person that you most admire do if he were in your place? For a Jew this means, "What would Abraham have done? What would Moses have done? What would Hannah have done? A Jew can go on and on, enumerating the many sages, heroes, religious leaders that have lived through the centuries.

It was said and still is being said that Abraham lived up to the entire Torah even though he predated it. The question then is raised, how could this be? Abraham, when he was about to do something, would ask, "Will my act make God happy?" If it did, he knew that it was right. If it didn't, he knew that the act was wrong.

I admit it is not always easy to decide what is right and what is wrong. But if you sincerely want to do the right thing, these four simple guides will be a lot of help along the way. Of this you are certain; it is always better to do right.

The writer refused to lend money to a friend. Now her conscience bothers her and gives her no peace.

– 18 –

You Are Half Cured!

THE PROBLEM

Perhaps my letter will inspire those men who close their eyes to duty and harden their hearts to their needy fellowmen to give more help and have more understanding. Unfortunately, I am one who did close her heart and therefore come within the class of worthless people.

I know very well that charity is the main foundation of Israel's pre-eminence, and that the basis of the law of truth rests upon help to fellow human beings. Yet, I failed to practice good deeds and my conscience kills me. I feel unworthy.

A friend of mine asked me for some money. She needed it desperately and she promised to return it as soon as she got a job. I promised to send her the money but I never did. Since then I am sick and heart-broken. I am ashamed before God. I avoid people as much as I can.

I am guilty and I committed the biggest sin. I just don't know how to make my bitter mistake good. I am a widow with a teenage daughter who is still in school. My income is very small. I live on a modest budget and have to struggle with the high cost of living. My husband was an excellent business man and everyone believes that he left me a great sum of money. Even had I told my friend the truth about my situation, she would never have believed me.

Please, give me a remedy for my sick conscience. I deeply appreciate your help.

THE REPLY

If you were to ask me what was the greatest thing a person could have, I would reply, "It is not money because money is slippery and you can't hold on to it. It is not fame, because you can be a hero one day and a forgotten man the next. The thing that counts is peace in your heart; that's all that really matters when all else is gone."

Your letter indicates that your peace of mind is shattered and all because you did not keep a promise to lend money to a needy friend. She had asked you, you had agreed, and then you never sent the money. When all this took place I don't know. How much money was involved I don't know. Whether or not she still needs the money is also in doubt.

At the same time, your letter speaks about your own difficult time making ends meet with a budget that is just inadequate. Between the written lines is the idea that you don't have the money, that your husband did not leave you the wealth people feel he left you, that in all reality, if they did know your financial plight, they would not ask you for loans. Both of these ideas stand side by side in your letter.

Suppose you begin by making one thing clear to yourself— you did or you did not have the means to make the loan. If you did not, set pride aside, call your friend on the telephone, and tell her how your conscience is eating you up because of a promise made you could not fulfill. If she is a fair, understanding person, she will quickly forgive you and set your own heart at peace.

If you do have the means to make the loan, without hurt to yourself and your daughter, make the loan. You can tell the lady that you were pondering your ability to lend the money. Again, if your friend needs the money she will be very grateful to receive it even at this time.

There is no sense in torturing yourself and spoiling your life and the life of your daughter worrying over what you believe to be a past wrong. If it is a wrong, correct it. If it isn't, forget it. Remember, God has already forgiven you. Now you go ahead and forgive yourself.

A devoted daughter has a problem with her 71-year-old father who lives with her, has the run of the house, and is still unhappy.

– 19 –

What Else Can I Do for My Father?

THE PROBLEM

I am fifty-two years of age, am married. My two sons are married and have children of their own. My daughter, 12 years of age, is with us. I must say that my husband is a wonderful father, and a most understanding mate. He has made me happy through the years with his attention, his affection, and his interested attitude in our home. So you see, I do not have a marital problem, nor do my children give me any real difficulties.

My father, who is 71 years of age, lives with us. Believe me, he is an accepted member of the family, accepted by me, my husband and my children. He is Grandpa to all, and the greatest courtesy and deference is given to him. He has his own room though he is certainly free to roam through the house. I cater to his every need and whim. My husband is absolutely careful not to ever ruffle his feelings.

With all this my father is unhappy. He looks for small incidents and builds them into huge issues. He has become ultrasensitive and is constantly hurt. If we ask him to go with us when we leave for an evening, he declines stating, "Three is a crowd." If we leave him behind, we are looked upon as if we did evil, as if we abandoned him on a desolate mountain.

I am at my wit's end. I don't know what to do with him. He is in good health, is in command of all of his faculties, yet he murmurs, growls, complains, and walks around with a constant chip on his shoulders.

My friends consider me a devoted daughter. Frankly, I feel that I am doing my very best. I have become so irritated that I now am short with my husband, something he surely does not deserve.

Where am I failing my father?

THE REPLY

Today man lives at least twenty years longer than his grandfather. Yet unfortunately, happiness does not automatically follow life's extension, and in fact, the extra years present an urgent and as yet unsolved problem. There are problems that come with age. It forces men to withdraw from activity, it lacks youth's vigor, it can be devoid of pleasure, and, finally, it is darkened by approaching death.

You find the unhappiness of your father inexcusable. In worried conferences you ask one another, "are not all of Grandpa's needs being met?" You feel that you have given him shelter, that you show him affection, and that your own children are devoted and loving.

However, in the eyes of your father, all these comforts and endearments are but dust and ashes, since in retiring from responsibility and retreating into age he has suffered in his own eyes a crippling of his ego. Believe me, he would be happy to be less loved and less secure if only he could feel himself still himself, playing the role he once played, and not being just a kind old grandfather. You see, your father needs not only that others love him, but that he love himself. To accept love one must feel worthy; self-respect includes both self-esteem and the esteem of others.

At this point in your father's life, his own self image does not coincide with the image society has of him. He'd like to feel young, but others make him feel old. He senses pity where there is concern. He would like to play the role consistent with being vigorous, ambitious, and aggressive, but society offers him a rocker, a sweater and a shawl. He may be conforming outwardly, but he is fuming inwardly. This, in turn, makes him grow sour and bitter. He feels himself misunderstood, though in reality, he is the one who misunderstands. Society gives him social security because he is an old man, but it does not give him self-esteem because of what he can still contribute.

Believe me, this feeling of being useless can be crippling. It can disturb sleep, slow digestion, ruin an appetite and even make one quite ill. Some day, psychiatrists will dignify with a name, that syndrome which occurs to men and women of advancing age who suffer a loss of self-esteem. A self-image is something each of us treasures throughout life.

Your father resents his old age because he dreads the emptiness of his life, what with his work done. He does not want to congregate with other old men and pitch horseshoes or swap stories. He hates sitting on a porch rocking chair, rocking away and getting nowhere.

I do know of a few old men and women who experience the pleasure of being wanted and needed. They are the people who educated themselves from their youth to be agreeable old people. They are still full of zest and because of it their advice is sought. They are resourceful because they are interested in living. You can find them on the Boards of Directors of schools and hospitals. You will always find them working, being active. To them, Time is Not Money, it is Life.

Your father needs friends, friends of his own. He must not be permitted to sit around worrying about himself, his aches, pains, and frustrations. He must be made to feel useful, adequate, and contributing. He must start a new life, one where he has retired from work but not from living. I hasten to point out that his new life just can't be one completely devoted to hobbies, laudable as that might be. His new pursuits must have value to him and must give him a chance for fullest self-realization. He must not sit as if his play is really over, that all that remains is for the final curtain to come down. He can be retired but must not be made to feel that he is superannuated. Within the limitations of his ability and health, he must apply himself eagerly to meaningful challenges. He must be made to realize that there are potentials of great significance in later years.

Your father, because he lives in this generation, has been given bonus years to live and he must be made to live them. Don't cripple him with over-attention, with constant reminders to him to take it easy, and that he isn't as young as he used to be. Point out to your father that he is lucky indeed, that there are enjoyments that come with golden years. Tell him that he can now enjoy freedom from routines. He can sit up as late as he wishes to finish a book, knowing that he does not have to be in the city by eight in the morning. Tell him that he now has the freedom to select his social appointments, and that there are fewer boring demands made upon his time. Tell him that he no longer has to live for the future, now he can live fully each day. How happy he will be if he can learn to fill the cup of the present.

You ask me what is wrong? Nothing with you, but a great deal with society. They have, through advanced medical skill, added years to life, but have neglected to add life to the years. This, then, is what you must do for your father. Don't be his nurse-maid, nor his valet. Give him responsibilities; ask his advice. Consult him if you will on family problems. Get him to run important errands. Again, I repeat your father must be made to feel certain of his own worth in old age. If he realizes that he still has a role to play, he will play his part at seventy and eighty, with dignity and with self satisfaction, and to the applause of those who love him.

You are a wonderful daughter and may God bless you. You have a sincere and devoted husband, and courteous and understanding children—the environment needed for happy living. Keep on caring for your father, but make him do everything he can do for himself. Encourage him to take vacations apart from the ones you take.

A daughter complains about her sister who is fresh and impudent to her parents, and gets away with it because she is considered the prize scholar in the family.

– 20 –

They Call Her "The Educated One"

THE PROBLEM

Unfortunately, formal education today has turned into a sort of god. It pains me to see how a person can cover all his faults and be seen as a different person all because he has somehow acquired a formal education. I hold no esteem for an educated person, if his character is weak and he is not God fearing. Of what use is education if it does not strengthen?

I have an older sister who hopes to get married soon. At home, she has been given the title of "The Educated One." True, she possesses more knowledge than I, but her character is bad. She has no heart and never feels the pain and sorrow of other people. She believes herself to be always in the right. She has hurt me many times, though it doesn't worry me as much as the lack of respect she has for our mother. I, too, in the past hurt my mother but I cried night and day to God for forgiveness. But she hurts mother all the time and doesn't even know it.

My mother is not an educated person, but surely that doesn't make her some sort of machine. She has feelings and I know she must cry all through the night because of the many hurts inflicted on her.

What bothers me is that my father doesn't do anything about it. He just sits there, quietly and doesn't say a thing. I cannot understand why. Is it because he just doesn't know how to teach us? Does he just permit my mother to be ridiculed because he doesn't think it is too bad? If he doesn't know how to teach us to stop hurting our mother, he is at fault because what is a father for if not to teach respect? If he agrees with us, he is absolutely guilty, because it indicates he is not loyal to his wife. If he is just indifferent, then his sense of values is all wrong because he is not teaching us the importance of respecting parents.

How often I pray to God that He give him wisdom, and I hope my father prays for wisdom as well. I know one day he will wake up to the realization that he has not taught his children anything. Then, perhaps he will start teaching us just what a father must teach his children. We are all grown up children now, all over the age of thirteen. If he doesn't teach us now our house will just deteriorate.

I write this letter mainly for my older sister and my father. My older sister was the one who taught us all how to find faults in my mother. She set the example for ridiculing and criticizing her for her mistakes. My father is the one who should have done something about it a long time ago, but unfortunately, never did!

Please help us all with your answer.

THE REPLY

How right you are! Mere knowledge is not education. Collecting a series of diplomas does not entitle one to the name of "The Educated One." A wise philosopher once pointed out "A knowledge of our own ignorance is the first step toward true knowledge." Solomon taught: "A wise man is strong: yea, a man of knowledge increaseth strength." The great poet, John Milton, wrote: "The end of all learning is to know God, and out of that knowledge to love and imitate Him."

Any person, your sister included, who lacks respect for his fellow human beings, who looks down on the one who gave her life, who insults, hurts, belittles the one God commanded to love and honor, is not an educated person.

When asked about the value of knowledge, Farrar replied, "Knowledge, without common sense, is folly; without method, it is waste; without kindness, it is fanaticism; without religion, it is death. But with common sense, it is wisdom; with method, it is power; with charity, it is beneficence; with religion, it is virtue and life and peace." It is evident that your sister fails in several of these categories.

If your father permits a member of the family to belittle and humiliate another member, he is making a grave error of omission. He should stand up and demand that every member of the family respects the other, especially is respect due to a mother and father.

Who says your mother is not educated? She may not know ancient history, nor the causes of the Boer War; she may not comprehend Einstein's Theory of Relativity, nor may she be acquainted with the Sunspot Theory of Business Cycles; but she realizes the value of raising children, carrying on a good home life, being devoted to husband, and family. If anyone is uneducated, it must be your sister, "The Educated One." I hope she gets wise to herself before she marries and has children, because she will receive no better treatment from her children than she gives to her mother.

A 40-year-old bachelor, whose life is being run by his elderly mother, asks how he can make a meaningful life for himself.

– 21 –

Did My Mother Crush Me?

THE PROBLEM

I am forty years of age and live with my widowed mother; my father died 4 years ago. I earn about $150 a week and give this to my mother to run the house. My married sister doesn't help with the finance and so it is all up to me. This I do with no regret. What bothers me is that I have no life of my own. In fact I never did. My mother controls every move I make. If I go out by myself, she worries or is lonesome. The result is the same—I have tremendous guilt.

At my age, except on my job, I have absolutely no purpose in life. I think very little of myself, have never been able to determine or define what makes a person, "a person." I know I'm not. How can I be?

Would you believe it, I've had a date about 4 times in my life. Every time my parents counseled what I should do, where I should go, how much I should spend. Dire warnings were given to me about girls demanding too much. I don't have a single friend in the world—neither male nor female. I'm alone, tremendously and completely alone. I work, eat, watch television, and go to bed, and the next day begins the exact repetition of the routine.

I'm intelligent, reasonably well-read, can carry on a conversation. What is wrong with me? How can I be an individual in my own right? I guess half of my life is over; I would like the second half to be more meaningful.

THE REPLY

If your mother has this tremendous hold over you, examine your own short-comings in permitting her to dictate to a forty-year-old man. Honoring and respecting your mother is one thing, living in her image and according to her pattern is quite another. If your mother and father ran your life when you were 6 or 8 or 13 or 17, it was their error. When you permit this to continue through the years, when you get your allowance from your mother at your age, blame yourself. You must like the safety of the relationship you are permitting to exist.

You ask me to define an "individual." An individual is a person with character, a man who has purpose and endurance, a man who is self-contained, able to feel and think for himself. He is one who, having a sense of responsibility toward himself, is able also to make up his own mind and carry out his own ideas. He does not lean on others. Though he seeks advice from experts, he weighs the advice and makes his own decisions. An individual has social responsibility. Because his emotional security centers within himself, he is not afraid to be an individual and disagree with majority opinion. He is not a rigid conformist. Knowing his inner values and having a healthy respect for his ability, he meets each day with anticipation.

I don't believe you should turn over your entire pay to your mother. On the contrary, you pay the rent, the gas, telephone, and electric bill, give her a generous amount for table money—but you run the show with dignity and with honor. You must act your age. How long will you continue to blame your mother for your own unwillingness to accept responsibility!

Begin now to do the things you should have done many years ago. Carve out a social life of your own. Join several organizations where you will have opportunities to meet people and at the same time exercise judgment. Become active; do things. Whether or not you are living now is open to question. You are breathing, eating, working, and sleeping, but there's more to life than just that. You must do something constructive for yourself and for others. This will help you feel more comfortable because it will give you a feeling of accomplishing something worthwhile. You have some constructive traits, use them.

Don't cling to pain and unhappiness, to dependency and inadequacy. Think, plan, and work. Let the real, inner view emerge. This life can be beautiful if you make it so. May your mother live to be 120, but you need more than her to make your life meaningful and rewarding. Your mother would be the first to admit it.

A woman, bored and unhappy with her status as homemaker asks how she can be made to feel more adequate?

-22-

Find the Time!

THE PROBLEM

I don't seem to be getting too much out of life. To others it would seem that I ought to be happy and contented with my husband and two children. My husband has a fairly good position and my children both attend school. Yet, to me, each day is just something to be lived through. It seems that I am busy all day long, seven days a week, and when it is over there is little to show for it.

Unfortunately, neither my husband nor I belong to any organizations. It seems that we are content with watching television every evening and then going to bed. There must be something more to life than merely being a homemaker, feeding a husband and raising children. To tell the truth, there are times I just don't even manage to get through my housework, to say nothing of even attempting to work for organizations.

What is wrong with me? Other women have as many children and seem to have time for many activities. I don't have time for either. All this makes me unhappy which is reflected in my home and in the attitude of my children. What do I do wrong?

THE REPLY

Many people do not have enough time; others have too much, and do not know what to do with it. Now, this is a fact, there is just so much time in the world, and this time is divided equally. No one has more time than anyone else. Each day has twenty-four hours, each week has seven days. It takes 30 days to make up a month, and twelve months to complete a year.

What then is the difference in time? The difference is, one person uses time wisely, and when so used, there is not enough of it. Another uses it unwisely, and wastes it, and finds too much on his hands.

To some extent this is true of you. You have no time for leisure and not enough time to make a home for your family. You are bored and unhappy. This leads me to believe that there is a deep sense of disappointment and frustration with your daily living. You do not feel fulfilled and realize that something is missing from your life. You notice that other women have enough time to do many things and you don't.

An eighty-year-old man kept a detailed record of what he had done during each hour of every day. When his diary was discovered and a careful check made of how he had used his time during the entire period of his long life, the following was found. He had spent over twenty-six years in sleep, twenty-one years working, two hundred and twenty-eight days shaving, and one hundred and forty days paying bills. He had also spent over twenty-six days yelling at his children, two days yelling at his dog. Of the total, only twenty-six hours were spent laughing.

What a waste of valuable time!

Each day is yours but once. You can fill it with good deeds, fruitful actions, and kind performance. These will be accomplishments that will endure in your mind and in the hearts of people around you. Time cannot take them away. You can do nothing in the past; you can do nothing in the future. You have only the present moment. Today, you have the time, and today is when you should make time count. Your best recipe for a better tomorrow is to give your best today.

There are valuable ideas to be learned that will make each day a full and complete one. "Learn to laugh; it is better than medicine. Learn to attend to your own business; few men can handle their own. Learn to say kind words; nobody ever resents them. Learn to avoid nasty remarks; they give neither the hearer nor the speaker any satisfaction. Learn to stop grumbling; if you can't see any good in the world, keep the bad to yourself. Learn to hide aches with a smile; nobody is interested anyway. Learn to keep your troubles to yourself; nobody wants them."

Simple advice, isn't it?

You say you are quite young. Good! All through history, men proved that if they used the present they could accomplish many things even during their youth. Demosthenes was the greatest orator of Greece at twenty-five, and at the same age Cicero was Rome's greatest speaker. William Gladstone was a member of the British House of Commons at twenty-four. Benjamin Franklin was a writer at fourteen. At eight, Beethoven created astonishment by his musical genius; at thirteen Mozart was unequaled in music. Ruskin was an accomplished art critic, and had written Modern Painters at twenty-four. John Wesley was a polished and forceful writer and skilled logician in his youth, and at twenty-four he was a professor of Greek. William Cullen Bryant wrote Thanatopsis at seventeen. Tennyson's first volume of poems appeared at twenty-two. Poe's first volume was written at twenty. Byron's appeared at seventeen. Burns was a poetic genius at twelve, and a brilliant and gifted writer at sixteen. The list can go on and on.

These people all had one thing in common, they used time. It is a fact that the men and women in this world who really count are those who cash in their daily receipts of twenty-four hours, who do not postpone responsibilities and tasks until tomorrow, who do not wait for the future. They never state they are too young or too old or too busy to accomplish anything. On the contrary, they open their eyes each day to a world of interest and activity, to a world of challenges to be met and successes to be achieved. They seem to be chasing through life as if they understood that there was insufficient time to do all they wished to do before being called to their Maker.

"Millions of money for an inch of time!" cried Elizabeth, the Queen of England, upon her dying-bed. Reclining upon a royal couch, with ten thousand dresses in her wardrobe, and a kingdom on which the sun never set, she, who has wasted more than half a century, would now barter millions for an inch of time.

You complain of two things, insufficient time and insufficient accomplishment. Probably, the second makes for the first. After all, as stated before, there are only twenty-four hours in each day and every person under the sun receives this similar daily allotment. No one, prince or pauper, receives more or less.

Stop complaining about the shortness of time and do something about it. Plan out your day properly. Surely, at least your evenings, need not be spent in front of a T.V. screen. Discuss events with your children. Become interested in your husband's position. Try to do something in your own way to make the plight of others easier to bear. Rise a bit earlier if you must and get through with your daily chores with dispatch. Join an organization, accept a committee post. Raise funds for your local hospital. Do something that lasts—just don't kill time. Remember:

> Soon will arrive another clear day;
> Don't permit it to slip uselessly away.

BOOK TWO

THE SEARCH FOR LOVE

THE SEARCH FOR LOVE

Introduction

Everyone has an inner desire, a need for love, and the fulfillment of this need adds warmth, richness and beauty to what may otherwise be a very dull life. If we remain unloved, we live in a vacuum into which are sucked lonesomeness, frustration, and unhappiness. These unhealthy emotions remain with us constantly, day after day, night after night, crippling the very basis of our existence.

Poets have gone to great lengths to describe love. Song writers have put to music the thoughts that run through the minds of men and women whose lives have been touched by this most thrilling and deeply satisfying experience in human life.

"Life is a flower of which love is the honey," wrote Victor Hugo.

"Love reckons hours for months, and days for years; and every little absence is an age," were the words of Dryden.

> "Love rules the court, the camp, the grove,
> And men below, and saints above;
> For love is heaven and heaven is love," proclaimed Sir Walter Scott.

But these are the words of poets—men, who themselves very often were seeking the essence of love and could find it only with words, but not with their own lives. In truth, real love has to be learned. It is not acquired in any other way. To be really in love means to accept and enjoy life, and all human activity: work, play, poetry, music, art. It is being in harmony with ourselves and the world. It is making ourselves feel that we have something to give, and wanting to give it.

Genuine love establishes a positive tie between yourself and the person you love. It flourishes on esteem, admiration, common interests, shared feelings and experiences. It is, in a sense, a feeling of belonging to one another. When you are in love, you want to give without preconceived thought of "what will this get me?" A writer once compared love with the beating of a normal heart, which does not stop to ask, "Shall I beat again?" It beats because it must; it has no other choice. But with each successive beat it brings a return of new, fresh blood. So, giving is the lifeblood of love. It replenishes itself.

We all want to be loved. History tells us of kings who lost their thrones, great leaders who betrayed their followers, ordinary men and women who wrecked their lives, all in the name of love. Was such sacrifice justified? Some found what they were looking for, but many felt they had been deceived by a mirage.

Love needs companionship, not mere physical gratification. Love satisfies our need for emotional security. Love gives us a purpose to go on living. How clearly is this emotion explained by our poets.

"Mutual love, the crown of all our bliss," wrote Milton.

"Love looks not with the eyes, but with the mind," wrote Shakespeare.

"No cord or cable can draw so forcibly, or bind so fast, as love can do with a single thread," wrote Burton.

And who can criticize the composition of the young twelve-year-old who said, "Love is something that makes two people think they are pretty when nobody else does. It also makes them sit close together on a bench when there is plenty of room on both ends. . . . Love is something that young people have in greater quantities than the old, because it is all about dimples and star-like eyes and curls. It is something that makes two people very quiet, and when they talk, it's all about dreams and roses and moonshine."

For centuries moralists have attempted to distinguish between love and sex. Love was regarded as spiritual and virtuous, and when it became contaminated by sexual desire, it was regarded as wicked. Most of us have rejected this type of thinking.

What, then, is this thing we call "love?" Certainly, it is not another name for sex. Love is the strongest of all emotions and can cause hatred, jealousy, disgust, disappointment, frustration. All other human feelings, by comparison become unimportant, fade, or die.

In all forms of love there is, to some extent, a blending of two or more personalities into one. The person loved becomes a part of the one who loves. The person who loves another, no matter how little or how much, places the needs of his beloved one above his own. The other person's needs become his.

There is much pain and suffering, much disillusionment and disappointment on the part of men and women who seek love. Unfortunately, many have reconciled themselves unwillingly to a life without genuine love. Many, who confused romance with love, can not adjust the one to the other. And there are those who are still waiting for their hearts to be stormed by love.

Millions of people "suffer" from love, millions are stricken by the plague of jealousy, are disappointed and disgusted with their mates, unhappy in a joyless marirage, or lonely and loveless in empty solitude. What a pity! It could be such a complete satisfying experience.

How beautiful are the words of Carl Sandberg:

I love you for what you are, but I love you yet more for what you are going to be.

I love you not so much for your realities as for your ideals. I pray for your desires that they may be great, rather than for your satisfactions, which may be so hazardously little.

A satisfied flower is one whose petals are about to fall. The most beautiful rose is one hardly more than a bud wherein the pangs and ecstasies of desire are working for larger and finer growth.

Not always shall you be what you are now.

You are going forward toward something great. I am on the way with you and therefore I love you.

A woman, married only 2 years feels that romance and glamour have disappeared from her life.

–1–

What Is Love?

THE PROBLEM

My second wedding anniversary was celebrated only last week, and already I am disillusioned with marriage. It just isn't what I expected it to be; my disappointment keeps growing daily.

When I first met my husband, I found him to be attentive, considerate, romantic, understanding. Believe me, I loved him with all my heart. My thoughts were about him almost every minute of the day. How I ached at that time to build a home for both of us. I was 21 and a school teacher; he was 26, and in business for himself.

Every date we had was a wonderful experience. His thoughtfulness was genuine and complete. He remembered me with candy, flowers, perfume. When he came for dinner, he was the perfect, attentive lover. Never did he fail to be solicitous about my welfare.

Now, after two years of married life, things have changed. He is not always eager for romance. His telephone calls do not convey words of love. He does not shake off his business worries but rather permits them to ruin perfect evenings. My own life has become humdrum because my husband doesn't make it exciting.

To be fair, I must say he is generous, helps in the house from time to time, visits my family. His voice is always modulated and he does tell me he loves me. However, his words of love have lost the electricity they used to have. How I would appreciate a well written love letter, or a poem dedicated to me!

What happened to our love? Or should I ask you to explain the meaning of the word love? I expected so much from marriage and I feel that I have been short-changed. Perhaps, I am riding a cloud which is slowly disintegrating. Something is wrong. My husband says he is not at fault. I don't feel at fault; yet I feel our marriage isn't what it should be.

THE REPLY

To many people, the word LOVE suggests paradise. Such individuals spend their lives seeking the heaven they are convinced must be right here on earth. They, and you too, are deluded. A meaningful, intimate relationship is the source of many moments of joy and many hours of gratification, it is true. Yet, the very same partnership also provides a full portion of unhappiness and suffering. That, after all, is what life is about, a variety of happenings that range from ecstasy to agony.

Partners who stick together through tears as well as through laughter for a decade or two, may find that the beauty and depth of their involvement with each other's destinies matches any love story portrayed in song or film. However, this beauty is both invisible and secret. To the onlooker, their marriage may appear to be as humdrum as paying the monthly bills. To the two married lovers, however, it feels like the mysteries of love coming to life.

Love is expressed between a man and woman who care what happens to each other, now, as well as in the future, who enjoy satisfying each other's spiritual as well as bodily needs. Love is "care, concern, understanding, anticipation, and responsibility." It is feeling happy that you have an important role to play in your partner's well-being; and wanting to do your utmost to help him enjoy a good life. If what you want is only "love's delights and none of its torments," marriage may not be for you. If all you want is heightened stages of romantic hours, marriage will be disappointing.

While courtship and romance may indeed be jammed full of rapture, the realities of any long-term intimacy (and marriage is just that) include feelings of anger, guilt, resentment. Disagreeable reactions to your mate rise from time to time and may throw you into some sort of conflict and turmoil. To pull you through such cycles requires knowledge, intelligence, insight, maturity, and the willingness to succeed.

You write that your husband is generous, cooperative, and expresses his love for you. However, you are disappointed with the words he uses. You want him to be a poet and compose beautiful poetry dedicated to you.

Elizabeth Barrett Browning once wrote: "How do I love thee? Let me count the ways." But not all of us can catch the romantic imagery of this gifted poetess.

Each man as well as each woman creates his own style of expressing emotions and feelings. Some men do it with flowers and gifts. You cannot expect all to be great writers. Words are not always meaningful. Saying "I love you" while you refuse to cope with marital responsibilities is of no value. At the same time coping with responsibilities but condemning your mate verbally day and night is neither the story nor the glory of love.

It might be that you have been watching too many T.V. programs, or reading too many love stories. Each person has his own distinctive notion of what love is all about. They are the product of years of movie-going, novel-reading, from what our friends tell us, from our own observations, and from our fantasies dating back to early childhood. As we mature and have more experiences with actual human beings, we hopefully modify our outlook until it corresponds more with fact than with fancy.

Marriage takes a lifetime; it is never quite finished. It demands of us our sincerest efforts, our noblest qualities our stubborn persistence through trial and error, our hopefulness. It requires the vision that love is a goal worth achieving, and that it is up to us to learn how to reach this goal.

This is what you want; now how do you achieve it? To begin with, resolve to become more aware of your deeper needs, your hopes, and dreams. Then try to make it your business to fulfill as many of your desires as is possible within the framework of REALITY.

You speak of his shortcomings in the field of love, but may have failed to mention your own. Did you ever hear that "love never reasons, but just gives; gives its all and then wonders if it gave sufficiently." Forget the books you have read. The whole business of love and love-making, is painted by the novelists in a monstrous disproportion to the other realities of life. To really love is to place your happiness in the happiness of another. The happiness of married life depends upon making sacrifices with readiness and cheerfulness.

Stop thinking of "I" and start thinking of "WE." What greater thing is there for a man and woman than to feel that they are joined for life—to support each other in all undertakings, to give comfort when that is needed, to minister to each other in pain, to suffer together through hardship, to share moments of despair as well as moments of happiness.

You ask me what is "Love"? Let me tell you that there is a difference between "LOVE" and "Making Love." Don't confuse the two. Love is the deeper and more lasting relationship. Marriage is an art. Be patient; you cannot learn any art if you are after quick results. There may be instant tea, instant coffee, instant mashed potatoes, but there is no instant love. To master these arts, you must devote your entire life to them. You've only begun. A successful marriage is an edifice which must constantly be kept in repair.

If you want to be loved, then love and be lovable. Dedicate yourself to the task of making your marriage a lasting one. You have the proper ingredients—a husband who is generous, cooperative, understanding. Share his problems as well as his joys. Listen to his tales of woe as well as his words of love. All sugar destroys a cake.

She feels she has waited
too long for her mate
and so she's soured on
love and marriage.

-2-

This Thing Called Love

THE PROBLEM

I've been misled. All my life I waited to love and be loved, but evidently I've missed the boat. I was waiting at the marital station but no trains arrived, or at least none that I could board. Here and there I thought I was in love only to be rudely reminded that it was so different from what I had pictured or seen portrayed on the screen.

There has been too much emphasis placed on love. It is my feeling that one can live a full, useful, adequate life without this romantic bosh about dedicated and devoted love. Let's face it. I'll never be waiting at the gate for my man to arrive. In any event, most men are selfish, egocentric, weak and completely unromantic. In reality, they can't discuss any subject except their business or profession. To me all this adds up to the fact that I've lost my love for love. Am I a neurotic? Am I really a nut when I say this?

My own feeling is that "there is no such thing called love." From now on let men go their way and I'll go my way, and never shall the ways meet. I'm not going to let any weak-minded, weak-willed male tell me that without loving I'll become a dried-up prune. And you should take a quick glimpse at those who tell me this.

I've tried to give love and it has been rejected. Enough is enough! Love is like an itch, the more you scratch it the more uncomfortable it becomes. At last, I've learned my lesson. Come on girls, join my group. Love is for children, mothers, grandmas, and people on rocking chairs.

What do you think Dr. Mandel: Is love a necessary ingredient of living?

THE REPLY

Movies, magazines, novels and television teach us the joys of love and of making love. Advertisers insist that we must look good and smell good in order to escape loveless solitude. Poets, artists, and philosophers urge their particular version of love, and frankly, most psychotherapists hold that the ability to love is a sign of good mental health.

The person who is incapable of giving love probably has a low image of himself. You understand that love flows in many directions: the love of parents for children, the love of patriots for their country, and very important, what we have come to call romantic love.

Corny as this may sound, I nevertheless venture to state that "love makes the world go round." It helps make life worth living and conquers many frustrations. We live in a society beset by competition and insecurity. We need acceptance and justification, and so we become very pleased when we meet someone who shares our beliefs. Such a relationship gives us a feeling of self-validation which incidently is one important basis for love.

There is a wonderful feeling in being able to say: "He loves me." Of course, we do not fall in love with everyone who shares our beliefs. There are other needs in us that clamor for satisfaction. The more needs one person satisfies, the more likely are we to fall in love with that person.

We live in a society that is love-oriented. From early childhood we hear about the beauties of love, the warmth of love, the need for love. You surely are a member of this society.

Don't close the tap because at the start some rusty water came flowing out. If you are thirsty, let the water run, and when it is clear take a good, refreshing drink.

Love is here to stay. Love is what this world needs. Love strengthens relationships. To say that lack of it makes one neurotic would be sheer arrogance, but love sure helps make life interesting and beautiful. I'm all for it! Believe it, I AM!

At 36, she asks if she should marry a man she doesn't love with the hope that love might come later!

-3-

I Fear Marrying a Man I Don't Love

THE PROBLEM

I am thirty-six years of age, single, and work for the United States Government.

Of course, you are aware that it is time a girl of my age was married, and obviously, this is my problem. Frankly, I admit I am very frustrated at this point. It does get more difficult each year to meet eligible men.

My friends consider me attractive and tell me that I have a nice personality. Earlier in my life I rejected several eligible men. I guess I was not ready for marriage then, but I am now.

Eight years ago I took a three weeks' vacation in Israel. There I met a very handsome Israeli. We enjoyed ourselves tremendously. I realized I liked him more than most other men I had met. To this day I am obsessed with the memory and just can't seem to forget him. I think I fell in love with him. Now I am in a quandary and don't know what to do.

I feel lost and lonely and I don't like living alone. I wish I could meet someone so that I can forget all about him, but this is beginning to look hopeless. I know it was nothing serious because I wrote to him once and he never answered. It could be, though, that he never got my letter.

It has gotten to the point where my feelings for him might interfere with opportunities to meet another prospect. What bothers me is that I have a fear of marrying a man I don't love. What shall I do?

THE REPLY

Stop living in the past and get down to some basic facts. For 8 years you have been waiting for a certain good-looking Israeli to answer your letter. You refuse to believe that he just is not interested in you. Instead, you question the reliability of the post-office departments of two countries. So, you sit at home, alone, dreaming of that exciting three week vacation in Israel. You relive the 20 days of love and romance and hopefully wait for the Israeli to jet to your home town and claim you as his own.

Stop dreaming! That Israeli of yours might just be the happy father of four or five children. Right now he may be employed in an orange grove or is cutting hair in a Tel Aviv barber shop. Your three weeks with him is at best a vague memory, and as he sits holding hands with his wife, you sit holding your head in your hands. You're not a teenager now, waiting for a dashing male to sweep you off your feet. You are thirty-six and getting older each year. The fish in your pond get fewer and fewer and those you threw back years ago are no longer in the swim.

What are you waiting for? Love? Romance? Security? Get away from your T.V. screen and as difficult as it may be, give up this concept of romantic love. Stop waiting wistfully to have your soul conquered by some mysterious force. Remember, in the end every flower loses its perfume.

Do you know what you are looking for? You state that you fear marrying a man you don't love. Your problem is "To choose or not to choose." If you are emotionally mature and do not fear marriage you will find a mate. Life offers plenty of opportunities to meet people, but it remains for you to make proper use of them. Only wrong attitudes and expectations are responsible if you find either no one at all or meet only the wrong people.

It may be that you fell in love with one who offered the least possibility of a harmonious union, and that very good marital prospects were neglected and are still being overlooked. Perhaps, two secret tendencies are chiefly responsible for this: the desire to maintain your superiority, and the hope of suffering. You claim you are attractive, have a good personality, and enjoy professional status. In the same breath you speak about your loneliness. You feel superior and miserable at the same time.

Could it be that you are running away from marriage? Could

it not be that you fear marriage as a test which you do not expect to meet successfully? Perhaps you demand love and security from your future mate because you have none within yourself. Aren't these the bases of your hypercritical attitude and short-lived interest? It is absolutely wrong for you to go on loving your romantic Israeli and to go on waiting for his letter. He is thousands of miles away and you will never be called upon to make a choice.

You seek perfection in a man and so have turned away several earlier proposals of marriage. This attitude of yours is well expressed in the following episode:

Two women met on the street. "Hello, Clara. What's the matter with you? Why do you look so down in the mouth?" Clara confessed she had just met the ideal man, the one she had been looking for. She raved about his looks, charm, intelligence, good nature, understanding, and modesty. And he was wealthy, too." Finally the friend interrupted. "What's the matter, then?"

"Nothing's wrong but my bad luck," was the response. "He's looking for the perfect woman."

Perfect men and perfect women just do not exist. At least, perfection does not exist in reality but only in dreams. Seeking perfection in a mate is a subconscious method of avoiding marriage. Examine your own conscience; review the men you have turned down. Ask yourself why you love a man you met 8 years ago for about 18 days.

This I can tell you, failure to choose a mate always results in personal unhappiness, frustration, and self-isolation. Remaining single is disappointing and discomforting. You claim to be good-looking. Then, take advantage of this present advantage. Reconcile yourself to this formula for finding a mate. Reconcile yourself to the fact that whoever you find is as good as you deserve. The problem is less the adequacy of the other person, than your own ability and willingness to do your best with what one is and what one has.

Poetic, romantic, and religious concepts tell you that "marriages are made in heaven." So recognize your destiny when he arrives. The main factor for proper choice is your willingness to choose at all—plus common sense and determination to make the best of what you get. If you act accordingly, you will discover that you have found the right mate. The less courage you have the poorer will be your choice. Remember, no person is utterly bad and nobody is the perfect ideal. All depends upon what you see and bring out in your partner.

Get to understand what it takes to live together. Take a good healthy realistic look into the mirror and a second glance at your birth certificate. Forget the mail-man and sunny Israel. Get into your best "going-out" dress, your flashiest pair of shoes, your best smile and make certain you *mix* and *mingle*.

Whatever you do, do something! Make a choice and learn to live with it. You will find that it will make living more worthwhile.

> *Married only 5 months she is most anxious to preserve her husband's love in marriage and avoid the pitfalls of other young couples.*

–4–

Can Love Be Defined?

THE PROBLEM

Some five months ago, I gave up college to assume my duties and responsibilities as a wife. I ought to tell you that I have just reached my twentieth birthday. Were it not for my "falling in love," I would now be in my junior year at college.

My husband is exactly two years older than I am. He is still a student though he earns enough to support our home. He is so engrossed in his studies that sometimes I feel he just doesn't love me. This is a painful admission to make since we've been married only five months.

I want desperately to build a good marriage and a good home. I want to be happy, to be loved, and yes, to taste of romance. Am I wrong in trying to find romance and happiness? Am I wrong in attempting to define love?

I know I am young, but just because I am young, I don't want to fall into the mistaken paths others have taken. I'm not concerned about money, furniture, furs, or diamonds. They are all meaningless, but my heart is filled with concern for the future. How well I know that the future is composed of many todays. I need help. I must know just what love is and how can it be expressed? Is it possible for one marital partner to love the other more than is reciprocated? I fell in love and don't want to fall out of love.

Help me, won't you?

THE REPLY

A person who tries to analyze love can be compared to one who attempts to reduce a wedding cake into calories, or a cup of tea to grams of tannic acid. To try to define love would be stripping it of its warmth and beauty, and placing it under a microscope to be scientifically observed. The word "love" is used and misused in many ways. It has become a meaningless expression covering a multitude of activities. During any day of listening you can hear the following uses of the word "love."

"I love hot-dogs with mustard."
"I love mystery stories."
"I love lima beans and brussel sprouts."

Thus the word "love" is carelessly tossed around and misinterpreted. How can the word describe the powerful emotional force in human relationships and be used in connection with some favorite dish or pastime?

Artists have tried to capture this emotion on canvas, poets have put it into metre and rhyme. Lovers have sought it and mothers have lived it. And because people hear so much and expect so much of this emotion, almost everyone makes some attempt to understand its relation to his own life. Young and old, men and women discuss the question, "What is love, is love all that matters? Is it possible to love someone you do not respect?"

Dozens of pamphlets, tons of books, numerous lectures have all dealt with the subject of love. Interesting to point out, that since practically all human beings love and are loved to some degree, it may be said that in a limited sense, all may claim to be authorities on love. You, too, are an authority, since you have been made aware of the nature of this emotional force.

Today, people associate love with sentimental and romantic feelings alone. But love is much more. Love which is physical vanishes with the object. The act of love brings the entire human being into play, his intuitions, his emotions, his mind and heart. Love brings to life everything that is dead within us. Love is extremely complex. Its ingredients vary not only in kind but in proportion. Love includes respect, admiration, tenderness, compassion, and physical attraction. It must be pointed out that the ingredients which go into love are likely to vary with age, sex, and personality.

It is no secret that women love differently from men, though it is unwise to generalize in this fashion. Suffice it to say that love is a growing and a changing emotion. Dr. Karl Menninger, a great psychiatrist, expressed it this way: "We do not fall into love; rather we grow into love." Thus a man may love one way at twenty, in a deeper way at thirty, and still more devotedly at sixty. A spiritual adviser once said of his wife, "I thought I could not love her more than when we were first married, but now after being married for many years and having three children, I do not have words to express the depth of my love."

Sometimes two people feel a strong first attraction toward each other, an attraction which subsequently grows into love. This may give the impression that their love was at first sight. But actually it did not spring suddenly into being. It grew.

The kind of love that is the basis for lasting marriage has a very special mixture of ingredients. Though they vary to some extent with different couples they do include: friendship plus companionship plus understanding plus respect plus physical attraction.

Actions speak better and louder than words in communicating love. This in no way eliminates words. "Sit, I'll get it for you." "No, you take the better slice." "Stay in bed until I get the coffee up" all represent efforts to demonstrate by action and deed, the affection and consideration for a loved one.

It is important to point out that the capacity for love varies with individuals. Some individuals are able to give and accept love more easily than others. A few people seem unable to love at all. Since human beings are imperfect, they love imperfectly.

Flaws and disappointments creep into the finest of love relationships. It is unrealistic to expect to be loved as completely as we would wish. To expect constant unqualified love is to demand more than human beings can give. It can be said that repeated inattention, continued neglect, cool indifference take their toll of love relationships. It is these little slights and oversights that cause love's casualties. Real love can better withstand an argument than repeated neglect.

Believe the man who tries hard to communicate his words in love. "I just can't put it into words," he pleads, "or it's hard for me to describe my feelings for you," he says and means that.

Adelaide Love put into words her great love in a poem she called, "Walk Slowly."

> If you should go before me, dear, walk slowly
>   Down the ways of death, well worn and wide,
> For I should want to overtake you quickly
>   And seek the journey's ending by your side.
> I should be so forlorn not to descry you
>   Down some radiant road and take the same;
> Walk slowly dear, and often look behind you
>   And pause to hear if someone calls your name.

A 37-year-old man, lonely and unmarried, finds living alone unbearable.

–5–

Have You Heard of Love?

THE PROBLEM

I'm unhappy, and that's it! I could write at great length and describe days at work and evenings at home—both filled with monotony. I have been unable to find interest in family or friends. Life just is dull and drab and I keep thinking that living is some joke played upon humans by eternal spectators.

Perhaps, I should tell you that I am thirty-seven years of age, unmarried, and am a successful certified public accountant. I have an excellent professional reputation and I certainly am in no great need for additional clients. Financially, I am quite secure; my investments have always paid good returns.

All this should give me an incentive to life and to living but it just is not so. There is no great motivation for me. Something seems to be missing in my life. What it is I have been unable to determine. But this I know: I am unhappy, lonely, and at times pretty miserable.

So, I turn to you for help and guidance. I imagine you meet only unhappy people and so you have some experience with their problems. What is wrong with me? Why don't I have a zest for life?

What I would not like having you do is to pass off some psychological jargon about my parents, grandparents, and environment and tell me that's what's wrong. It won't help me. I just want to know what is missing in my life. What can I add to make my life complete and happy?

THE REPLY

I read your letter and one question kept running through my mind: "Have you heard of love?" You are successful, have money. You have made wise investments which earn satisfactory dividends. Yet, you are lonely, unhappy, unmotivated, and miserable. Read your letter and perhaps you, too, can see that you never said a word about LOVE.

Loving and being loved is an important ingredient in life today. Current literature is occupied with this emotion. It has been a theme for artists and writers since the dawn of history. It fills television and movie hours. It makes life possible even during its darkest moments.

Love can work wonders. It can fill days with beauty. How many times have you heard that love makes the world go round? It may sound corny but it is the truth. It has been my conviction that with love anything is possible; without it, nothing. It is a tonic that strengthens human beings.

For some time, perhaps, you have been in love with yourself. Now this has become monotonous. You became a good accountant, a wise business investor, a good business man—all to no avail. Your life was still empty, it did not include anyone to love.

Why are you unmarried at thirty-seven? Why haven't you enriched someone's life with the love you could give? You feel no closeness to friends and family. In fact, you are a modern hermit.

Your feelings of emptiness have brought you to write to me and announce your insolvency, if not bankruptcy. Well, you certainly can salvage much of your life yet. There is, at thirty-seven, much living that you still can do. In your present state, it gives you a sense of value and worth; builds up your ego, and makes present and future secure.

Unfortunately, we live in a busy, materialistic world, a world with great demands on our time. It seems to be a world of constant strain and of nagging pressures. This rushing way of living often furnishes excuses for neglecting friends and family. In the rush to accumulate material wealth, love of family, friends and mate is often neglected. However, the time comes when the need for love catches up with us.

You are at that point now. You realize that professional and financial success just don't fill the void in your life left by the absence of love—love of the opposite sex, love of friends, of neighbors, even associates. Now, you must stop for a moment the hurly-burly of life and give love its proper due.

Take a week off from ledgers, journals, balance sheets, and trial balances. Forget, if you will, schedules of accounts receivable and accounts payable. Instead of preparing a comparative balance sheet for a client, make a tabulation of your values and joys in life. If you do this honestly, you will see that you are on the loss side, not the profit side.

But enough of finding fault with you. You are asking for help and I should, in all fairness tell you that you still can work to make your life enjoyable. What I want you to do is to take the prescription and follow it carefully! I hope you will.

To begin with, scrape off the frost from your heart. Scrape it all away! Defrost it! Look at women differently. Make up your mind that one of them can offer you a great deal in life. Don't suspect each female as a plotting woman who wants a free meal ticket for the rest of her life. Get that out of your system! Forget it! Once again, scrape it off! Mix and mingle and understand the value of companionship and friendship.

Permit love to get to first base in your life. Remember, I

am talking about love, and not "making love." There is a great difference between the two. Get the satisfaction of doing things for people. Feel the warmth of satisfaction from an act of yours that is completely unselfish.

I guess I could rush this a bit, push the point a bit deeper, when I say, "Go out and get married." Certainly in this great City of New York, there must be at least one intelligent, cultured, good-looking woman who can help you be happy.

I'll tell you what's missing in your life:—a wife and children. It's not too late but it is getting later every year. Living together will bring you happiness. Sharing problems, accepting challenges together can go a long way in making years happy and productive.

You see, you may like ice cream, and you may like chocolate syrup, and you may like whipped cream, but you would not sit down to a bowl of chocolate syrup, nor would you eat whipped cream from a pot or pan. However, when you pour the syrup over the ice cream and top it with loads of whipped cream and consume the delicacy together, it tastes delicious and delightful.

Life is that way. Work alone is tiresome. Recreation alone is boring. Counting money day after day is monotonous. Constantly being with friends is not the answer. But when your life is composed of work, recreation, finance, friends, it has meaning.

So, once again, I ask, "Have you heard of love?" You have! Then where have you been for the past 10 years? Where have you been hiding? Whatever your answers are, get out and meet people. If you have any trouble meeting wonderful cultured women, drop me a line and I will try to help.

Though she is able to classify men into all categories, she herself is an unhappy married woman.

-6-

What Is Man?

THE PROBLEM

Just what is a man? I don't mean what is his chemical composition, nor do I mean to question the religious definition of man. I merely ask the question about the trouser-wearing, pipe smoking, gift to the fair sex.

To me, a man is many things. He is an individual who suddenly desires to make love to women, and finally marries one of them. True, he has two feet, two hands, two eyes, two ears, one head, and one idea at a time. Frankly, all men are made of the same material, except that some come better disguised than others.

Generally speaking, they can be divided into three classes: husbands, bachelors, and widowers. A bachelor is one who just won't take yes for an answer. He is one who claims he hasn't made the mistake once, and believes that he is a thing of beauty and a boy forever.

Husbands are of three general varieties: prize, surprise, and consolation. Making a husband out of a man is one of the most skillful plastic arts known to civilization. It requires faith, hope, wisdom, charity, and common sense. If you think it over you will agree that it is a psychological miracle that a soft, velvety, tender, sweet-scented thing like a woman should really enjoy kissing a big, awkward, tobacco-scented thing like a man.

If you flatter a man, it frightens him to death, and if you don't, you bore him to distraction. If you permit him to make love to you, he gets tired of you in the end, and if you don't, he gets tired right at the start. Either way you seem to lose him.

If you are the clinging-vine type, completely dependent upon his masculine strength, he begins to doubt that you have a brain. If you are the modern, advanced and independent woman, he doubts whether you have a heart. Again, you score no hits; just errors.

If you are quiet, he longs for a bright mate, and if you are brilliant, he longs for a playmate. If you are popular with other men, he is jealous, and if you are not, he hesitates to marry a wallflower. If you please him, he seldom mentions it, but if you displease him, he never fails to tell you about it, especially if you are his wife.

And by the way, Dr. Mandel, before you think the wrong things, I am married. I don't venture to say I am happily married, but this I know: If my husband would only meet me half way, an effective, meaningful relationship might result. I've spoken to my husband many times but his words are always sharp and meant to hurt. So, where do I go from here?

THE REPLY

There are many things I could tell you, but frankly I just don't know where to begin. With the image of a man you have in your mind, I just wonder whether I can ever be of any good. Someone has compared marriage to a dollar bill. You cannot spend half of it when you tear it in two. The value of one half depends upon the other, and so it is with regard to husband and wife. You claim your husband is surly in his comments to you. You ought to know that if a husband's words are sharp, maybe it's from trying to get them in edgewise.

My question to you is, "Why did you ever marry any man—what with the picture you have of men?" You, like many a wife, have made your own marital grave with your series of digs. If you like to be humorous, write gags for second-rate comedians, but don't use them against your husband. Your wedding license is not a certificate that gives you the right to drive him. You remind me of the boy who was once talking to his father.

"Papa," he said, "how much does it cost to get married?"

"That, my son, depends on two things: How much you've got, and how long you live."

You ask, how can this marriage be successful? To begin with, the secret of a happy marriage is: Just keep on being as polite to one another as you are to your best friends. Then again, there is one word above all others that makes marriage successful and that word is "ours."

Your husband isn't perfect, but neither are you. I venture to say, had he been perfect he would have selected someone else. You ought to bear in mind that marriage is an arrangement like a booking of movies, in which a number of less desirable pictures must be accepted in order to obtain one or two major attractions. Certainly, there must be some good in your husband. FIND IT! It just can't be that everything is wrong with him. You remind me of the woman, who when her husband claimed that she had overdrawn the checking account answered: "You say I'm overdrawn—I say you're underdeposited!"

Marriage is a career. It takes work to make it work. Happiness or unhappiness has nothing to do with it. Of course, this is a mutual task. As Alexander Dumas once wrote: "The chain of wedlock is so heavy that it takes two to carry it—sometimes three."

You certainly have taken men apart and so you just can't put your marriage together. When I read your letter I thought of the comments of Solomon, the wisest of all men. Certainly, his wide experience in the field of matrimony qualifies him to speak on the subject of marriage. One day, irritated by one of his numerous wives, Solomon took refuge on the roof garden of his house. Looking down on the tenements of his subjects, he saw a man sleeping contentedly on his mattress in a corner of the housetop; and taking up his quill, Solomon wrote this proverb: "Better to dwell in the corner of the housetop, than with a brawling woman" (Prov. 25:24).

On another day, a day when it did nothing but rain, hearing the dripping of the rain, Solomon had another idea; and, taking up his quill, he wrote another proverb: "A continual dripping on a very rainy day, and a contentious woman are alike" (Prov. 27:15).

Instead of attempting to perform word autopsies on the men, why don't you use some plastic surgery on some of your ideas? Instead of spending so much time determining what is wrong with women, why not spend at least half of the time trying to better yourself? No woman can love a man having previously derided him. Build him up in your eyes by changing your opinion of men in general.

Be like the woman who was standing before the Justice of the Peace.

Said he: "Do you take this man for better or worse?"

Said she: "He can't be worse, and I don't know how he can get better, so I take him as he is."

A bachelor worries about the risk involved in marrying a divorcee with children.

-7-

How Much of a Risk Do I Take?

THE PROBLEM

I am 42 years of age, a bachelor and have gone out and kept company with many girls in the past.

A few months ago I met a divorcee who is 37 years old. She is an amiable, ingratiating and pleasant person. I realize that I have acquired an affection for her and would like to marry her. However, she has two children from a previous marriage—a boy of fourteen and a girl of eight.

Although I have never been married, I do not object to acquiring a wife with children. I earn a modest yet comfortable living and am able to support them.

My parents, however, to whom I am very devoted and whom I love dearly, object violently to my marrying a woman with young children whom, they contend, I will have to raise as a step-father. At their insistence, I inquired and was told by the young woman that she sought and secured the divorce because her husband was an habitual drunkard. She added that she had lived with him for fifteen years and that he had been a drinker at the time she married him, and before the children were born.

Now I find myself in a serious dilemma. I do like this woman very much, but I love my parents too—and am reluctant to cause them undeserved misery. They have made many sacrifices for me and have always given me readily things that I wanted.

My problem is what to do. Shall I marry this likeable divorcee with two dependents, or listen to the protestations of my parents? Having never been a father, I may find difficulty in undertaking the role of a step-father. I am also aware of the many obstacles I will have to face and overcome, regardless of my sincere and good intentions. Moreover, I would feel like an ingrate toward my loyal, but nevertheless, adamant parents. They would surely disown me, although I do not seek to incur their wrath.

As an adviser in human relations and one who has encountered and helped solve such problems, would you please advise me in my predicament? I assure you that I would treasure any counsel you render.

THE REPLY

You are a bachelor, 42 years old, and have kept company with many girls in the past, though you have walked with none of them to the altar. From your letter I cannot judge whether the ladies did not meet up with your ideals, or you weren't what they had in mind, or perhaps, your parents did not offer their enthusiastic approval.

You wonder if you should marry the mother of two children, though you find her an amiable, ingratiating, pleasant, and charming person. You fear that you will incur the wrath of your parents.

To be a loving, devoted husband at the same time you are a loving, devoted son is not an unheard of feat. If you truly love this woman, you will make your parents see things in the right light, unless, of course, all this talk about causing your parents misery is just another excuse you have contrived.

I am afraid that your problem is not your parents, or their wrath, but rather your own immaturity. You must grow up and learn to make decisions. If you were really mature, you would spend less time worrying about the obstacles you have to meet, and devote more energy to overcoming the obstacles you already have. A marriage must be entered into with confidence in its success, and you have it shattered before you even muster up enough courage to ask the question.

It would seem that before thinking of marriage you must overcome more than the fear of your parents' wrath. You must overcome your dread fear of marriage itself. You must overcome your fear of the challenges which life presents us. You cannot be a pawn in life's game of chess. Rather you must move ahead on your own, when it is your time to do so. If your parents are, indeed, putting obstacles in the way of your making a decision, then they are, in truth, keeping you from marriage and potential happiness, for there is hardly a greater joy that I can conceive than sharing one's life with the very special kind of friend the right husband or wife can be.

Your parents, like most parents, have made many sacrifices to "give things readily." Don't you think it is high time they let go of you, and instead of giving you things, permit you to grab a bit of happiness for yourself? Your anxieties regarding your parents are far too great. If they are the loyal parents you say they are, they would never disown you—at least not for trying to do what is every man's right to do—marry and establish a home for himself and the wife of his choice.

You need not be a step-father at all. You can very well be a father to these children. It has been done before, and successfully. People adopt children of whose background very little is sometimes known. The adoptive parents, who offer a home to orphans, find in later life the rewards of parenthood to be very sweet indeed.

It isn't difficult to be a parent, in spite of the great responsibility it carries with it. Just love those two children and be willing to listen to their problems. You cannot expect to get anything without putting something in. If you want children to call you Dad, then you must treat them as if you had actually sired them. They need a good father, and they shall love you in return. Believe me, the love you give is all the magic that is necessary to open all the doors necessary to build a happy family, ready-made or otherwise.

You are 42 years of age, bear this in mind. Your vintage girls are now few in number. The best choice you can make is to marry a woman who has been previously married, and if she comes with children, GOOD, consider it a real bonus for you.

If you don't make a decision soon, time will remove the problem for you completely. You will get older, and the fountain of youth will not be discovered. You will become less and less of a bargain to a worthwhile female. You will be even more set in your ways, and the choice of a partner will no longer be yours.

At 42, it is high time you emerge from behind Mama's apron, cut the Gordian Knot. Love your parents! By all means, love them always! That's a God given commandment. But stop loving them as a child and start loving as a man. Only then will they cease to stand in the way of your making decisions; they will then know that you are capable of choosing a course for yourself.

An unmarried girl, who loves a divorcee 15 years older, lost him and finds life no longer worth living.

-8-

Without Love I Die!

THE PROBLEM

I'm only 24 years of age, and I have no genuine desire to live. I'm considered attractive, have some college background, and generally make an excellent impression with the men I date.

Some time ago, I fell in love with a divorcee 15 years older than I am, and the father of an eleven-year-old boy. We dated almost every day for 3 months. I loved him and showered my attentions on him. He loved me as well, else, why the steady dating?

A few weeks ago, he told me I was not for him, that I was too young in years and too immature in thought and activity. I thought he was joking, but little did I know then that he meant what he was saying, and that he would not date me again.

My life is now shattered. You see, I, too, am a divorcee, though I have no children. I loved my first husband but he just did not love me and told me so. Our divorce was by mutual consent and neither of us has hard feelings. Nevertheless, I was rejected by my first husband, and now by my love.

Had I the courage, I'd end my life. Don't worry I won't; I'm the type of coward that will hang on even though I am miserable. Yet, I go through life listless. I'm without feeling, without emotion, without desire and will. Every day seems to be a routine experience in monotony. I wait to go to bed each evening, and hate the thought of arising in the morning.

I know I can't go on this way. My family is after me to change, to snap out of it, to get on with life. But I don't have the strength or the desire to start all over again.

THE REPLY

Sometimes, rejected by the one we love, we may wish to put an end to life. However, these thoughts of suicide take on a rather passive form. We withdraw from our friends, withdraw from social activity, and become preoccupied with the memory of the wonderful times we had with our beloved one. We feel miserable, filled with self pity, as if the world had come to an end.

Right now, with this disappointment fresh in your mind, you sit and think of the places you used to go with your lover, the songs you sang together. You keep dwelling on the love-filled moments you spent in his company, and just cannot believe that this is all over. Every once in a while, you feel tempted to call him on the telephone, but pride and the feeling that it is hopeless deter you from this act. It's all over, you know.

Sometimes you entertain thoughts of vengeance. These thoughts are dismissed quite quickly. You day-dream about some action you might take that will attract his attention to you. You go through mental gyrations, become an actress, a senator, a great physician. For a minute in your daydreams, you see him begging for your attention, but soon you snap back to reality and everything seems hopeless again.

Of course, it is natural to feel hurt over lost love, and to miss the closeness of a relationship. But the mature person avoids wallowing in his misery. Rejection of your love by a man does not make you totally undesirable, unworthy of having anyone love you. If you feel this way, it is because you hate yourself and so cannot see anyone else love you. These are self-destructive thoughts.

You are young and attractive, and surely not the only divorcee on the horizon. You must help yourself out of your depression by becoming interested in other activities, things which will bring you into contact with other people. In this way, you will be able once again to regain your self-esteem. Participating in group activities where you will be accepted by others will do much to restore your own belief in yourself. Even more important, you will then be able to see your previous love relationship in its proper perspective—as an experience in life which should help you grow and mature.

Love is a vital element within each of us. It is a beautiful, happy, exuberant force. But merely being able to feel love is not sufficient. Only when you are at peace with yourself, your intellect, and your emotions can love bring you a sense of inner unity. Believe me, you are not compelled to play the role of Juliet in a death scene. She was young and immature. YOU have a lot of loving to give and receive, so get emotionally ready.

MARRIAGES ARE MADE IN
HEAVEN BUT LIVED
ON EARTH

BOOK THREE

MARRIAGES ARE MADE IN HEAVEN BUT LIVED ON EARTH

Introduction

It has often been said that marriages are made in heaven. The special department in heaven that is concerned with marriage must be working overtime, because more and more Americans take nuptial vows each year. No doubt this fact makes florists, photographers and caterers deliriously happy. However, it is rather disappointing to note that it did not make the brides and grooms as delighted as they had expected to be. In fact, in one out of three instances, the participants were so disappointed they rushed off to a divorce court, begging that their vows be dissolved.

Americans, who talk about marrying for love more than any other people, also break up more of their marriages. Today, unfortunately men and women study each other for three weeks, love each other for three months, fight for three years, and sometimes tolerate the situation for thirty years, and after that often rush to get a divorce.

What happened to make all these marriages end in the divorce court?

Why are so many men and women disappointed?

Many reasons have been given. Perhaps, reading the letters

that follow, a good idea of what goes wrong might be formulated. However, it is safe to say that somewhere love disappeared. One writer indicated that love eludes marital partners because they are unable to respond properly when things don't seem to go just right. True enough. Husband and wife ought to learn how to take one another in stride, whether their opinions are similar or not.

Love eludes marital partners because they don't communicate with each other. Communication signifies the desire to achieve mutual understanding, the desire to help each other live more happily. The need for communication is obvious in the story of the young married woman who was busy knitting "little things" for a blessed event which was as yet unknown to her husband. "Do you know," she began, "I visited the doctor today." "You did," replied the husband with his nose glued to the T.V. set, "and how does he feel?"

Love eludes marital partners because they demand that their check be paid in full. "I love you. Now, what are you going to do for me?" This demand, C.O.D., never works. The deepest reward for loving is the genuine joy of knowing a person like the loved one and in being grateful to God that you both exist at the same time and that He brought you together.

We have been sold the idea of always getting the best. We demand the best seats at shows, the best education, the best neighborhood, the best home, the best position, the best children. And since we have been thoroughly indoctrinated by T.V., movies and romantic fiction, many of us will settle for nothing but the best in marriage.

We proclaim that the Declaration of Independence states that the pursuit of happiness is our inalienable right, and that it includes the pursuit of a happy marriage as well. Granted! I go along with this! But if we expect to have a happy marriage as a constitutional right, without any effort on our part, we are doomed to disappointment. We certainly must realize that everything worthwhile in this world has to be worked for and earned, and to expect marital success without the exercise of effort is expecting the impossible.

It is interesting to point out that no matter what we purchase, be it a package of Uncle Ben's rice or an automatic cooking range, a booklet with instructions, carefully compiled and illustrated, is given to us. No matter what article we purchase, directions for its use are included. Business and professional or

ganizations demand that we go through a period of job orienta-
tion. But to marry all we need do is pay the appropriate fee
and say, "I do," and, presto, we are partners in a marriage
without the slightest preparation for this vital and dramatic
change in our way of living.

Society makes no demands, sets no standards, administers no
tests to people who are about to embark on the sea of matrimony.
Usually, there is more time spent in selecting the menu, ar-
ranging for the musicians and similar details than there is in
marital planning.

How strange, when you consider that marriage implies the
beginning of a new home, a new family, a new generation. Isn't
it ludicrous that we receive instructions, and take a test to obtain a driver's license, but require neither to obtain a marriage
license? Two people, barely out of their teens, unable to earn a
living, completely unaware of the challenges of marital life,
decide that "this is it!" Within a matter of weeks they are led
down the aisle to be pronounced man and wife.

Marriages fall apart because of impossible expectations and
demands of the partners, fail because neither party knew what
to expect, and very often, never expected what they got.

Marriage is more difficult in our culture today than in the
past. The changing roles of husband and wife have made it so.
The roads to follow are not clear cut. Wives now, not only care
for their homes, but attempt to carve out a career of their own
choosing.

It takes more than a marriage license to make a successful
marriage. It takes patience, understanding, communication and
compromise. Above all it takes preparation. Problems present
themselves that cannot be solved by the book. On the contrary,
the couple must face and resolve the conflict. Sometimes, they
can do this themselves. Sometimes they need the help of a marriage counselor or psychoanalytical therapy.

Read now about the problems of those who have been ill-
prepared for marriage. Are any of their problems your problems?
What is wrong in their marriages?

An unhappily married man asks how he can continue to live with a wife he can't stand.

-1-

Marital Danger Signals

THE PROBLEM

Let me tell you my story. The past 30 years of my life have been spent with a nagging, jealous, opiniated boor, who feels she knows it all and that the whole world should revolve around her. She has made and continues to make my life miserable. I have to be at her beck and call, always ready to cater to her every whim. Believe me, not even an emperor in former centuries enjoyed the fantastic luxuries demanded by this egocentric woman.

She struts around the house as if the Almighty created only her and presented her as a gift to mankind. Conditions in the house must suit her every neurotic need and wish. Things are always too noisy for no radio can play, no television can be heard, the hi fi must be silenced. "I cannot think when there is noise," is her comment, just as if she were pondering the landing of a man on Mars.

She is devoid of warmth and affection, is constantly criticizing my every move, is completely domineering, demanding, demanding, demanding. When she is not demanding she is finding fault.

Inwardly, I hate her, hate her with every fiber in my body; yet, I cannot seem to break out of this emotional prison. Talk about mental cruelty—if this were a criminal wrong, my wife should get a life-term sentence.

All through my marital years, I have suppressed my true feelings. I have dared not speak out about what bothers me because my wife explodes at the slightest imagined threat to her security. To secure temporary peace, I play the role of yes-man, and I pay a terrible price for this false truce. I have forfeited my self-esteem, submerged my ego, sunk my spontaneity. I have substituted a hollow illusion of a relationship for its reality. How I would love to take off with someone else—a mate to whom I can relate and who will relate to me.

I guess I neglected to say that I have two married children and 4 grandchildren. It is my feeling that both my daughters feel that I have been pushed around long enough. I doubt that they would hold it against me if I left my wife to find some happiness with another woman.

The most terrible part of all this is that my wife wears a halo that fits tightly around her head, a halo she keeps polishing day after day. She imagines herself to be the model of goodness, a prize among prizes; she constantly talks to the Almighty, and from time to time imagines that she gets answers. Don't for one minute think that she is insane. Nothing like it. She makes everyone around her insane.

It is time that the women of the world stopped thinking that they are constantly sacrificing their lives for men, that they are constantly on the giving end. If men do not live as long as women, it is because women insidiously and cleverly, shorten the lives of their mates. Whoever says they are the weaker sex? Nonsense! Rot and rubbish!

Tell me, good Doctor, how do I solve my problem? How do I change or get rid of a nag? How do I convince her that I, too, have the right to live in my own little place in the sun?

Marriages may be made in heaven, but to secure true happiness, we first must meet our true love. I didn't even meet a reasonable facsimile.

THE REPLY

Nobody loves everything about everybody all the time, but you've reached the unhappy point where you can't tolerate anything about your wife. She doesn't act right, doesn't speak right, just isn't right. Maybe it's time for a change. In any event, and whatever the reason, somebody is doing something wrong. The question is: can that somebody be you? Must it, indeed, be your wife?

Where have you failed her, if failed her you have? Why must she go to such lengths to be certain that you love her? You did fall in love with her many years back! After all, there was some good you saw in your mate before she said, "I do."

Today we know that nothing in the world is static: not the stars, nor the cells in our body, nor our cultural values, nor concepts of truth, nor our relationships. In our parents' youth, *they* may have believed that once marital vows are exchanged, both partners can relax. After all, they and their traditions agreed that they were stuck together for better or worse! But our generation knows better, knows that the law of human development calls for continuous change, expansion and evolution of our personalities, for as long as we live.

How can this be done? By being ready to respond creatively to the new and unexpected. This means to develop the capacity for changing according to the needs of the situation, and to keep improving upon the past.

You cannot allow yourself to be submerged. You must labor to arouse the interest of your mate. After all, you did at one time capture the interest of your mate, and she yours. What happened? Remember, no marriage can prosper on past glories. And I sure hope your wife is reading this article as well.

Believe me, if you try and have tried to do this; if you have brought variety, purpose, vigor, excitement, as well as tenderness, concern, understanding, and affection to your marriage, and your wife has not responded, then you will have to proceed along other lines.

If your wife suffers from chronic irritability, if she is cold and nasty, if she has assigned to you a single task "Pleasing me;" if she has issued one commandment before you: "Thou shalt have no other gods before me," with her accepting the leading role, then make an end to this marriage before you find yourself on top of an emotional volcano.

It's natural to try to gratify the one we love. But it's unnatural to do so by abandoning our own personal style of life in favor of hers. Why you have done this is a question you must answer for yourself.

You have a right to enjoy life. Now get the courage, imagination, and determination to do just that. Sit down with your wife and tell her clearly and firmly that the dictatorship has now fallen, that no longer will she be the sole voting member in the household, and that if she persists she will have to live alone, that you are abdicating your position as husband. This might be the shock therapy she needs.

Of course, it is my hope that by talking this over with your wife, a common road can be found. Both of you can try to become so inviting and responsive that as the years go by, you and your wife will experience continuous surprise and appreciation, and often joy.

Marriages are made in heaven. But true happiness is manufactured right here on earth.

How can she go on living with a man she considers mean and hateful?

-2-

Marital Patience

THE PROBLEM

Though my problem is involved, I will try to make it brief and to the point. My husband is the meanest and most spiteful person that lives. Everything must be the way he wants it. I have absolutely no say and must never expect anything good for me or the children. When I speak to him, he walks away and that's that. It's like I was speaking to the wall. If it sounds good to him after some thought on his part, he'll repeat it to the children as if it were his idea, never giving me any credit at all.

He is just self-centered, comes first, second, and always. For me there is never a thought. From the very start of our marriage 45 years ago, he never gave me any money. He was the shopper, the buyer, and the doer. He bought what he thought was necessary and the fact that he was stingy made it very difficult for all of us. He always beat the children when they were small. He cursed them then and curses to this very day. He's an angry man. One word of mine and he flies off the handle and mistreats me terribly.

Our two children are now out of the house and he has become worse. He must have the last word on any subject. He speaks and he knows and he cannot be told anything different. He's constantly finding fault with me.

At the present time, I'm not well and I just can't take his anger or his screaming. I just don't know what to do. If his neurosis gets any worse and I understand it does with age, I'll just go to pieces. I might add that his own family doesn't care for him because he was an angry, self-centered man even before his marriage. Please tell me what to do.

THE REPLY

The picture you present of your marriage is one in which your husband is an aggressive, sadistic individual who makes life miserable for you. He controls the money, never has a good word for you and constantly pours out his venom against both you and the children. He is insulting, never listens, and is abusive both in words and in deeds.

At the very outset I must state that either you are a saintly person, or one who should be given a Good Housekeeping Award for patience. I say this because you have lived with your husband under these conditions for more than 45 years. Now, in the so-called golden years of your life you ask what can be done. The answer forty years ago would be quite different from the answer you will receive today.

Where were you at the very start of your marriage? Why did you suffer in silence? How come you permitted your husband to treat you with so little respect? It must be that you either were very much in love with him, or that you were extremely patient because you lacked self-confidence.

Generally, where there are marital difficulties several solutions present themselves. The injured mate can attempt to understand the situation. Why does my marital partner act this way? Why all the hostility? How do I contribute to the unhappy marriage relationship? Obtaining answers to these questions gives the husband or wife a better understanding of the problem, and offers ways of changing the situation. The unhappy mate can

attempt to alter the environment so that the actions of the partner can be modified.

Secondly, the husband or wife who feels hurt, can decide that
this marriage cannot be successful and so move for a separation
and a divorce. The tremendous divorce rate in this country at-
tests to the great number of people who move in this direction.
The men and women who end up in the divorce court indicate
they have made an error in their selection, state that they see no
way of changing, and want the marriage dissolved.

You have lived with your husband for forty-five years, attended family simchas, nursed him when he was ill. Together, you
raised children who now have homes of their own. During all
this time you steered clear of lawyers and divorce courts. You
endured where other women long ago would have decided to
terminate so unrewarding a marriage. To think of divorce at
this time is just out of the question. Both of you will remain
together until the Almighty will see fit to call one of you to Him.

Then again, to think of attempting to change your husband
at this time is equally out of the question. His behavior is rigid
and stems way back to his early growing years. His way of
handling people has been reinforced over the years. The chances
are that he will end his years with the same personality he has
today. He will bully, complain, belittle, humiliate, and think
only of his own comforts.

The best thing for you to do at the present time is to understand his own difficulties. If you succeed in understanding them,
you might find living with him a bit easier, even though not
happier.

There are many reasons why some people find it difficult to
treat other members of the family with proper respect. Generally,
it can be traced to personal fears and inferiority feelings. We
all are inclined to be more critical of the shortcomings of our
mates because we identify ourselves with them. Their shortcomings reflect on our own values and status. If we are more
sure of ourselves, of our own value and position, we could accept our own shortcomings and those of our close associates more
readily, because we would not consider them as expressions of
our value and significance.

A self-confident person is able to regard faults, limitations, and
shortcomings in their proper perspective, without unduly making them tests of special value. Respect for members of one's
family is, therefore, closely linked with self-respect. He who

fears disgrace and humiliation in the world at large becomes over-sensitive of his relatives' imperfections.

That your husband has been the tormentor is clearly evident in your letter. Yet, you are equally guilty. After all, no relationship is created by one side alone. Both parties continuously play into each other's hands, regardless how active the one and how passive the other may seem. The tormentor is no more guilty than the martyr who permits the cruelty to continue, the torment to recur. Tyranny in marriage cannot be maintained without indulgent submission; courage and self-respect always stop it.

At this stage of your life with your children out of the house, with your duties and responsibilities somewhat decreased, you have the opportunity of doing more on your own. Why not become active in organizations where your help is needed and appreciated? Why do you remain at home to be insulted and belittled? Could it be that you somehow like the position of martyr? Does it present a better picture to your children? Does it make your own inadequacies easier to live with?

Unfortunately, your husband will continue to be what he has been. He isn't going to change much during the remaining years of his life. He isn't going to change because there will be very little motivation around to get him to change. Accept this fact! Now, get out and live, do something on your own. Prove to yourself that you are worthwhile and adequate. Visit your children, but don't tell them of your years of hardship and sacrifice. Attend ladies auxiliary meetings. Go to the nearest yeshivah and help in the lunchroom. There is great satisfaction in helping to feed children. Don't spend the greater part of the day at home so that you can be insulted. Since your husband will not change, you just might change by introducing new activity into your life.

I am reasonably certain that both of you will remain married to each other to the end of your days, that you have been meant for each other, and that some good did come out of the marriage.

She recoils at his sexual advances and does everything to discourage physical intimacies.

–3–

My Wife Is Frigid

THE PROBLEM

I am married to an ice-berg, a woman who just never experiences any sexual desire. She does everything to avoid being made love to, complains constantly of headaches, backaches, indigestion, just anything to discourage my advances. It would be almost impossible for me to describe her deliberate attempts to make herself as unattractive as possible when evening rolls around. She winds a couple dozen rollers into her hair and looks as if she is wired for sound. A thick mask of cold cream is then applied to her face that makes her look like a waxed clown, to say nothing of the pair of men's socks she puts on her feet. To make the picture even more complete and more repulsive I might add, she gets into a high-necked, long-sleeved, flannel nightgown. In that outfit, she immediately extinguishes any fire that might have been burning in me.

From time to time she sleeps in another room. "Your snoring bothers me," she replies when I lift my eyes in wonder.

This lack of love and affection is undermining our marriage. A smoldering resentment is building up in me. I am beginning to hate everything she does, the way she dresses in the morning, the loud noises she makes brushing her teeth, how she sips her coffee; her very voice makes me want to commit homicide.

It is getting so that I like to remain in my office hours longer than necessary. Taking another woman out is always on my mental agenda. After all, when I don't eat at home I must eat elsewhere—and I am not talking about food either.

What bothers me the most is that during our courtship she gave me no indication of this deficiency in her make-up. She was the most adoring, most affectionate, most clinging female I ever dated. What happened to that lady who could kiss for hours in a cramped parked car? I know I am not to blame. I am as eager to make love as I ever was.

THE REPLY

The term "frigidity" is employed too loosely by too many people, husbands especially, and has been used to describe women who have never experienced sexual desire, and who do not respond to any form of stimulation. It can also be applied to unsatisfied wives whose emotions are stirred but who never experience real fulfillment in their sexual play. In a book of marriage, a noted doctor wrote: "The frigid wife is an artificial creation of unnatural circumstances."

I am not going to go into too much detail about the facts surrounding a woman who avoids sexual contact with her husband. There are many excellent books in the library that you might consult. Yet, I do wish to cite one reason that might prevail in your case.

You state in your letter that during your courtship days your wife indulged in petting and enjoyed the experience. The question that might be asked is—"What brought about this change in her?"

Today, women expect pleasure and release from tension when they indulge in sex. When a woman finds neither, she suffers nervously from her inability to attain fulfillment or, if she is never aroused at all, she is certain that something is wrong with her. With this her husband quickly agrees. A combination of these facts will cause her to develop a sense of defeat, inferiority, guilt, or failure as a woman. All this will make her recoil from her husband's advances.

This type of negative reaction eats away at the husband's life as well. He finds little joy in forcing himself on a cold, withdrawn, reluctant woman. When he does, he finds the experience belittling to himself. All this can grow and grow and grow, and if permitted to continue, the marriage is soon headed for the divorce court.

What you ought to do at the present time is to deal with the so-called frigidity before it becomes a cancer whose metastatic growth invades every part of your marriage. Don't sulk, argue, bemoan your fate. Act! Believe in the fact that doctors, who have studied this problem agree that every normal woman is able to respond warmly in her sex life. With one single exception there is no such creature as a frigid wife. That exception is the woman who was born without any genital corpuscles. This handicap is so rare that it is scarcely worth mentioning.

Havelock Ellis, in *The Sexual Impulse and the Art of Love,* advised husbands as follows:

> The main part of the task in curing sexual anesthesia in a woman must usually rest with her husband. He is by no means always equipped for this purpose. One fears that there is still too much truth in Balzac's saying that in this matter the husband is sometimes like "an orang-utan with a violin." The violin remains "anesthetic" but it is probably not the violin's fault. This is by no means to say that husbands are consciously or intentionally brutal. Certainly much brutality may be exercised by a husband in sheer ignorance from a sense of conjugal duty. But often the inexpertness is combined with a real desire to be considerate. The sad thing is indeed that the awkward husband is, in a great proportion of cases, awkward simply because he is virtuous and high-minded, has tried to live a life of chastity before marriage, and has never learned to know the nature and needs of woman. It is quite true that the very happiest marriages, marriages of life-long devotion on each side, have sometimes been made by young people who have never known anyone but each other. But this innocence is a two-edged sword and in many cases it is the other that cuts. Then the man who has faithfully lived by the rules of morality he was brought up in may find that he has thus wrecked his own domestic happiness and his wife's.

Frigidity is the end-product of any number of demoniac forces that are found in marital relationships. Included are fear of unwanted pregnancy, fear of disappointment, fears that are carried over from childhood, a sense of guilt, and sheer ignorance.

Sooner or later the people who come to my office to discuss their marital problems tell me that their sex life is not going very well. One woman indicates that her husband wants more sex than she is willing to give. Another confides that her husband doesn't make love to her enough. Husbands tell me that their wives are never really interested, that they submit to intercourse with reserved acquiescence. Some wives are shocked at what they feel are indecent proposals from their husbands, and others weep because they have been rebuffed by a puritanical man for acts which seemed both natural and fulfilling. Every couple has its own story of sexual disharmony.

You feel your wife is frigid. She may feel you are about as romantic as an ice cube. You want her to be warm, yielding, and exciting. She may say that never have you expressed any love for her, just a desire to make love. You claim she gets dressed to go to bed. She may insist that you do not bathe too often. You complain she is disinterested. She defends that she is not motivated. And both of you may be right.

Neither of you should try to sweep this situation under the rug. The more you try to hide your feelings the worse the marriage will become. And don't go in for quack remedies, old wives' tales that imply that eating garlic and gulping eggs will make your spouse more inclined to indulge in sexual activity.

Improvement in your sexual relationship rests with both of you. Neither is all right or all wrong. Something has to be done to make this facet of your lives more meaningful. If you really love one another, each of you will find the way. With this attitude, the problem aspects of your sex relationship will disappear. What you both need is professional advice, patience, understanding, and a willingness to make the marriage work.

*His wife complains that
he has no technique in
his love making, that he
is just usual and me-
chanical.*

-4-

My Wife Claims I'm a Lousy Lover

THE PROBLEM

The following poem tells my entire story. It may sound as though I am joking and treating the subject lightly but believe me that is not so. The reason for the poem was that I once attempted to discuss the problem with my wife and sent her the poem. She read it, smiled, and told me that I was right—I was and still am "a lousy lover."

So, here is the poem and my problem at one time:

I treat her kindly; wash the dishes.
On her birthday I send best wishes.
I do her shopping; prepare the dinner.
Remark to her "You sure look slimmer."
Love words to her I sweetly whisper
Even when her manner's crisper.
I feed the children; keep them quiet
Disturb the lady and I have a riot.
I never read while at the table,
Speak lovingly as I am able.
Praise the dress that she is wearing
Her eyes, her figure, and her bearing.
I say, "My darling, you're looking younger,
Even though she looks from hunger.
I'm faithful ever, always praising.
Into her eyes I keep on gazing.
I keep repeating how much I love her;
Never a glance I give another.
I groom my hair; use Karate lotion

I'm careful of my every motion.
Though hard I try, it's no use brother
I still remain a lousy lover.

That's it. No matter what I do, how hard I try, how considerate I am, when it comes to making love, my wife rates me a
failure. It's getting so I try to avoid any and all love-making
sessions, but this doesn't help. In fact, I get into more serious
trouble. What do I do?

THE REPLY

No one can deny that you are a cooperative, helpful, considerate husband. Your poem lists all your excellent qualities. Yet,
by your own admission, despite your favorable personality traits,
when it comes to the art of making love, you rate a failing mark.
But brother, this need not always be so! Since love is an art, it
can be learned. Stop washing dishes, slow down on the shopping,
cut down preparing meals. Use the time you save in consulting
some excellent books on the art of making love. I am quite
certain your wife will gladly trade in your assistance for the
new information you will pick up.

First of all, be honest with yourself. If you have a problem,
you must be sure that you recognize it. Is your problem ignorance of all the facts connected with the sexual relationship? Are
anxieties, prejudices, or tensions not permitting you to relax?
The second step is to make up your mind that you definitely
and honestly will do something about your handicap. If you
are to create the beauty of sexual love you must learn your part
and perform it with excellence. This is your personal responsibility. You love your wife and want to make her happy. Her
delight and happiness should be yours.

At the very start you must know yourself and your wife as
well. This requires experience but you can do it. It takes effort,
patience, and a keen desire to succeed. The husband who applies
himself to the task of finding out how to make his wife completely happy in his arms, builds for himself an earthly Paradise,
one that draws dividends again and again and again.

A doctor once compared sexual love with a mountainside
which a husband and wife must climb together. They climb
the mountain because they want to share the adventures along
the upward path and the superb view from the summit. Both

make the climb helping one another, adjusting their pace to one another, ascending the last steep slope side by side, and then share the sudden beauty of the valleys and skies at the moment they reach the peak.

Sexual sharing is like this. Each experience involves a great deal. Once husband and wife have learned how to help each other in sexual sharing, the fundamental harmony thus attained keys every aspect of their lives together. Remember that each person is different, with different needs and different responses. After all, you chose her because she was different from the other women you dated.

Begin with the ABC's; have a working acquaintance with anatomy. Understand that sex is beautiful.

You need not remain a "lousy lover"—not today, when there are doctors you can consult.

Should twenty-year-olds without any means of support get married?

–5–

"Look Who's Getting Married!"

THE PROBLEM

I attended a wedding ceremony the other day, sat in the chapel and observed two immature children going through the proper religious marital routine. The bride, a recent high-school graduate, was all of eighteen. The groom had only recently blown out the twenty-one candles on his three-layer cake. He was ending his junior year at one of the city colleges, with four more years of academic study ahead of him. I knew he had no visible means of support.

These two over-indulged, over-protected youngsters looked like teenagers acting out roles in a mock-marriage. They were in love, so they claimed, and had read many times that "love conquers all." Didn't T.V. scripts, night after night, portray how love and faith won over all odds?

Whenever the question of finance was brought up, the groom offered a stock answer, "My father promised to help us." The father would only smile at this and reply sheepishly, "After all, that's what a father is for."

The attitude of both makes me ill. To enter into a married relationship without assuming its responsibilities is indeed the height of immaturity and unmitigated gall. It actually negates the purposes and aims of marriage.

What has happened to the men and women of today? Where is their backbone? When will they stop imposing on parents?

THE REPLY

I go along with the idea of that parents ought to lend a hand in launching a new marriage on peaceful waters, protected from immediate financial stress and storm. However, for parents to assume the total financial burden is an act that hurts more than it benefits. Character is not molded this way, nor is bride or groom being prepared to face and lick life's challenges.

I've listened to all sorts of excuses in regard to this type of marriage.

"Why wait until he finishes school?"

"She's young and I want her off the street."

"I want to be a young grandmother."

"The kids are so much in love."

To this I give a one word answer, *humbug!*

In most cases, very little good can be found in a young man who demands that his father support his bride. He seeks a long honeymoon with his father picking up the tab. He yearns for love and romance devoid of any responsibility. Such a marriage is based upon a precarious foundation, one that is erected on a sandy insecure base.

The sudden serious illness of the sole-supporter can smash the romance to bits, ending love, romance, the home, and the marriage. How can a young man demand that his parents underwrite the total cost of his married life?—rent, food, clothing, education, insurance premiums, medical expenses, and pocket money. A marriage that requires nothing, demands nothing, and costs nothing is worth nothing—no responsibilities are exchanged, only small talk, small interests, and stale sex.

A man once told me that when he was learning to play the cello as a child, he found that it was very difficult to play the "thumb position." It hurt and he suffered pain. But he went for his lessons regularly and had to show progress. He kept practicing despite the pain. Finally, one day a callous formed on his thumb, and just in the right place. Then he was able to play it without pain.

It is very noble of parents to offer children a "start" in married life, to help out with the purchase of furniture, kitchen utensils, and other household necessities. Parents have followed this procedure for hundreds of years. Today, with children spending anywhere from sixteen to twenty-two years in school, they require this type of help even more.

Married to an attorney for eighteen months, she feels he looks down on her.

-6-

I Feel Inadequate as a Wife

THE PROBLEM

I have been married a little over eighteen months, and it seems as if my marriage is foundering. I am a high school graduate. My husband is an attorney. I never believed that my not attending college could so alter one's opinion of me, but I have found recently that my mother-in-law feels I am not really good enough for her son. My husband has never agreed with her, but neither has he taken my side. Instead, he has insisted that I defend myself, and there is no need, at any time, for him to have to defend me. But when I did, my mother-in-law was insulted.

Now my husband wants me to apologize. My problem is aggravated because my parents live on the other side of the United States. I have no one to confide in. They have advised me to join organizations, to meet friends. To some extent, I have done this. But when I ask my husband to accompany me, he refuses, saying that he is ashamed to go because we are childless.

This is my first marriage and my husband's second. At the time of our marriage my husband lied to me. He lied about his age and about his first marriage. He lied about his father being dead, when in reality, he was divorced. He led me to believe that his first marriage was childless, when in reality there is a daughter living with his first wife. When I called these things to his attention, he said that it should not matter to me whether he has lied or not.

I know that I am not perfect. I have my share of faults. I am sensitive, somewhat dependent, and have a bad temper. I am not easy to live with but I do want to save this marriage.

THE REPLY

There are many reasons why people so often find it difficult to treat other members of the family with proper respect. Whatever the reason is, it can be traced to personal fears and inferiority feelings. We are inclined to be more critical of the shortcomings of relatives because we identify with them. Their shortcomings reflect on our status. We feel ashamed of their faults, as if they were our own. If we were more sure of ourselves, of our value and position we would accept our own close associates more readily. A self-confident person is able to regard faults, limitations, and his shortcomings in their proper perspective, without making them tests of social value. Respect for members of one's family is, therefore, closely linked with self-respect.

Your in-laws have had an unsuccessful marriage. Your husband has had an unsuccessful marriage. Both have had their effect on him. Both have decreased his self-evaluation. Both you and your husband suffer from inferiority feelings. You are constantly overwhelmed with thoughts that your mother-in-law thinks little of you because you lack a college education. It might be interesting for you to determine how much of this you believe. Do you think you are inadequate? Do you believe that there is a lack in your life?

If a college education still makes a difference between your husband and yourself, then other important factors in the marriage are lacking. Perhaps your sensitivity and dependency make you less appealing. Perhaps your temper has added to your marital difficulties. A wise man counseled, "Mind your marital tongue so that your marriage is not wrecked on verbal rocks." Defend yourself if you feel the need, but insulting your mother-in-law goes beyond defense. If you permitted your temper to gain an upper hand, perhaps you owe her an apology.

She is married to a devoted, understanding man who works hard but is dull and wants to know what to do.

–7–

I'm a Bored Wife!

THE PROBLEM

My problem is rather an odd one. My husband is very steady, works hard, is devoted to the children. He is not too demanding, that is, no more than he finds necessary. Generally, he eats what I prepare, even though he makes his displeasure mildly known. He likes his home; in fact, I think he likes it rather too much.

You might, therefore, want to know the reason for my writing. Well, let me tell you. When my husband returns from his business, he wants peace and solitude, by that I mean he wants to be left alone. I want to discuss things with him, tell him what I've done during the day, ask him questions about his business. He keeps on telling me, "just leave me alone, I want to get the hum out of my system." It seems that I am spending my evenings helping my husband get the sting out of his system, and I don't like it.

What worries me is why he wants to be alone. After all, I am his wife and I want him to share things with me. If he wanted to be left so much alone, he should never have been married. Don't you think I'm right?

Frankly, all day long, I talk with friends and neighbors. When my husband finally comes home I want to talk with him. Is this such an unreasonable request? Don't think I haven't discussed this with him. Again and again, I say, "J, why can't you have a conversation with me?" That just makes things worse. He never talks after that.

My husband knows I am writing to you. In fact, he suggested it, saying that surely you would understand his point of view and make it clear to me. So I am writing now and I do expect an answer that will at least teach him to share time with me.

THE REPLY

You are right; your problem is rather an odd one. You have a sincere husband, a real friend, and yet you sign your letter, "Bored Wife."

You complain that your husband wants some private time to unwind when he returns from a day at business. Believe me, there should be a quiet time in every day for every person. In every relationship between people, there comes a time when privacy is essential. In some families in fact, a member will lock himself up in the bathroom for his private thoughts if there is no other space available.

During these private moments of thought, a person catches his breath, sort of relaxes and slows up the passing day. Private moments such as these will lessen the chances of angry words and hurt feelings because tension is decreased.

My advice to you is to coax your husband to take a 15 minute nap before dinner so that he will be in a better mood to enjoy the meal you prepared. A 15-minute breather will do wonders. He will get up refreshed, ready for you and conversation.

You must understand that your husband is silent because he wants to remove himself from the battle line. He doesn't trust his temper, is afraid he will become upset too quickly so he withdraws for an hour of privacy.

Greet your husband when he returns with a smiling face. Taking two minutes to brush your hair, redo your makeup, and greeting him cheerfully and understandingly might just set him at ease—and this is what he needs most of all.

Once again, I urge you and all married men and women to allow marital partners private moments to lick their wounds, get over the battles of the day, and do some very personal private thinking. You see, you do get this when he goes to work. He never does.

He is steady, devoted, understanding, so what if he isn't a tremendous conversationalist. Love him and live with him.

Married for twenty years she finds her home a morgue and her husband a solemn undertaker.

–8–

Twenty Years of Nothing!

THE PROBLEM

I've been married to my husband for twenty years. He's sixty years of age; I'm a young sixty-three.

From the beginning I saw peculiar traits on the part of my husband. One that bothered me the most was, that for him, there was no difference between week-days and Saturday, Sunday and holidays. They were all alike. To make matters worse, there are periods of time when he just doesn't talk to me, doesn't talk, that is, for months at a time. At my age, I just can't take such treatment any longer.

Years ago, he worked in the post office. However, since we were childless, I, too, went to work. When he was fifty-six years of age, he returned one night and said that he had quit his job. He never explained the reason to me, nor do I know why to this very day. When I asked him why, he gave me the "silent treatment," and so I stopped asking.

When he had no job, my troubles really began. He actually haunted me to give up my job. I was very happy working. The money I made helped me to accept my situation and my thoughts. After fighting me for three years to give up my job, I finally consented. Now I am a housewife.

I never realized how bad things at home were till I saw how my husband spends his time. He's in bed at 8:00 in the evening and he is up at 5:00 in the morning. I have absolutely no married life with him at all, not even simple companionship. Night after night, I face bare walls. My house is not a home but a morgue. There is no conversation and every once in a while he begins screaming so that I am ashamed to face anyone in the hall. We live in a very large apartment. I hate to walk out on him, but I can't stand the mental strain any longer.

I love life and people but my husband can't see my point of view about living. He keeps on saying that we need no other interests or people, just the two of us. But he never shows any interest in me anyhow.

My question is: Should I leave him? He's so lost in his own world he won't miss me. Should I go back to work? If I did I'd be running away from reality. When I ask him to go with me to a doctor, he says he's not sick, but I am.

He has two brothers and one sister living in different states but since they don't write to us, I don't know where to go for advice. Won't you please help me?

THE REPLY

Facts and feelings are all mixed up in your tangled marital life. Both of you entered into marriage at 40 or more years of age. In fact, you were 43 and your husband was forty. You became husband and wife with fixed ideas as to what marriage ought to give you. You wanted warmth, friendship, affection, security. From your letter it would seem as though your husband wanted a woman around the house who would make him as comfortable as possible with as little activity on his part as possible. He wanted no undue stress, no excitement, no involvement, no competition.

But you lived with this for twenty years, working part of the time, doing little for the rest. Now you ask me whether you should leave him. You, and he, too, ought to stop to think how utterly empty living would be for both of you if suddenly you did not have each other, and suddenly didn't have this center of living which is your home. At 63, I don't urge divorce, though I do counsel you to seek a job, maintain outside interests, become involved in institutions. Don't let yourself down so dreadfully. Put pleasure in your daily life. If you like people, mix with them. God has given you a great gift of a personality that is agreeable, patient, and dutiful.

Getting a job is not running away from reality, it is, rather facing it. You obtain for yourself what your husband cannot or does not give you. In your case, "diversion," not "divorce" is the answer. Diversion, that is, that purports to be interesting, productive, and socially and morally acceptable.

She fell in love with a man because of his love letters and now finds herself married to a tyrant.

–9–

My Husband: Cold, Selfish, Tyrannical and Stingy

THE PROBLEM

I married my husband in a very foolish way, so I can only blame myself for my unhappiness. He was in Europe, and through friends' recommendation, they "knew this nice woman who has a brother—etc."; we started corresponding, and for seven months letters came and went. It is my feeling, even after all this, that your letters reflect your inner life. Am I right saying this?

His letters were just beautiful. What else can I say! I went to Europe, not exactly to meet him, I did not decide it then. I had cousins in Hungary I wanted to see. I met him; he would not let me go. He cried like a baby and that also impressed me. But a man never cries like that, this I know now. Afterwards I realized that his friend's wife wrote me those wonderful letters. He did not.

Well, a man can be good without an education—sweet and loving. This man turned out to be cold, selfish, tyrannical, extremely stingy towards his own home. His whole line of family is the same. They are all selfish and stingy. If you know one, you know them all, I always said. His sister, a greedy person, put herself up as the head of the entire family. Everyone agrees with her to humor her. She lives in another city. Many times she came to us and took over the house, being very handy and efficient. I put up with this for 20 years, but thank goodness, finally too late though, I told her off.

My husband lives in a fool's paradise. He imagines himself to be a good business man, borrows money from the bank to build up a stock. He has a few stores, has a good line of work. In five years he could have a gold mine if he didn't borrow, build, and continue to buy.

He gives me $150 a week for the house which covers fuel, doctor bills, blue cross, and all the things imaginable. I must be a magician to be able to manage. Ever so often, when he doesn't like a meal, he exclaims, "I give you $150 a week and this entire meal didn't cost you two dollars." No matter how I explain it, he complains I am not spending enough for food.

I have two boys. The younger one is more like his father than the older one. He wants business and at 19 has a business of his own. The older boy, 22, is impossible to live with—selfish, indifferent, self-centered, disorganized. Both demand everything and hardly tolerate me. The older one is a free loader, taking but never giving.

My husband is living in a world of his own, in a sense of grandeur, false prosperity. I am trying now to build a fund for myself. For the past 2 years I've worked in an office. I'll be 60 at my next birthday.

I feel that every door is closed for me, and my only escape is if I die. I have forgotten how to laugh, and my children never even learned that. You see, he was not a good father either. He used to go to business daily and even on Saturday, though his religious partner remained at home. My children never enjoyed their father. My older son wanted him so badly; it was heartbreaking to watch him.

What do you advise me to do? How can I help myself and make the most of my remaining years?

THE REPLY

Of all human relationships, marriage is the most complicated. Few relationships can produce such extremes of emotion or can so quickly travel from extreme bliss to ice, with each side blaming the other. Each partner strives to improve the other; yet does not seek self-improvement. I wonder how much more meaningful marriage would be if there was some genuine, deep self-examination.

Now, won't you please re-read parts of your own letter. You received beautiful love letters from your husband and accuse him of having them written for him. Does this fact make the letters false, unreal, without feeling? If this is so, not one of us should ever purchase and send a printed birthday, anniversary, father's day, mother's day card. He did ask, plead, coax someone to express his love in better language. Looking down at this effort of his puts you in a bad light.

He is interested in business, borrows money to increase his stock, is attempting to expand. You belittle his efforts and attempt to substitute your business judgment for his. What makes you believe that your judgment is superior to his, his accountants, and business partners?

You call him and your sons selfish, inconsiderate, cold, self-centered, disorganized, to list but a few of the adjectives you use so freely. Are you in any way responsible for the way your sons have turned out? You claim that he spent little time with his children. How did they take on the very characteristics that are so hateful to you? Where was your influence, your motivation, your teaching, your guidance? How come your children barely tolerate you?

You claim he is stingy giving you $150 a week for a family of four adults. He claims that your dinner meals do not indicate an expenditure of two dollars. Surely, something is wrong with your budget (income or/and expense) if you cannot prepare one good, nutritious meal a day. In every area you claim the men in your home to be in the wrong and you are in the right. My own feeling is that there is a great deal of misconception on both your parts. Let me explain.

All through your marriage you have felt that you "married your husband in a very foolish way," whatever that might mean to you. He was impressed with you, of this there is no doubt. He professed his love with great sincere emotion, and finally you accepted his proposal of marriage.

Where did things go astray? What made him cold after marriage when he was so warm prior to marriage? As our youngsters would say, "What turned him off?" How did you disappoint him?

I bring all this up because I feel that both of you, having invested so many years in this marriage, ought to work hard to salvage what is left. I know you agree because nowhere in the letter do you suggest even a thought of divorce.

To begin with it might be wise for you to determine why you are in total disagreement with your husband, your sons, and your husband's family. They are all "real and alive" and have to be lived with. Turn the magnifying glass on yourself, be frank, honest, and objective, and then change if you have to.

You feel your husband is stingy; he feels you are not giving him an even break with meals. Why not change the budget where all expenses are paid for by him and you get a generous allowance for "table money." This will allow you to prepare better and more adequate meals, and at the same time demonstrate to him that you cannot have steak and chops with an insufficient allowance. You will benefit in either way.

Don't interfere with his business acumen. In fact, I would praise him for his initiative, strength of purpose, devotion to his business. Why belittle him, shatter his financial dreams when you yourself believe he does have a gold mine! In other words, communicate with him on a higher level. This in no way implies subjugation, subordination, or self-denial. It is an active way of communication which deals with the wishes of another person. Love in this sense is not surrender but lively participation. Harry Stack Sullivan defines love as the ability to consider the satisfactions and security of another almost as important as your own. There is no higher level. Blessed indeed are the marriage partners who can function on this level!

You don't have to die, not at all. There is so much you have to live for—engagements and marriages, being a grandmother and feeling fulfilled as a human being. In other words, there is more to life than being a wife, mother, and grandmother; a very important facet of living is being yourself.

Now go out and improve yourself first. It is high time you did learn to smile. Who knows it might become contagious in your home and will spread to your husband and sons. It is worth striving for.

For 24 years my husband keeps threatening that he will divorce me because he claims that I lied to him.

– 10 –

It's Spit, Not Rain

THE PROBLEM

I am married almost twenty-four years and have three children. From the first week of our life together my husband has wanted a divorce and it was only because I went to our Rabbi that he stayed with me—but my life has been most unhappy.

His charges against me have to do with things that had their origin before we were married. He says I lied to him about a former boy-friend and gifts he had given me. My husband had compiled a list of questions—all pertaining to this former friend and my relationship with him, and wanted me to answer them with my hand on a bible. Dr. Mandel, for the sake of keeping this marriage together I tried, but everything I said made him question me deeper like a district attorney trying to prove that I am a liar. Finally, I said I would answer no more questions and he should leave me alone. He calls me a liar and a cheat constantly.

My husband has a very responsible position which pays adequately but for the past ten years he has worked at night too, Monday through Friday. No matter how much I pleaded that the children need a father at home, he said the second job was his *security*. He would accumulate enough money so he could leave me, whenever he felt like it.

For the past few years he has taken to going out with the boys on Sunday nights. At first I didn't care because I work too, and I can't run with him—and he said he needed this relaxation to enable him to work on two jobs. Now, for over a year he goes out with the boys Saturday and Sunday nights. He says he has wasted enough of his life with me—he does not enjoy my company and will not spend time with me. So I sit home every weekend. The few friends we had together I have lost contact with. If I say anything, he answers, "You made your bed, lie in it." If I don't like this arrangement he will MOVE OUT.

He has never developed any type of relationship that has a deep meaning with the children, though when it comes to money he gives them whatever they want. All their heartaches and frustrations they bring to me—and believe me, there have been many. If I say anything to them about going to their father, they answer, "We can't talk to him." The children are extremely bright in school, but I feel they sense things are not right between us, and now they are most unhappy, especially my daughter.

Now, let me tell you about myself. I am a college graduate who has been teaching school for the past few years. All the money I have earned has been used by the family for private colleges, furniture, camps, and other such necessary luxuries. At one time I was pretty, but now the years have taken a toll of me.

I don't want a divorce but my husband doesn't want to have anything to do with me. I just don't know how much longer I can stand to see my husband get dressed up in his finest clothing and go out by himself until the wee hours of the morning. I ask you: "What should I do?"

THE REPLY

A sailing vessel without any destination just drifts; it is carried along by the tides and winds, sometimes high, sometimes low. It groans and creaks in the high seas, and remains almost stationary in the calm. It follows the actions of the seas, doing what the winds, tides, and seas do. They are its master; it is their slave.

Your marriage is just like this. It remains afloat but has no direction, and having no direction, it goes nowhere. It is subservient to the environmental factors that prevail. You are more concerned about what other people will say than about yourself and your family. You lack self-respect and find it hard to tell the difference between "rain" and "spit." You have failed to set up a set of private personal values and so you end up disillusioned, disappointed, frustrated, and in emotional debt.

The success or failure of a marriage depends very largely upon the personalities of the husband and the wife—their dispositions and patterns of behavior, the maturity of their thinking, the amount of love they have for one another. People with neurotic personalities find it difficult to make a good adjustment in any human relationship, especially in marriage. When such people marry they carry over their neurotic form of behavior into their marital association.

Your husband's actions are those of an immature person, who cannot think logically and cannot control his expressions and actions. One of the signs of maturity is the ability to share love and affection, to actually care for someone; a genuine desire to share with another person, to share thoughts, feelings and possessions. There is the desire not only to be happy but to give happiness, not only to obtain satisfaction but to give satisfaction to a mate. A mature person is able to cooperate with other people, to make the necessary adjustments and adaptations to life.

Without such deep feelings between husband and wife no genuine marital relationship can develop. Without love there can be no marital happiness, no marital satisfaction, no satisfactory living together. Love calls for a genuine concern for the other person's welfare, a deep abiding desire to contribute to the other's emotional needs, to help a mate grow and develop.

You have nothing at all. You are a slave to the idea of "just being married." It is not possible for you to happily accept a position of subservience. You cannot live fruitfully if your husband rules and forces and you just obey. No person can bear a position of inferiority without anger and disgust. No son or daughter can adopt proper marital attitudes if one of the parents is being mistreated. To have a marriage you must feel needed, worthwhile, and that you are a full, active partner in a meaningful relationship. You have none of this!

You are making things too simple for your husband. He really has his cake and eats it too. He has a family, a home, even a willing wife; all this he has without giving up his independence. He goes out on the town every weekend and leaves you behind, adding insult to injury by telling you "that's how it is, if you don't like it, I'll move."

Make him move! Don't be his substitute wife, his servant, his housekeeper, the guardian of his children. Demand your rights or ask him to live elsewhere. Surely, somewhere in your makeup you can find the strength and courage to defend and protect your self-respect. Just being married for the neighbors' sake is senseless.

If you were once pretty, you'd better see to it that you are good to look at once again. To let time take advantage of your femininity is to permit yourself to be robbed in broad daylight. Today, no woman has the right to look plain, not with what can be bought in jars, tubes, and bottles, not to mention wise investments with the beauty-parlor and a few good dress shops.

You are a teacher; why don't you use some common sense! Skip a summer camp for your college children, and spend your summer check on yourself. Dress better, look better, and perhaps you will even get to feel better. The thing you cannot do is to continue feeling sorry for yourself. Only you can make yourself unhappy, and surely you are unhappy if you permit yourself to be the punching bag. Stop complaining and do something. Your husband has no respect for you. He has demonstrated this all through the years of your married life. Perhaps he does this because you show no respect for yourself.

I recall the words of a writer who exclaimed: "O marriage! marriage! what a curse is thine, where hands alone consent, and hearts abhor."

A married woman who finds married life dull and monotonous, and the woman's role insipid.

– 11 –

Marriage Isn't Everything!

THE PROBLEM

I'm mature enough to understand that romance isn't lasting, that being married isn't the sum total of a girl's happiness. There was a time when I believed that should I find a mate and a decent married life, the world would belong to me. That's what I thought years ago.

Now, I am thirty-nine years of age, married and the mother of two young children. My husband is no better and no worse than the average married man. He has his good points and his variety of quirks. I've learned to live with him and accept all the little things about him that irk me. We go out once in a while, though a good deal of the time he reads a book as I watch television programs.

My children are growing up. I'm not the kind of a mother who believes that a life should be lived only for children. I care for their needs, send them to school each morning, and await their arrival home with cake and milk.

My house is neat and clean. I'm not a bug about cleanliness because I believe a house is a home, and a home should look as if it is lived in. Yet, each morning I dutifully dust, sweep, put things away, prepare meals, answer telephone calls, take messages, and then think.

I think about the monotony of married life, the dull regularity of daily living, the insipid role of the woman and I want to scream out in protest. "Is this living?" I yearn to proclaim, "Can't life be made more interesting?" I demand. Unfortunately, I get no answers.

Frankly, since you are a male, I expect no help from you

either. I find myself writing to you because you seem to have all the answers. Do you have one for me? But whatever you do, don't tell me how fortunate I am to be married and have children. If you do I'll scream!

THE REPLY

The world is conquering space, of this there is no doubt. Only recently man walked on the moon. An American flag has been planted in moon soil. We, the men and women of this century, were not content to think about space. We wanted landmarks in the great wide expanse of the heavens, platforms for our satellites, visualized our space ships soaring about. We demanded to comprehend space, to define it, and in the greater sense, to use it.

Now, our problem is to conquer time. This we know. To us, time is limited. Each of us is given a ration of time to use in whatever way we see fit. What we do with our allotment of time is our concern or should be. I am not referring to the overall large amount of time, but rather with the smaller units of time within our grasp: tomorrow, next week, the next hour, or the very present.

Living a life is like building a house. You have a certain space in which to build it. Some people do much with the building lot, make their houses beautiful places, warmly furnished. Others use no imagination and the result is box rooms. Life is like that, except instead of building with feet and inches we build with hours and days. How meaningful the words of Disraeli: "Life is too short to be little."

If your life is monotonous, blame yourself. If your frustration is great because your life is filled with dull little things, take careful inventory of how you fill time. All of us dread throwing away our lives, yet we do this by wasting days, or in other words, using up our lives by throwing it away piecemeal.

An American educator once asked the question: "Is your life a brush-pile or a tree?" The contrast is apparent. The brush-pile is a heap of cut and broken branches. From a distance it may look like a tree, but its branches have no communion with the living stem. They are in the process of decay while the tree is still alive, its branches vitally related one to another. They feed upon soil and sun and bring forth flower and fruit.

You feel your life is empty. You are hungry for recognition.

You ask yourself, "What shall I do next?", or, "How do I bring a bit of excitement into my life?" It could be that being a wife and a mother is not enough for you, though I know it would make thousands of women happy and vibrant. (Go ahead and scream if you wish.) However, you need more.

I find no fault with your great desire to do more, to produce, to create, to find additional meaning and purpose in life. What I abhor is your doing nothing except complain, and looking to others to find something for you to do. You have control over a good deal of the time you are using. You have the power to so structure time as to give you ample rewards.

You might develop a few relationships with interesting people. Give and share the spontaneous expressions of joy. This will make you feel free—free to accept the duties of wifehood and motherhood minus frustration, that is. Getting to know people is an interesting experience because it makes for an exchange of interests and ideas. Together, you might explore the city, browse through museums and libraries, walk through parks, visit famous landmarks.

What you must understand is that time itself is nothing. It is what you put into time that counts. Again I repeat you are master of some of the time during the day; use that part in such a way as to pay you the greatest dividends. I say to you what one man said to another: "Your calendar shows the passing of time. Your face shows what you are doing with it."

A wise man once wrote: "Keep forever in view the momentous value of life; aim at its worthiest use—its sublimest end; spurn, with disdain those foolish trifles and frivolous vanities, which so often consume life, as the locusts did Egypt; and devote yourself with the ardor of a passion, to attain the most divine improvements of the human soul." "There is a time to be born, and a time to die," wrote Solomon, and it is the memento of a truly wise man; "but there is an interval of time between these two times of infinite importance to all of us."

What a fortunate woman you are, to be blessed with a loving husband and two healthy children! You are indeed rich and don't know how to use or count your wealth. Now, stop killing time. Did you ever come across this notice in the lost and found column of a newspaper: "Lost, yesterday, somewhere between sunrise and sunset, two golden hours, each set with sixty diamond minutes. No reward is offered, for they are gone forever!"

What time of the day is it now? And what are you doing?

Have your children gone off to school? Is your home neat? Have the beds been made and the dishes put away? Is the dinner ready for final preparation? If you have answered yes to all of the above, then part of the rest of the day belongs to you alone. Can you imagine? You are the owner, the king, the dictator of that time! In a few hours that time will be lost, gone forever. How you fill it belongs to you.

There are elderly lonely people in hospitals and senior citizen homes. Why not visit with some of them and bring a bit of sunshine into their dull lives? It makes no difference that they are not relatives of yours. They are human, created by the hand of God, and need a bit of warm sunshine. There are telephone campaigns to be helped, solicitations for schools, hospitals, synagogues.

You have two eyes for seeing, two feet for walking, two ears for hearing. Jump for joy, sing a song, offer a prayer of thanks. You have "all this and heaven too." There is much you can do to change each day. To begin with, you can try to change yourself, for the better, I mean.

Dear wife and mother: I don't have all the answers, but I do know what ails you. You're doing nothing with your legacy of time and you feel guilty about this neglect. So, get out and use it. Remember, "he lives long that lives well, and time misspent is not time lived, but lost."

Her husband hates to part with money, never takes her out, always finds fault, and shows her no love. Can she be helped?

– 12 –

My Husband Doesn't Love Me!

THE PROBLEM

I am married almost twenty-four years, have two children; one of them goes to business. My problem stems from my husband. I really don't know where to begin. He is a hard working man, never gambled nor drank, but he has a terrible temper, and is also very stubborn. He is very nice to other people and gets along with everyone, but to me and the children, it is just the opposite. He insults us, never has a kind word, refuses to take me out. I would be satisfied with a ride in his car, or a visit to relatives, but he refuses. His excuse is that he works hard all week. Or, he just refuses, gives no reason at all.

I have a nerve condition and it seems to be getting worse. The doctor said I must go out and be with people. All day long I am in the house, alone, as I don't go out alone. I also don't feel well. I went through plenty, such as surgery and other trouble. Where I live I have no friends. Most of them go to work. I can't go out or travel alone as I panic and tremble.

I take care of the house and make the meals. The house is kept clean and I am very particular about my appearance. I am in my forties and look much younger, even with all my troubles. I am considered nice looking.

My husband won't allow me to buy anything for the house or for any of us, even the smallest item. There are always arguments. He gives me table money and that is all. He pays the rent, etc. He hates to part with a nickel.

I am not extravagant, but I would like to go out; maybe my nerves would get better and I would have peace at home.

He is always finding fault and yelling. I know my husband is not in love with me. I have spoken to him about it and he keeps saying I am not well.

My life is very dull. I go to sleep crying and get up crying. I don't feel sorry for myself, but I would like a little happiness. I have spoken to my Rabbi. Many years ago, we went for counseling, but it didn't do any good. Now he refuses to go for help and won't talk to my Rabbi. He says I can do whatever I want, he won't change.

I have no family here, but his family has told me to leave him. I don't know what to do in my condition, which way to turn. I will do whatever you tell me.

THE REPLY

There are many things you say about your husband. At the best, he is hard-working, and neither drinks nor gambles. After that, he is stingy, doesn't want to go out, has a terrible temper, doesn't permit you to buy things for the house, belittles you and the children, and argues constantly. You have come to the conclusion that he no longer loves you.

Now, what about yourself? You claim you are neat, attractive, keep the house in order, prepare the meals, though you suffer from a nerve condition. You indicate that you are doing your job; he feels you are not well.

There is something wrong with facts as they are given. Why doesn't your husband want to take you out? After all, you are not demanding much—a ride in the car, a visit with relatives. As tired as he might be, there is always one day a week, or one hour for that matter, when he could feel sufficiently rested to take you out, especially if you are well dressed and good to look at. Again I ask: What is wrong?

There is an old-time riddle which asks: "Which came first, the chicken or the egg?" I now ask you, which came first: your constant crying, nervousness and complaining, or his desire not to leave the house? If going out with you means listening to a long account of your aches and pains, your sufferings and hardships, I understand his wanting to remain at home, eyes glued to a television set. It is simpler for him to turn off your complaints at home, than in a car, and it is less expensive. In other words, tensions spring directly from the impact of two personalities upon one another.

Every husband, as well as every wife, harbors a long series of wishes which he strives to fulfill, and a number of sensitive areas which he must shield. Marriage entails the sacrifice of many, of these ambitions and the exposure of some sensitive areas. You have a marriage of 24 years duration. How well do you know your husband? How well do you understand his needs?

I cannot excuse the behavior of your husband in yelling, being stingy, arguing with you and the children, belittling your endeavors. He is absolutely wrong with this type of behavior. Perhaps in your former counseling sessions, you discussed this with the therapist. I do believe counseling in regard to these items can and will produce improved conditions.

Though there is little doubt in my own mind about your personal unhappiness, yet I feel your account of your married life, though accurate as far as it goes, is not the complete story. There are discordant elements in your marriage. Internal circumstances have separated you from your husband and very often you make each other miserable. Nevertheless, you have remained together for 24 years. Whatever your married life is, it is evidently more satisfying than any other. What you would like to have is a bit of social life, and this you can have. Social evenings can be arranged by the woman in the household. If your husband does not like to leave the house, then you invite company to the house. This brings up another matter. How come you don't have a single friend? It is rather strange for a woman to be so friendless. Look into this odd situation, and correct it. Are people shying away from you because of your panicky attitudes?

What can you do to relieve the tension and the monotony of your marriage? Right now you and your husband are constantly intensifying your difficulties with your course of action. Both of you can attempt to understand one another and then work toward a fruitful compromise. This is better than an intensification of antagonism. No program for handling marital difficulties can be successful unless it takes into account the meaning of the difficulties to the particular people involved— you and your husband.

If I were treating you, I would try to help you understand the meaning of your difficulties in terms of your deeper needs and desires. In this way, you (both of you) would be in a position to work out an intelligent, workable compromise between the conflicting aims of your husband and yourself. Without a spirit of sympathy and understanding, very little can be accomplished.

Try to believe that your husband does love you. Going out often does not by itself indicate love, nor does the lack of going out indicate an absence of love. Try to stop complaining about your varied aches and pains. Greet your husband (do it even if it hurts) with a smile when he returns from work. Be well groomed, as if on a first date. Look feminine, and act feminine.

The worst thing you can do is to divorce your husband. Relatives and friends who advise you to shed him are completely unfamiliar with life as a divorcee. Why amputate when you can do some doctoring!

So, I end the way I begin. When a man doesn't want to take his wife out at least once a week or once a month, the woman ought to look to herself for the cause. Do some self-examination and come to some genuine realizations. Your marriage will improve, believe it, there is great hope for it.

A final word—make some friends on the street, and when you do, remember an age-old adage. When you smile, the world smiles with you; when you cry, you cry alone. Don't swap emotional symptoms with friends and neighbors—recipes, yes, but not frustrations, disappointments, and animosities. That, most people can get listening to the news of the day.

It's all up to you! The strength of a woman is unbelievable, when she has the motivation to begin and the patience to see it through.

*My husband tells me he
no longer loves me the
way he used to, and has
fallen in love with a
more exciting woman.*

-13-

I'm Losing My Husband

THE PROBLEM

My husband and I have been married a little more than 12 years. We now have three children, and he says he doesn't know me and can't talk to me. He says he no longer loves me the way he did when we first married, wants to recapture the magic, but it just doesn't return.

About 5 months ago, he said he had to go out alone at night for a while to clear his head. He went out regularly from 8:00 P.M. to 12:30 or 1 A.M. When he returned I was not supposed to ask him where he had been, nor what he had done. I never could go to sleep until he returned.

In May I noticed he was very disturbed and I questioned him about it. He wouldn't talk then, but two months later, he said he'd been having an affair with a non-Jewish girl. He indicated that he loved her the way he once loved me. She had brought the magic back, but he still loved me as a mother. He didn't know what to do. He loved her but felt he owed the children and me some responsibility. He said I was too good for him, but at the same time made him feel guilty by not demanding too much from him. He told me that if I would forgive him, he would not see her any longer. I did because I really love him. He still goes out but he doesn't see her though she has called him at the office. We have tried to make a go of it, but he insists it isn't working out.

This weekend we had an argument because I complained about his leaving me 6 nights a week alone. He answered: "Tough luck. That is how it is going to be." We argued back and forth. I was crying, which he says he hates, because he's not worth my tears. He then went to our room, packed a box and a suitcase and said he was leaving.

Just then my father and my children came into the house, took notice of what was going on. My 11-year-old son asked him where he was going, and my husband answered that since we did not need him, he was going away for good. Both my father and my son told my husband how much he was needed in the house.

Later, my husband took my father home. He said he'd be back in a little while. He returned five hours later and told me that he would stay but only on his terms. He unpacked and told me he wasn't ready to leave now, but had he had lots of money he would have left long ago. He even named some bachelor friends of his who would be glad to marry me. I told him I wasn't interested in his being a "Shadchen," I was happy with him and thought he was happy with me.

Unfortunately, I can't talk to his father who tells me I should give my husband time for himself. He never even said a word to him. Please advise me what can be done. The children and I really love him. I told them that Daddy is nervous and that they should not yell in the house.

I did many things in the house: recovered the chairs, bought an old piano and scraped it down and refinished it all alone. It means nothing to him. I hope you will give me a directive because I don't believe he really wants to go, or change anything. He's striking out because he's unhappy in his work but won't leave his father to work for someone else. He feels he has been good to everyone but that no one appreciates him. He's disappointed he hasn't made it big like some of his former friends. When he was young he always had things his way. What can I do to keep this marriage alive? Please help me.

THE REPLY

There are several things your husband has said which clearly spell out the truth. I agree with him when he says that he's not worth your tears. I concur with him when he says you're too good for him. I'm even of the opinion that had he had the money months ago, he would have taken off with his girl friend, taken off, that is, to locate and recapture the magic that he finds missing in you. The truth is, your husband has not grown up yet. He wants his cake and wants to eat it as well—wants his freedom and his dependence, both at the same time. That he has not left you is not an evidence of love but rather a fear of not making the grade with his second.

A person is like a steam boiler; he can contain so much before he blows his lid. In order to avoid an explosion, there is some kind of valve on a boiler which permits the steam to escape periodically. Your husband is not a boiler; he is a human being and therefore has no valve in his head. He is a disgruntled, disappointed individual who, like anyone else, must let off steam from time to time.

Some men who are disappointed with life and some of the frustration it deals, turn to drink. Some turn to cards, and still others turn to women. Your husband chose the latter. Any one of these vices is difficult to lick, but the hardest one for a wife to swallow is the other woman. Not only does she miss having his companionship, intimacy, and all the other pleasurable things that come with having a man around the house, but she feels ashamed of his behavior in the eyes of people, as well as the terrible pain of rejection.

Your husband is certain of your love for him, and perhaps he does love you. Can you think of a better person to whip for one's personal failures, for feelings of inadequacy than the person who loves you unfalteringly, the person who loves you despite the shame and pain inflicted upon you? Why shouldn't he pretend to be leaving when he knows you will plead with him to stay? Why should he not go out night after night, coming home at whatever hour suits him, when he knows for sure that his ever-loving wife will forgive? He is punishing you because he knows he can get away with it. I wonder how your husband would react if the situation were reversed, if you packed your things, took the children, and left him an empty house. You know, he might just forget the "magic" he is obsessed with and come pleading for wife, children, and a home. Did you ever think of the results that would follow if you were a bit firmer with him? It is a thought, isn't it?

Love is a very beautiful, gentle thing and must be nurtured and fed daily so that it can stay alive. Somewhere along the line both you and your husband failed one another. I cannot think of a wrong and right in such a situation. Perhaps, one is more guilty than the other, but there are two of you. The action of one brought about what may have been the wrong reaction of the other. Your husband is not successful and so he takes it out on you, the patient, loving, dedicated, hard working wife. Sometimes too much acceptance gives the other partner just too much guilt feeling. Of this you can be certain, complete compromise on your part is no solution—begging a man to stay is just not worth what you get.

I imagine you are both still young, since your children are young. I doubt that you can settle your differences alone. I don't believe either his father or your father can or should interfere. Your marriage is sick and you need a doctor, one who can tell both of you where you are failing one another.

Of this be certain: you cannot allow yourself to be humiliated. You cannot allow your husband to be both married and single at the same time. He cannot have his pie and eat it as well. There is no marriage if you have to purr when he pats you on the head as you lick his feet. To be a mother, wife, shopper, maid, cook, baby-sitter, and part time lover and get absolutely nothing in return is an act of bankruptcy. Stop it!

What should a husband do who feels his wife has no taste in her choice of clothing, nor a desire to dress up.

-14-

My Wife Doesn't Dress Up for Me!

THE PROBLEM

The only thing that kept me from writing to you was the fact that so few letters are published in your column that are written by men. I don't know whether you favor the women, or that men feel less inclined to write. However, this doubt will be cleared up in my mind if I see my letter published in your column.

My problem is a simple one though quite serious to me. We've been married five years and have one child. My wife keeps a good home, is a good mother, and I think she is devoted to me, as I am to her. I can't complain about the meals nor her attitude to my family. All is well.

Yet, there is a serious fault in her behavior that sometimes just turns me off. She doesn't dress tastefully, nor is it as feminine as I'd like it to be. I can't understand her because her friends always look as though they are in the height of taste and fashion. My wife is quite content to wear the same "going out" dress week after week, nor does she bother to change her shoes. Inwardly, I dream of her dressed the way I'd like her to be. Going home on the train I compare her to other women as far as clothing is concerned and she comes out second best.

There is no doubt that I love her, but I wonder if my love will diminish because of her attitude toward dress. Is there anything wrong with me if I want a beautiful aroma of perfume around her? Is there anything wrong with me if I want her to be attractive, feminine, and well dressed? And if there is nothing wrong with me, what in the world is wrong with her?

Please don't minimize this imperfection in her behavior and don't tell me to be satisfied with her other good qualities. I'd go with less food, with a house that isn't perfectly clean if I could get my wife to dress the way I want her to dress.

THE REPLY

There are a few things that never go out of style and a feminine woman is one of them. How beautifully have poets and writers described women:

"A handsome woman is a jewel."

"Women are the poetry of the world in the same way as the stars are the poetry of the heavens."

"Without women this world would be drab indeed."

I agree with all and would include a hundred other descriptions of my own because I feel that the Almighty has placed the genius of women in their hearts, because the works of women are always works of love.

Generally, women are very concerned about their appearance. Isn't this a major reason for the success of the cosmetic industry, to say nothing about dresses, shoes, perfumes, hats, hair-pieces?

In fact, any woman who is less than attractive and feminine to-day has herself to blame. With all this I have heard it said that beauty is the first gift nature gives to a woman.

The question in my mind is, why doesn't your wife take advantage of what can be purchased in a bottle, a jar, a tube, or at the dressmaker, perfumery, or beauty parlor? Several answers come to my mind. She doesn't have the money. Or, she doesn't have the motivation. Or, she doesn't have the taste. You have the power to clear up each of these situations.

Increase her allowance and indicate that it is to be spent for clothing. I can hardly think of the woman who will turn down the statement, "Honey, here is $100, please buy yourself a new outfit." It takes money to be attractive in the manner you hint at. Beauty parlors demand payment. Perfumes are expensive. Shoes and boots, if they are fashionable and feminine, go at high prices. Demanding that she have these things without making them financially possible is asking for the impossible. So, dig down into your pocket and give the love of your life the means by which she can satisfy your taste.

What about the motivation? You do know what motivation means, don't you? To make it even clearer I'd like to put a few questions to you. How are you dressed? Do you take her to a Saturday night movie, dressed in an old pair of pants, and needing a shave? That's hardly motivation for her to spend an hour before the mirror. And how often do you praise her, praise her for her natural good looks? You know, it has been said "Beauty is in the eyes of the beholder."

And now let's get to understanding your needs. Have you told her that you would like her to be dressed more fashionably, that it is important to you for her to wear the type of clothing you like? It doesn't belittle you one bit if you clearly and definitely tell her the type of hat, the type of dress, the type of shoes that you would like her to wear. Most wives would be delighted to be made aware that their husbands are that interested in their wearing apparel.

Which really leads me to the final thought, that she doesn't have the taste. You might just take exception to what I am about to suggest, but were I in your position, I would not hesitate. You have the faculty of admiring clothes on others and you know what you want to see. Be practical, be realistic, be smart—go shopping with her. Your wife would be delighted especially if you pick up the bills. Then you can help your wife select the things you would like her to wear. Your going with her would be the right motivation. She would understand your needs and you would make all the purchases financially possible. A practical solution, isn't it? Then, go ahead and try it. And when she is dressed the way you like, remember to tell her how lovely she looks. Telling a woman she is beautiful will help add perfume to the flower.

The mother of 5 children, she yearns to make something of herself.

– 15 –

I, Too, Am a Human Being!

THE PROBLEM

I am a young-looking, well-educated mother of five lovely children. Only two attend school. Thus I am at home with the two toddlers and the baby. "Boys will be boys," and they certainly are. I am kept on my toes constantly, for they are alert, active mischievous children.

Somehow, insidiously, during the 11 years of our marriage, I have slowly been divested of my self-respect. Though the children have been taught to respect my husband as well as the strap, they managed to walk all over me. I realize that I do too much for everyone, especially the two in school. I take a great deal of interest in their school work, because, after all, I am a teacher as well as a mother. I constantly feel that everyone is making demands upon me. Most of the time, I'm not a "person," not a "me," but a "thing," a piece of machinery that sees to it that meals are served, laundry is done and time schedules are met.

Does it sound strange to you that I have needs too, that are not being met at home? I must be myself again. I have rather sadly, or is it wisely, come to the conclusion that I must satisfy my needs away from my family. Why must I manage the house without household help, or help from my husband, and enjoy my chores because my husband says I must?

Doesn't it make a lot more sense for me to return to teaching on a part-time basis and to hire a woman to care for the apartment as well as the children? I delight in teaching and working with children. I know that I can enjoy my own children more when I've been away from them for part of the day.

My family needs to know that I am a person, too. I feel that I must resume teaching, either part-time or substituting. I'm fortunate that I have "something" to return to. What do the "poor" mothers of large families do in such circumstances where their husbands either ignore their essence as a human being, or pretend that the problem is non-existent? Do most husbands feel that a good sexual relationship is enough to obliterate everything else?

My husband does not agree with my solution. I should appreciate your counsel and advice.

THE REPLY

Recently, I came across the story of a Muslim anthropologist who came to America. When he returned home, he was invited to address a group of eminent anthropologists on the subject of American marriage practices.

"In the United States," he said, "they have a peculiar custom of marriage where one man and one woman live under the same roof all their lives. They call it 'monotony.'"

Isn't that your problem at this time? The Almighty has been very good to you and blessed your marriage with five children, yet leaving you with good looks and an education. You now resent the time you have to be with your youngsters, three of whom are still at home. You feel trapped, unfulfilled. Your marriage at this time is not giving you the stimulation and satisfaction you want.

You have taught your children to respect your husband. Well, teach them to respect you. Asking you to help them with their homework is no lack of respect. Expecting you to have their food and their clothes ready is not indicative of lack of respect. A mother has a role to play in the home, and the father has a role to play. He, too, must understand that it is required of him to go to work daily to support his family. Your share is taking care of the children and the home. It is evident that you are jealous of the role he plays and do not enjoy the role you must play.

At this time you have the tremendous urge to go out to work. You want to turn over the care of your young children to a woman so that you can take a part-time job. Of course, if your husband is not making enough to support the house, work for you becomes imperative. However, if you seek the job because you feel your role as a mother and wife is too passive for you, a new area of competitiveness arises. It is only too true that when a woman unconsciously feels "pushed around," inferior to men, she begins to resent her household duties.

You are wise enough not to suppress this emotion, this feeling of discontent. It is important for you to remember that as long as hostile feelings are kept on the surface they are not so difficult to eliminate. Now, you ought to talk out these feelings with your husband. Discuss them with him as calmly and objectively as possible.

What bothers you a great deal is that you feel you are being taken for granted. You are not getting enough attention. Perhaps it has been some time since your husband complimented an outfit you wore, or told you that you look pretty. It seems to you that he and the children ask but do not give. You resent the fact that he does not help you with any of the chores. Surely, with five children your husband ought to realize that fathers, too, are parents. He must accept responsibility for them and help you help them.

I surely agree that you have the right to be a human being, to love and be loved, to feel accepted, to feel free to express yourself as an individual, and to be recognized, not as a piece of machinery but a human being. Only then will your life become richer, freer, and more meaningful.

Yet, I must caution you that false pride can only lead to unhappiness. Certainly, you should feel pride in helping to create such a wonderful family. Certainly, you can take great pride in being both a mother and a wife. You have the right to take pride in your daily work, in the home you are building, in your children, and you must know where to draw a line between pride and an inflated ego.

I agree that your husband's behavior toward you is important, and that he is not as solicitous as he might or could be. It is not realistic for him to pretend that you do not have a problem. Frankly, if he were more concerned about you and your problem, you might not have to solve the problem in the way you have selected. If he exhibited more tenderness, he might get you to feel needed, not as a valet but rather as a life companion. He will some day learn that whatever affects one partner in marriage inevitably affects the other.

If you believe that a stint at teaching will give you back some of your feelings of adequacy, go to it, but make certain that your children are provided for. I'd prefer, for your children's sake, that you do substituting rather than take a regular part-time job.

*He has one big headache
—his wife who likes to
be miserable and wants
him along as company.*

– 16 –

She Wants to Be Miserable!

THE PROBLEM

At the very outset of my letter, permit me to tell you that I love my family. I have two married children, and bless them five grandchildren. This makes me happy as it should. My problem is my wife and I are very opposite in our likes and dislikes. I am an extrovert and my wife is an introvert. But let me tell you my story.

At the present time I am a retired man. I like to do the things that I missed doing when I was young. Of course I do them with reservation. This may surprise you but I was an orphan, the youngest of 9 children, and so there were many things I could not do as a youngster which I do want to do at this time.

I do want to point out that I don't mind doing odd jobs in the house, when I feel like it. However, there is a great deal of argument over silly things that really don't mean much. I love to kid around in a sensible way; so I don't do that anymore. I try my best to overlook many things.

But still there is a cold blood feeling in our house. I want us to be happy. Of course my wife works and she thinks she is the only woman in the world working. The doctor said it is good for her. So what should I do if she works, commit suicide? Should I commit suicide because she wants to be miserable? If she wants it that way I let her live that way. But I want to live a little. I don't gamble except once in a while on a good fight or sometimes on a baseball game. Why not? I can afford it.

I would appreciate your answer. You might make me a better retired husband. Who knows?

THE REPLY

You write to me as a husband, father and grandfather, and as one who loves his family. You claim to have one big headache—your wife. She wants to be miserable and you want to live it up! You are retired; she is working. Every once in a while, when you feel like it you do some odd jobs around the house.

There are many questions that come to my mind as I read your letter. Why must your wife work? I don't go along with your statement that the doctor ordered it. You claim you gamble once in a while and that you can afford it. Can you afford it because your wife works to keep the house going or are both of you comfortably set financially? You claim you are an extrovert and she an introvert. Could it be that she must do the thinking and the planning since you are bent on capturing the fun, the excitement, and the activity you missed while you were an orphan boy? The cold blood that seems to prevail in your home, and which emanates from your wife, can be the result of deep resentment at being compelled to rise early in the morning to get your breakfast before she departs for a day at her job.

You indicate that I might be able to make you a better retired husband, and at least, it is an indication that you do believe that you are partially at fault. A long time ago, wise King Solomon (and certainly he was a married man of wide experience) said that there is a time and place for everything. I go along with the wisdom of this ancient philosopher. I go along with it because it is just as true today, and very true in your case.

First of all, remember that you are a father and a grandfather and the fun, excitement and activity you missed when you were twelve, eighteen or twenty-two, you cannot make up at this time. Forget it, it wasn't meant for you. In fact, you may look very silly trying at your age, to indulge in teenage activities, or in attempting to recapture teenage feelings and emotions. If you must indulge, try to live them in the experiences of your grand-children. Give them opportunities to enjoy those things you were unable to enjoy when you were their age. Continue to do this as you grow older. Again, remember that you are a grand-father. I don't mean that you must walk around with cane in hand, but I certainly don't infer that you jump on a bicycle, dive off a high diving board, or go around in T-shirt and shorts. You must learn to grow old gracefully.

A man who can retire from his place of business has a thou-sand advantages. He can now be master of his own company, his own pleasures, his own time. He can view nature with an unhurried look, can enjoy his children and grandchildren, can become better acquainted with his wife. He can read, travel, plan, and even project into the future. However, a foundation of good sense, and a cultivation of learning are required to give the proper seasoning to retirement.

In every man's life comes a day when he must stop trying to act like a youngster. He must try to push around his mind, not his body. He can be aggressive, dynamic, and even extro-verted in fighting for a cause, in righting a wrong, in correcting social abuses.

I recall a wife leaving this poem to her retired "youth-seek-ing" husband:

> King Solomon and King David
> Led very merry lives
> With very many concubines
> And very many wives.
> Until old age came creeping
> With very many qualms
> Then Solomon wrote the Proverbs,
> And David wrote the Psalms.

This is certain: Few men can build a happy retired life by themselves. You claim you are happy, but you are not. You indicate your wife can be miserable as she chooses, but you won't. Yet, you realize that you are not as happy as you can be. You miss the warmth, the friendship, the understanding—the love of your partner in life.

It is my feeling that you are somewhat of an egotist. You want to have fun and you have it. You want to gamble and you place bets. You want to do things that you should have done in your younger years and you do them—all this to the consternation of your wife who is ashamed of your conduct and is hurt by your indifference to her wishes and to her problems.

To make your future years happy ones, stop being a guest in your own home. If your wife works, then you must help in the house; help on a permanent basis and not when the spirit moves you. The woman who complained, "I don't like my husband's retirement because I have twice as much husband on half as much pay," spoke a great truth.

So, stop chasing after your youth; it is gone forever. You are now a ripe, mature human being; act like one. Stop exploiting your wife. She is a full partner in the home and is entitlted to full rights, privileges and considerations. As you grow older you need many things if you are to realize rich, happy future years. None is more important than a philosophy of life suited to mature people. Such a philosophy is the culmination of a man's or woman's experience, a diploma from the school of life and proof that he has lived long and that he also has made good use of his time.

The longer you live, the more experiences you have upon which to reflect. The result is a growing concern in spiritual things, a desired closeness to God and to His way of life. You must constantly seek to become not only more useful to yourself but more useful to others. You must learn to appreciate the value of beautiful, meaningful relationships.

*She cannot tolerate a
marriage where only
she is the giver!*

-17-

Must I Keep on Giving?

THE PROBLEM

I am sick and tired of hearing people say, "You made your husband what he is today, and you can only blame yourself." I deny this most vehemently. I spoiled my husband? Never! If a man is a failure as a husband, he has never had much potential as a man. He was selfish and rotten to begin with. In good faith I offered to help him in times of financial crisis. I saw nothing wrong in that. What is wrong is that the helper is too often used, taken advantage of. There isn't an equal amount of effort or caring on the other side. And a "You have an endless source of energy" comment from my husband is a bitter pill I can't swallow. This sort of thinking has made my husband phlegmatic and has turned him into an overgrown "mama's" boy.

I shall never admit that it was wrong to start helping when we needed it. Where I made an error was in not recognizing his symptoms of self pity and self love.

I think that the most important thing in life is to be good to one another. One will overcome many obstacles to brighten the day of a loved one, to ease his pangs of loneliness, to encourage him to greater achievement, to strengthen his belief in himself, and to join the rest of the world when they shout bravo at his accomplishments.

No two people can be closer than husband and wife, and there should be no such thing as "you are doing too much," providing there is love, not affection, but deep mutual love. I did not say 50-50, I said *mutual love*.

Love is the original motivator for doing things for someone. When you love you seek to make life a thing worth living for yourself, but mostly for the one you love. However, there is no greater offense, no greater rejection of your love than to be repaid with "you enjoy doing things for people."

This type of response sends you off in a frenzied search for love that will equal yours. This type of response slaps you in the face, destroys the very core of your beings, rocks the very foundation of your trust in people. It floats the ship of matrimony on a sea of tears, despair and loneliness.

What can a wife expect out of married life? We cannot all be beautiful and capitalize on it, we cannot all be brilliant and achieve earth-shattering goals; we cannot all be born with talents to be developed. This we can write off as "shigzal," fate, as something that it meant to be, or just say, "gam ze l'tov." But we have the right to expect deep abounding love, respect, and consideration from our husbands.

How long must I continue to give without receiving? How much longer must I continue to live without love, to be considerate without receiving consideration, to be cooperative without receiving cooperation? Love cannot be a unilateral situation. And, dear doctor, if you use the word, "accept," I'll scream.

THE REPLY

I would advise you to reread your own letter, read it with both intelligence and emotion. Study your own definition of love. Try to apply it to your life. When you love, it motivates you to do things for the person you love. It is not accompanied with a price tag or with an exchange value. It is not as you clearly stated "a 50-50 proposition." After you have carefully reread your own words, ask yourself if you are in love. What ceased to exist in your love for your husband or his reciprocation to you?

Do you think you are alone in this feeling of rejection? Is there any one of us who has not at times felt the limitation of human response and longed for the satisfaction of a deeper, more meaningful understanding? Do not all of us at times find ourselves inarticulate in trying to voice the deepest feelings of the heart? Do we not find some dregs of bitterness in most cups of happiness, and long for some magical fountain of living water from which we can drink deeply? Yes, yes, and again yes, if we are maturing.

Love serves; it heals; it overcomes limitations between people; it reaches past self-interest; it finds a way when to common sense there seems to be no way. Love is present when a woman finds in a man the rest and satisfaction her heart has been seeking. When that type of love is present, that marriage is not a legal bond, but a divine one.

Marital happiness is not a bequest but rather a conquest. Love is a universal phenomenon, which we mistakenly feel has its source in ourselves and its satisfactions in others. Years ago, you felt the stir of love and interpreted it in terms of personal attachment. Now that the allure that first attracted you is tarnished, you have nothing left but bitterness and disillusionment. What you once fought to get (your husband), you must now fight to keep. Despite the assurances of novelists and playwrights, marriage is not an ultimate goal in human relations, but rather the beginning of a whole new cycle of life experiences in which the marital partners must work to preserve, strengthen and fulfill the romantic feelings that were present prior to marriage.

So as not to provoke you to scream, I will not advise you to "accept." However, I might add that the best time to avoid divorce is before marriage. That was the time you should have considered what you were willing to give. That was the time you should have weighed the factors that would make for harmonious adjustment.

Marriage is no game, so stop blowing the whistle and yelling foul. Marital responsibilities cannot be meted out on a pharmaceutical scale. Seek self-fulfillment in other areas as well as in marriage. Unite with your husband in a common purpose, the raising of your children. Do not compare your contribution with his. After all, you should give your contribution graciously and unselfishly. Remember, marriage is a sacred union where two souls become wedded to God to fulfill His purpose.

*He feels that many men
run from marriage be-
cause of unrealistic
fears.*

– 18 –

Are Men Afraid of Marriage?

THE PROBLEM

Why do men fear marriage? It seems to me that this fear is a common disease which has attacked males of all ages. I know of many cases, (myself included) where young men have cared deeply, have professed their love, and at the last minute decided that they just couldn't walk down the aisle.

A little over a year ago my close friend found herself in such a situation. The young man had fallen in love and wanted to marry her. He told her that soon he would announce the engagement. However, when the time for the announcement arrived, he informed her that he just could not face the idea of marriage, and that ended what could have been a beautiful relationship.

I know another young man who is in his early thirties. He is tall, handsome, professionally established, and financially secure. However, he can't face the idea of getting himself attached to any one young lady. Any time he gets close to a serious relationship (and I know of two such occasions), he turns tail and runs.

Just the other evening I heard of an extremely orthodox affair where the groom, evidently thinking it all over, just didn't show up. What made him run at the last moment, no one knows.

Just what is the matter with men? What are they afraid of? I refer to men from all walks of Judaism—the chassid, the conservative, and even the reformed. And I am not speaking of youngsters either, but men from 25 and up, all the way to thirty-five. These men claim they want nothing out of life but to find a mate, settle down and raise a family. They have the whole-hearted blessings of their family, are well established, lonely, eager for companionship, love and affection, but some-how cannot face marriage. I would like to get some answers from young men who range anywhere from 21 to 40, married or unmarried.

THE REPLY

"Why do men fear marriage?" you ask, and then you go on to explain how young men, who have been in love, have fled in haste at the last moment. These men are tall, secure, financially independent, and have one thing in common; they run from the marriage canopy. You know of many such cases because your friends and you have experienced them.

Of course you realize that not all men run from marriage. After all, half of all married couples are men—men who date, love, become engaged, and finally are married. Not everybody who says, "I love you," hesitates to ask, "Will you marry me?" Your friends and you have run into a great deal of hard luck. The young men between 21 and 40 have successfully avoided the all-important question, and this has made you conclude that men fear marriage.

Something must be wrong! Men are getting married every day of the year. Every day of the year and twice on Saturday evenings and Sundays, men and women stand under the marriage canopy and agree to love and respect until their days come to an end. You know that, don't you? Therefore, one of two con-clusions must come to mind: either there is something wrong with you, or there is something the matter with the young men who date you. Perhaps the wires are connected to a dead outlet and so no electric current is present.

It is to be admitted that some men will never marry. They are afraid of family responsibility and perhaps doubt their abil-ity to make a woman happy. These men will never admit this fact to themselves or to others. They keep talking about not meeting the proper female and keep searching for their intended mate. They waste a woman's time, spend her emotions, but al-ways manage to avoid the question. They indicate interest, display affection, seem to show understanding, but that is as far as they go.

Perhaps you should treat some of your men friends as the lady in this story. They had been sitting alone in the swing in the romantic moonlight. She had been seeing him for some months and felt that with a bit of motivation on her part he would pop the question. For more than half an hour not a single word broke the silence of the night. "Perhaps he is worried about money," she thought to herself.

She decided she was going to offer him the lead, get him to think. It was going to be tonight or never.

"Suppose you had money," she said, "what would you do?" She now awaited the answer that would make her happy.

He looked into her eyes, gave her hand an added squeeze, and slowly replied, "If I had money, I'd travel!"

Suddenly, she withdrew her hand, and then in a moment placed it back on his. A minute later when he looked up, she was gone. In his hand was a subway token.

It seems to me that you and your friends ought to hand out subway tokens to some of your frightened suitors. If you are interested in hearing from men up to the age of 40, I have the right to assume that you are no longer in your twenties. If this is so, and I think it is, you ought to take to heart the words of the poet:

> Gather ye rosebuds while you may
> Old time is still a-flying
> And the same flower that blooms today
> Tomorrow will be dying.

Stop shopping for men in the same market. What you will get tomorrow depends upon what you do today. I might add that you ought to change your lady friends as well. Why should you all be running into the same bad luck?

This you must realize: men are getting married, and on a regular basis! The question you ought to ask is not, "Are men afraid of marriage?" but rather, "Why are men afraid of marrying me?"

Once again I repeat it might be that you are being attracted to the non-marrying male, or that you lose the men to other women. In either case it is up to you to do something about it. Ask yourself some questions. Review your past years. Think of the number of times you have refused proposals of marriage. Have you been going only to the same places, meeting the same people? Iron rusts from disuse, stagnant water loses its purity, and in cold weather becomes frozen; even so does walking in the same ruts sap the fervent eagerness of the spirit.

I only agree with the second line of Samuel Hoffenstein's "Advice on Marriage." He wrote:

Men in single state should tarry,
While women, I suggest, should marry.

Get rid of the men around you. They are probably followers of Thales, one of the Greek sages. When his mother urged him to marry during his youth he replied, "It was not yet time"; when he had come to full age, he added, "that it was no longer time."

And by the way, take a good look at yourself. Do you look fresh and clean? Can you be an interested speaker and listener? Do you make a man feel uncomfortable? Are you cultured? Do you speak only about aches and pains or are you at home with topics of the day?

Freshen up! Dress up! Look up! Do this and more, and you will neither be concerned nor single for long.

The constant battle of "who" pays for "what" makes their marriage a series of disagreeable experiences.

– 19 –

Your Expense, Not Mine!

THE PROBLEM

Every now and then my household is disrupted over the question of money. My husband and I both work. I earn a little more than he does. However, I pay the rent every other month, buy certain items for the home, and also cover my husband's medical expense through my insurance coverage. My husband pays the telephone, gas; buys essential foods, and pays the rent every other month.

When we were married, he was not yet a citizen, and not doing well. I took a chance, and although he tried, he did not follow my advice—at any rate, he now holds a steady job. I therefore feel, since I furnished most of the home, that if something needs to be replaced, he should do so. He says I earn more and I should do so.

My feelings are that he is wrong. Suppose he had a bachelor apartment and a towel or sheet had to be replaced—he would have to do just that. I might add that except for a "very" infrequent gift, I clothe myself and take care of my needs. Please let me have your opinion.

THE REPLY

When husband and wife quarrel over money, "his," and "hers," then the entire relationship needs to be examined, because it is obvious that there is much more to the marital difficulty than the question of money. Marriage—living together with another person according to the rules set down by religion and society—living with understanding, love, appreciation and respect cannot be successful when a certified public accountant and an attorney are brought in to arrange the financial responsibilities of husband and wife.

The financial arrangement between your husband and yourself smacks of a too meticulous assignment of "who pays what." There is absolutely no togetherness here, but rather a practical, systematic business between two discontented people who wish to live together so as to split operating expenses.

It seems to me as if you and your husband have private, precious bank accounts which each one of you hopes to enlarge by attempting to minimize household contributions. He buys meat and fish; you buy fruits and vegetables. You cover his medical insurance; he pays the telephone bill, gas and some other assorted essentials; you bought most of the items for the home, therefore, you insist that he replace them when they no longer are serviceable.

It seems to me that in this marriage there is too much emphasis on "I" and not enough on "we." There are too many conflicting aims and anxieties in the marriage, too much competition, too much suspicions, too much hidden maneuvering for financial security. The marital conflict is being fostered because of the particular attitudes each of you have.

The first step toward a happier marriage is a reevaluation of the relationship. The fact that you earn more and he less should not enter into the calculation of the family budget, nor should there be a definite assignment of certain expenses to husband and wife. If the marriage is to last, then, let there be one pocket, not two. All monies earned should go into one bank, not two separate bank accounts. From this one collective cash reserve, all expenditures are to be made. This would indicate trust and increase the feeling that this is a permanent, meaningful relationship. It would help eliminate possibilities for marital conflict by determining who should pay for the purchase of a new kitchen towel.

Both of you are now courting the danger of the "mine and yours" marital syndrome, which most of the time leads to a separation between husband and wife. With a working wife, the danger is even greater. Since you earn more than your husband, his manhood is greatly challenged, or so he thinks. On the other hand, you, by withholding your salary, indicate your hostility, and satisfy your need to control. Neither of you does much to strengthen marital ties.

If your marriage were sound, it would be of relatively little importance who pays what expenses. In a good marriage, there is a minimum of "mine" and "yours"—almost everything is "ours." Your marriage is ailing; the money situation is only one of the symptoms. Why not get professional help before the marriage deteriorates and dies!

"Every other week my wife tells me to take my things and get out." Should he dissolve this marriage?

– 20 –

Take Your Things and Go!

THE PROBLEM

I'm married a little over two years, and in this short period of time we have had several hot arguments during which my wife has told me to take my things and get out.

The arguments always started because I saw things about her sister and the sister's son and daughter that upset me terribly. I'm not one to run for a divorce right away. How much can one take?

I was married late. I'm a man in my early fifties, never before married. She was married and left a widow, no children; age 40.

A short while after we were married, her mother, who was a very sick woman, became seriously ill, and went to the hospital. My wife paid all the expenses plus for nurses around the clock. A very short while afterwards, she passed on. My wife paid all the funeral expenses. After the funeral, her father just gave up living, and within a few months, he ended up in the hospital with a heart condition. Immediately my wife engaged nurses around the clock for sixteen weeks plus paying the doctor $150 a week. I kept telling her all the time to get rid of the nurses because it would break her. Her answer was that it was none of my business, that she was paying for it.

Her father passed on after the sixteen weeks and she paid for all the funeral expenses. Today she is broke. Her first husband left her in a very comfortable financial position. Her brother, who is a rich man, refused to contribute a penny. Her sister claims she has no money. The whole financial burden fell on my wife.

So, when I mention something to her about her family, she

says that I'm tearing them apart and follows with, "So you can take your things and get out."

There is a saying one never knows his partner until they live under one roof, then either happiness or disappointment creeps up. In my case, quite a bit of disappointment after being single so many years. People tell me that as long as there are no children, it is best to break it up. By the way, I would like to add that her parents were poor people and lived on a city pension.

THE REPLY

Marriage brings change. Change brings with it the inevitable necessity for making adjustments. Many of the problems, however, begin with small situations, which in and of themselves may not be major calamities, but which become crises because of their persistence. The emotional stability of the individuals who have to meet the problem is a very important factor. Thus, while any trivial situation might become a crisis in the life of an individual, the degree to which it is critical, depends on the extent to which he has acquired a personality capable of facing and resolving difficulties.

That your wife was left a large sum of money by her first husband is something you cannot deny. Rightfully or wrongfully, she feels that this money is all hers, that you have absolutely no say in the way it is spent. This was made quite clear to you when as a devoted daughter she sought to make her mother's remaining months as comfortable as possible. She refused to use her wealthy brother as an excuse for not helping out. With this point of view I have no fault to find. You, always practical, felt that she ought to watch her money. You kept on criticizing her devotion and dedication to her mother though you knew this always upset her.

When she lost her mother, her father became ill. Once again, your wife acting out of love, dedication, devotion, went all out to make her father comfortable. Once again, you warned her about financial expenses. Money was not important to her; her father's comfort was of greater concern. She felt that a good heart was more valuable than a large bank account. Your great concern was her decreasing financial position. Instead of offering her words of comfort, instead of making life for her easier (she did lose two parents in a short period of time) you kept pointing out the deficiencies in her family. I just cannot agree with your point of view. To discuss future financial positions when lives are at stake is to place money above love, parents, and even God.

Nowhere in your letter do you mention any other source of disagreement. Out of tremendous emotion, out of the feeling that you don't have compassion for her, your wife told you to get your things and leave. Of course, I don't agree with this type of talk in married life. But somehow I have empathy for your wife who was watching two parents die.

What both of you ought to do is to forget what has happened. You must make her understand that you appreciate her good heart, that you did not mean to prevent her from helping her parents. Finally, I caution you not to belittle her relatives. She may be aware of the pain they are causing her and needs no reminders from you.

My wife makes me miserable because she considers herself an expert on my shortcomings.

– 21 –

Paranoia For Two

THE PROBLEM

I am in a sad state, believe me, I am. I have been married to a woman for the past 28 years. We have two children, both married. There are four grandchildren. I might as well give you the facts without too much delay. I don't love my wife. Frankly, that's putting it mildly. If I were to be more accurate, I feel she is just a chain around my neck—a woman who is selfish, unproductive, frigid in every sense of the word, is completely wound up with her own petty, unsuccessful, meaningless pursuits.

As I look back now, we never had a marriage. I never should have married so lazy, so indifferent, so egocentric a woman. While the children were growing up, I didn't want to upset the apple cart. We stayed together, by force of habit. There were days we didn't exchange more than a dozen words. You see, I really find her dull and uninteresting. Interestingly enough, when she does go out to an affair, she gives outsiders the impression she is the life of the party. Her moaning, groaning, complaining begins the second she steps into our home. Off goes her glamour clothing, and on goes whatever comfortable rags she can find around. Don't talk to me about love, about masculine acts of affection, of giving gifts. I've followed the book until I'd like to commit two murders, the author of the book and my wife.

I feel my married life has been wasted, and the pity is, that she will probably outlive me by 20 years. Why not? With the care she takes of her precious body, science will do research to determine the cause of her longevity.

Now, we tolerate one another. I get the minimum of attention from her. Any attention I do get involves my shortcomings. She is an expert on that. It has gotten so that I just hate the sound of her voice. I have no interest in her or she in me, for that matter. Why do we remain together? Why am I permitting the remaining years of my life to go down the drain? I had so much love to give, but a neurotic wife didn't need it, want it, or take it. I sure am in a sad state.

THE REPLY

Though you and your wife don't love each other, you both have used any number of devices to keep your union together. All these bits of unconscious strategy are miserable, but evidently, for you and your wife a miserable marriage appears better than the admission of marital failure. Perhaps the fear of loneliness which follows divorce is keeping you two together. Of this I am certain, love is not keeping your union intact.

She is frigid; you are disinterested. She is egocentric; you do not exchange a dozen words with her during the course of an evening. She is neurotic; you are filled with hatred, hostility, guilt, fear and a few other unhealthy feelings. Over the years, you have managed to spend time with your work; she, with her petty interests. Neither one of you, unfortunately, is receiving the affection, the attention, the interest you require. This has been going on for so many years that by now both of you have a day-to-day existence. From time to time, you awaken from this lethargy and realize that your years are flying by, and that there is something missing in your life. I dare say her story is quite similar. She is accusing you of the very same faults you find in her. The result: paranoia for two.

If all love has disappeared, if there is no meaningful relationship between the both of you, if you are just killing time, if you are being deprived of the warmth and richness that should go with a marital relationship, my advice to you is to terminate your marriage. Why be miserable together and blame her? Separate and at least if you are miserable, you will have no one to blame.

Did I hear you say that "Divorce is out of the question!" I did! Well then, fill your life with interests, with hobbies—and of course, with friends. Attend club meetings, social groups. Build yourself a complete life, one in which you will feel fulfilled, not frustrated. There is little to be gained in continuing a paranoia for two.

Your marriage has been sick a long time; it's almost ready to die.

*Though I am quite at-
tractive, cultured and
educated, my husband
just doesn't make any
passes at me.*

-22-

One of Us Is Neurotic!

THE PROBLEM

I am considered quite attractive by my friends and relatives.
I know I dress well and in good taste. I have two college degrees
and am now working toward my Ph.D. This I do while taking
care of my home, my husband and my two children. At my last
birthday I was 28 years of age.

My husband is a quiet, weak individual who is easily manip-
ulated. Unfortunately, he has withdrawn from me in every area
of married life. He is considered by others to be friendly, warm,
pleasant, and soft-spoken. I have found him passive and inef-
fective. I must point out that my husband comes from a home
where his mother made great demands on him. His father was
and still is a nonentity. I don't believe my husband knows the
meaning of the word "love" since he never saw it displayed in
his home.

My own parents were quite demanding when I lived with
them. A sense of anger always prevailed in my home, and
frankly I think I married as quickly as I could to escape from
my own home.

I get some satisfaction out of my home, some out of my children, and from time to time a great need for my husband seems
to take hold of me. But, when I am at college, I feel like a college girl, act like a college girl, and relate to others like a college girl. Sad, isn't it?

I wish I could give you more information about my husband
and myself, but I honestly can't. There are days we don't talk
to one another; there are weeks where there is absolutely no
affection shown, neither my husband nor I make any attempt.

One of us is neurotic I am sure. Perhaps I rushed into this marriage. Perhaps I should have married a much stronger person. What I want to know is, can this marriage be saved? I should add that materially, I have everything any woman could want, including a beautiful suburban home.

Would marriage counseling help?

THE REPLY

There is quite a conflict raging in you. You don't know whether to be a devoted mother, a suburban housewife, or a college coed. At the present time you are attempting to handle all three roles, but your repressed rage and hostility makes this almost impossible.

To begin with, you complain about your husband's quiet nature. The fact is that you selected him because he portrayed that reserved personality you felt you could handle. Basically, you feel inadequate as a woman and so manipulate your husband to enhance your desire to feel superior to him.

It would be wise to understand your husband's needs. He desires the protective surroundings of a close family relationship. When he married you, he expected you to provide the warmth and love he needed. Instead you gave him a sort of intellectual acceptance, or plain anger when you felt disappointed and frustrated. You made him feel that he was on the outside of the family looking in.

You misunderstand his lack of aggressiveness as indications of his not loving or wanting you. Your anger is so great that you drive him away, for it reminds him of his mother's anger and his father's inability to stand up to her.

Both of you want love, yet neither knows how to give it. Because you doubt your own ability as a woman, you do not accept your husband. He reacts by being cold and indifferent. He does this to defend his own sagging ego.

Extensive counseling is in order so that both of you can be helped with your feelings of anger and inadequacy. Marital counseling might improve your communication and understanding. Your husband must be made to understand that his anger is a result of his dependence on your opinions. When he will be able to stand on his own feet and become indifferent to your opinions, his anger will diminish.

You must begin to feel adequate; he must feel independent.

It isn't a question of who is neurotic, but rather what are one's needs and how can they be satisfied. When this will be done, a happy marriage will result.

His suspicious wife looks for the other woman wherever they go.

– 23 –

My Wife Is Suspicious

THE PROBLEM

I never dreamed that I'd ever come knocking on your door for help, but time does things. Now let me come to my problem. My wife and I are around 40 years old and we have three children—10, 12, and 16. I married my wife for her charm, beauty, true understanding and deep love. The twenty years we are married, are to me a picture of joy and happiness. No one could ask for a better wife. She always keeps the house clean and the children spotless. In addition, she is very nice to everybody and is liked by everyone.

As for myself, I am rather quiet, hard working and manage to be home every day around 4:00 in the afternoon. I start working at 6 A.M. My wife and I spend a lot of time together and I also have more time for the children than other fathers have.

I've always loved my wife truly and deeply, respected and cherished her for being so devoted and good to me and the children. I have been the envy of all my friends. However, since moving to a new neighborhood, I have noticed a certain suspicion in my wife. It started as follows. Across the street there lived a woman who used to walk her dog each morning when I went to work. Many times in the morning I looked out of the window to see how the weather was, but my wife thought that

I was watching the woman. In the beginning I laughed at this nonsense, but it kept getting worse and worse.

Unfortunately, I blush easily, and every time my wife accused me, I became red as a beet. This made matters worse. She accused me of being friendly with the Rebetzin in the Shul, the sales clerk in a store, a neighbor, just anyone. We had many fights about this but I could not drive it out of her head.

It is ridiculous to feel that I just can't look at anyone. Because of her unfounded suspicion, we have lost many friends. Now that the woman with the dog has moved away, my wife claims that I am observing the widow and her two daughters who have moved in.

Believe me Dr. Mandel, my heart is crying. I simply can't take it anymore. It is a real tragedy and I am ashamed to hear the terrible things I am accused of. Something must have gone to her head and it is impossible to drive it out. We are strictly orthodox people, and I see no other solution than to seek a divorce. This thought makes me sick. It will be the greatest shock to my life and to my wife, too. But under no circumstances can I take these vicious, imaginative accusations any longer. Our arguments now leave us not talking to one another for two to three weeks.

THE REPLY

For a man, who most of his married life, has lived with a charming, beautiful, truly understanding, deeply devoted wife, dedicated to husband and children, you are considering the most drastic remedy for your marital woes—divorce. Though your wife has for the past 20 years been meticulous in her care of you and the children, you are prepared, if she doesn't desist from what you feel are unfair accusations, to amputate and end your marriage. This is like offering to have your hand amputated because you have been stung by a bee.

Nothing happens without a cause. The woman, who suddenly finds evidence that her husband is interested in other women, is not acting on a meaningless impulse. Long before she started accusing you, she must have been torn by inner conflict which she found even too difficult to admit to herself.

There are one of two assumptions you can make in regard to your wife's accusations. One, that she is emotionally ill, and her doubts about your fidelity are part of the symptoms. Second, your conduct, though innocent on your part, has given her the proof of your interest in other women. In either case, she needs help and understanding, needs reassurance and not threats.

At this point you ought to clear your own mind. Question your own attitudes and actions that have made your wife feel you are not faithful. How have you motivated her imagination? Looked at from this point of view the strange predicament in which you now find yourself may become more understandable.

When a wife begins to suspect her husband of being interested in other women, it may indicate a feeling of feminine inadequacy on her part. Invariably, she begins to doubt her husband's interest, counts the number of times he overlooks complimenting her, makes mental note of his decreasing conversation and attention. At this time she starts to feel that she is but another piece of furniture in the home.

Right now, your wife feels insufficiently loved, and so demands continued signs of devotion. Because of this hunger, she looks upon every outside interest which takes up your time and attention as a dangerous threat to her own safety. She feels she must guard your every step, becomes aware of every glance you direct toward another woman. All this because she is unsure of your continued love, and feels she has lost her glamour.

What can you, as a husband, do for your jealous, suspicious wife? How can you give her the emotional support she now needs? How long is it since you've told your wife you love her? Or that she looks pretty? Have you brought her flowers lately or taken her out to dinner? Given her money for a new dress? Helped her with the dishes or the children when she's tired? These are the times to be the lover and the friend.

In these and innumerable other situations you must fulfill the various facets of your role as husband in order to sustain the closeness you once had in your marriage. Remember, she needs help. Telling her that she is wrong is of no help or value. Her idea of feeling neglected is not entirely inaccurate in her own mind. As a sympathetic husband, you can do a great deal toward encouraging and providing a certain sense of security. Instead of arguing, threatening, just offer assurances of your love and affection. Whenever possible, show signs of appreciation and esteem. Let her know how much she is needed. All this may help her overcome her feeling of inadequacy.

With calm and tenderness, air your problems together. In this way you may find many facets about yourselves and your relationship of which you were unaware. These revelations and the way you cope with these problems can awaken you to unexplored strength within yourselves, create new closeness, and a renewed foundation for emotional satisfaction. The question now is: If you must be the stronger in the partnership, are you willing to be that, without feeling hostile or throwing it up to your mate and playing the part of the long suffering martyr?

In any event, divorce should always be the very last resort, after everything else has failed to readjust the marriage. Believe me, rebuilding ties between yourself and your wife is preferable to jumping into a new relationship which may prove no more satisfying than the original one.

You have had the love of a charming, beautiful, understanding, devoted wife for almost 20 years. Don't sell it short even though you feel the love market is dropping. Rather bear in mind that the heart of a woman is never so full of affection that there does not remain a little corner for words and signs of flattery and love. How true the words: "Love is like the moon; when it does not increase, it decreases."

We never know how much one loves till we know how much he is willing to endure and suffer for the one he loves. It is the element of suffering that in reality indicates love. The person who loves must be willing, patient, and strong to endure for others. To love is to place our happiness in the happiness of another.

There are popular slogans that advise you to see your dentist twice a year, your doctor periodically. To this I might add that marital partners ought to see a marriage counselor when they feel their marriages are getting weak. A marriage gets sick before it dies. Yours is sick now. Both you and your wife ought to do everything possible to save a relationship that has 20 years of wonderful memories. Go to it!

My husband is an excellent provider, a generous husband and a complete bore.

-24-

My Husband Is Steady But Dull!

THE PROBLEM

It is rather difficult for me to write this way about my own husband, a dedicated father and a devoted husband but he is just too dull for my blood. He is the type of man who is content at the end of the dinner meal to sit, read the paper, talk with the children, and then go to bed.

I can't find too much fault with him in most categories. He has an excellent position and is earning enough to support us in good style. My children have always had whatever they wanted, and from time to time, we have made trips within the United States and abroad.

Perhaps, most women would be satisfied with this type of mate. He is not too demanding, gives in most of the time, can always be counted on, helps with the children but he is no leader. He is not aggressive, does not really create an impression when he is in company. It's not that he doesn't make waves when he's around, he doesn't even create ripples.

Frankly, I know that the children don't think too much of their father. This I can see by their actions. They don't have the respect for him I'd like them to have. I guess they have read my mind because I find it almost impossible to respect such a man. What with the movies and T.V., where you see real men, it is difficult to compromise with a man who is a "wage-earner" only.

With all this there has been a deterioration in our home. No one seems to be paying attention to anyone else. My husband, good, steady man that he is, is unaware of all this. He eats his breakfast, goes to his office, returns at the end of the day to eat, help, converse, and go to bed.

How much longer can I live with such a man?

THE REPLY

Unfortunately you are learning about husband-wife relationships through the glaring eye of television. If you are watching the ads, especially those selling beer or smokes, you are apt to feel that the real masculine individual has escaped you, and that you are married to a tea-drinking mate. You forget that he is dedicated, devoted, and looks after the family, and see him as a hard-working dolt.

Of course, television has done the reverse as well. It has portrayed the husband as a dull, bumbling, clumsy individual who is scolded by his wife, insulted by his children, shouted at by his boss, and ridiculed by his mother-in-law. This husband, portrayed regularly on television, has become the source of jokes for the growing children of today. They see "father" as the titular, but not the actual head of the family. Again and again they are shown how easy it is to "put something over on Dad."

On the other hand, the female in the family is nearly always pictured as the crisp, intelligent, cultured, well-read, efficient manager of the home, who almost always maintains a martyred expression of pain over the antics of her ineffectual husband. She treats him like a household pet: silences him with a look, sends him off to work with a peck on the cheek, awakens him from the couch so that she can sweep under him, drags him from the corner bar or neighborhood poker game. She is always hard at work settling all the problems, managing the finances, guiding the children, and doing a hundred and one assorted jobs.

This is a daily diet to wives and children everywhere in the United States, with the result that homes are being shattered and family life is falling apart. As one jurist put it, "American family life is going to pot." Women have allowed their minds to become drugged by the shallow glamour they see on television. They fail to see the truth in the genuine facts that regulate and guide a happy married life. These very same women end up in Mexico for their quickie divorce, and by their action create heartbreak, add to disappointment and disillusionment. They are ready for the "Second Time Around" but no one around is doing much asking.

No one wants to live with heartbreak. All men and women entering into marriage seek a rewarding experience, something deep and lasting. This doesn't mean an endless series of incidents that make for fun, joy, intrigue, suspense. There is a difference between getting the "kicks," and experiencing deep and lasting satisfaction.

Make no mistake about this! All people marry in search of happiness, marry because they feel they're in love. Then, later, they translate happiness into their own way of life. The wise person understands what marriage is, realizes it is God ordained, that it is a holy union of two people who are going to build a new generation on earth. The Almighty Himself said, "It is not good that man should live alone."

You have a home, a decent, well-provided for home. You have a husband who is both devoted and dedicated. He goes about providing for his family without griping about his tremendous load. He reads, converses, travels with you on vacations. All this you admit, but he doesn't act like the horseriding, cigarette smoking he-man you see portrayed on television.

You loved him when you married him, saw something in him that made you want to spend the rest of your life with him. Why and when did he change? Could it have been that you caused this change? Could it be that you made him so timid and docile? Could it be that you have transferred to him a myriad of female chores? Has he become the errand boy? Does he do the sweeping, dusting, washing and drying as the rest of the family relaxes in the living room? Has he become an easy mark for all of you? Have you made him the quivering jello of a man you say he is? Ask yourself these questions, and give yourself some honest answers. Perhaps, after all, you have smothered all his initiative, crushed his desire to get even further ahead.

Respect your husband for what he is, and set the stage for your children, those who are still living off the sweat of his brow, to do the same. See to it that your family lives like a family. Evenings need not always be spent in front of a T.V. screen. In fact, try turning the set off just for once and so force the family to find some constructive topic which can be discussed.

By example, show how much you appreciate your husband's dedication to his family. Praise him to the children. Tell them how fortunate they are in having a father who is so devoted to their welfare.

Then, I suggest you fill your own days with worthwhile activity. You must have too much spare time if you find fault with your husband, that is, that he just doesn't deserve. I'd suggest that you bake a cake instead of buying one in the bakery. Take extra pains with the dinner some evenings instead of throwing some things together. Try applying as much time and effort in your job as he does in his.

Surely, you don't wish to become a statistic in the divorce court. Make no mistake about it, you can, if you continue your present line of thinking, shatter your life. What you will gain the "second time around" will be far less than what you possess at the present time.

You've got a great guy, not the smartest in the world, not the most aggressive in the world, not the most successful in the world, but a man who has given you a comfortable home, has permitted you to travel, has made a family live and prosper. Say this a hundred times a day. Make it a morning preamble for your children. Give a little to this marriage. Capitalize on your husband's strengths instead of emphasizing his weaknesses.

She feels her husband has not grown up and is just another one of her children.

–25–

My Husband, Too, Is a Child!

THE PROBLEM

I am married 20 years and have two children, ages 7 and 9 years. I should say I have three children, because I'm married to a 40-year-old mama's boy.

My husband is in business with his father and I say that with tongue in cheek. My husband is supposed to be a partner in that business but he is treated like an employee. He works over and above the call of duty, sometimes working 14 hours a day, 6 days a week. He only gets a 2-week vacation during the summer.

His parents take a 3-week vacation plus weekends whenever

they feel like it. They have been to Europe and Israel 4 times. They give expensive wedding presents to friends but to their son, nothing. My husband has a car from 1962, and needs a new one desperately. He tells me there isn't any money in the business to buy a new one. Yet his father just bought a new car and his old one is a 1964 model.

My parents, who only work for a living, purchased every stick of furniture in our house and the clothes on my back. Once in a blue moon, my in-laws throw us a couple of bucks. On the whole, they are stingy, selfish people who give to strangers, but take their son for granted. He works like a horse for them but his father won't give him a raise.

I'm not a spend-thrift. I buy only what I need, never have enough cash to buy something extra. I can't even go to the beauty-parlor once a week. I waited 19 years to buy a house because my in-laws didn't approve. My parents gave me the down-payment. I could go on and on about my in-laws' selfishness.

I have always been a good daughter-in-law. I respected them and did as they asked, and got nothing in return but a lot of unnecessary insults. Either I'm too skinny, not clean enough, my cooking is not tasty, the children are not being brought up right. I'm fed up and want my husband to get out from under his parent's thumb before it's too late. He has a Master's degree and can make something of himself. All he does now is work hard so that his parents can retire comfortably. My father-in-law is only 63 years old and has many years before he retires.

I'm on the verge of divorce. I, too, want to enjoy my life. I don't want to skimp and save every minute when there is no need to. The business is a fairly good one, and his father can give him a raise. If my in-laws would stop giving to every charity under the sun and to every stranger, they might give their son something instead. My daughter needs a coat and I can't buy it.

My in-laws are getting older but so are we. Am I wrong in telling my husband to get out of his father's business? I know that if anything happened to my in-laws we would be compelled to accept the burden of making a home for them. This I would do because I don't believe in old-age homes.

Dr. Mandel, please help me make my husband understand that he is supposed to cleave unto his wife.

THE REPLY

It would seem that you have three separate problems: your husband doesn't stand up for his rights; your in-laws give you

too little; your parents give you too much. With a bit of adjustment in the three categories, thoughts of divorce might disappear.

Let's leave your husband's weakness to the very end and begin
with your in-laws. They worked up a business and are now in
the sixties. They want to live, enjoy life, desire to see the world.
This they are doing by taking vacations, going on weekends,
visiting Israel, buying a new car, and giving charity to numerous
organizations. For all this I give them credit. I approve of their
taking care of their bodies and souls—enjoying themselves and
giving charity to everyone who holds out an open hand. They
struggled for their money, spent time and energy to obtain the
opportunities now available to them.

Surely, you have no right to begrudge these people the joys
that are still open to them. There is no need to wait to show
your kindness until one of them dies or is crippled, show it to
them now. Bear in mind that the money they are spending is
their own—not yours, and not your parents'.

In no way do I condone their fault-finding, their constant criticism of your home and habits. Your husband should calmly
and definitely ask them to desist from this hateful practice. I
know that you will not resent constructive advice from anyone,
even your in-laws.

Now, to your parents. I see them as a devoted couple who
want their daughter to be happy. With this in mind they buy
you clothing, furniture, towels, a new dress. They do this because
it gives them great joy to do it. They do not measure their gifts
to you with the gifts their *machotonim* are giving you. They want
to give now, while they are alive, and so they do. You don't
have to be a business man to urge presents on children and
grandchildren, you must only want to give of what you have.
This, they do. As for you, throw away the measuring rod, the
pair of scales that carefully measures what each set of parents
is doing. Weighing and measuring can only bring unhappiness,
and disaster to marital happiness.

Whatever you do, don't envy what your in-laws have, what
they do, and the charity they are giving. Envy is a social disease
and brings ruin to health and happiness. Not to envy is one of
the Ten Commandments. Envy will shorten your own days,
cloud your own sunlight, make you difficult to live with.

Now, your husband presents a different problem, and one
which you ought to move heaven and earth to solve. If he has

something on the ball and can do better elsewhere, motivate him to take a chance. Don't threaten to leave him unless he does; don't nag, don't nudge, don't clamor. Quietly and with assurance, point out to him that he has value to give to an organization and that you are right behind him in his every undertaking.

You have been married 20 years and it is unfair to blame your husband's weakness on your in-laws. There are many questions that have to be answered. Why does your husband fear to leave his father's business? If he is a partner, why doesn't he have the courage to assert himself? Are the profits large enough to warrant salary raises? What contribution is he making to the business? I am not impressed with the time he puts into the business, I'd be more impressed with what he puts into the time.

I am not minimizing your problem. You have the right to live, to give your children what they need, enjoy a vacation, go to the beauty parlor, wear fine-fitting clothing. All this should be yours. The question you must answer is, must it come from your in-laws? You see, there is a difference between generosity and responsibility. It would be wonderful if they were more generous, but you have no right to expect it. You do have a right to demand that your husband gets paid in proportion to the work he puts in. No person can question that. It is the responsibility of an employer to pay his employees. It is the responsibility of one partner to give the other partner his share of the profits.

Why think of divorce? If you had an ugly wart on your right hand, would you have the entire arm amputated? Because your husband fears asking for a raise, you are ready to deprive your children of their father. What kind of thinking is this?

If your husband is a mama's boy and lacks a strong ego, then you go ahead and help him build it. You cannot do this by belittling him, making him feel inadequate, tearing down his defenses, calling him names, deriding his parents. Rather do it constructively—do it with love, understanding, purpose, do it quietly and calmly—over a cup of coffee if you will.

However, separate all your problems and solve only those that are problems. Continue to be a good daughter-in-law. You will derive great satisfaction from this, and your own in-laws in time will treat you the same way. Keep on lighting the candles of others; it will not in the least detract light from your own.

When he courted her, he catered to her every wish. Now he wants to be the complete boss.

— 26 —

My Husband Wants to Be Boss

THE PROBLEM

I have been married seven years and it seems to me my husband is quite different from the way he was when he was courting me. Now he prefers to do things by himself. He goes to the movies alone; prefers to take long walks by himself and I feel left out of his life.

The greatest difficulty in our way is that he wants to be boss in the family. He feels that decisions about family budgeting should be his since he is the one who works for a living. I feel that I should have as much of a say as to expenditures as he has. After all, I too am contributing to the running of the household by shopping and by keeping house. In fact, in my family my mother always made the major decisions and my father went along. In his family, his father is the absolute ruler.

Unfortunately, I feel left out. He seldom thinks of my comfort though he goes out of his way to please his friends. When I call this to his attention, he really loses his temper, storms out of the house and doesn't return home for hours. When he does, it becomes my turn to let go. The effect this has on my two children only time will tell.

Frankly, I have thought of leaving him quite often and I suppose one of these days I'll do just that. I've told him this but it seems to go in one ear and out of the other. Believe me, it wasn't this way when he was courting me. At that time, he tried his best to please me. Whatever wish I made he quickly granted. I certainly believed that I was getting married to a prince. Unfortunately, my prince disappeared and instead I have a dictator.

Just what do I do to make my husband realize that I am around? I am at my wit's end.

THE REPLY

Some time ago a newspaper conducted an interesting survey in regard to family relationships. In an effort to determine certain facts of family life, it sent out a questionaire to school children containing this simple question, "Who is the boss in your home?"

Answers generally fell into two groups. Some replied that it was the father. A great many indicated that it was the mother. One reply really set collators on their heels. It contained this very honest observation: "I really don't know who's the boss in our house. My father and mother are still arguing about it."

Your children evidently have the same reaction since they are daily witnesses to your struggle for dictatorship in the household. Or at least, you resent your husband's running the household. There is a conflict between your husband and you. He, following the precedent set by his family wants to assume legislative, executive and veto rights. This irks you because in your family these rights were vested in your mother. This situation makes for dangerous and explosive ammunition. Very often a genuine explosion occurs.

Surely, there are areas in daily living where your husband should have the final say, just as there are areas where you ought to make all the decisions. I am quite certain that your husband does not interfere in the feeding and bathing of the children, nor is he concerned about the way you prepare meals. He is not interested in where you do your retail shopping. All this he gladly leaves to you.

When it comes to the raising of children both you and your husband should be involved. Neither one of you has the right to tell the other, "This is not your domain, please stay out." There should be no dispute, there need be no boss; harmony and understanding should rule. Neither you nor your husband should aim to achieve a point of vantage from which you can dominate, exploit, control, and intimidate the other. Neither one of you should be grasping and anxious.

The world is divided into two kinds of people—climbers and doers. The aim of the climber is to get to the top of anything that can be reached. He is the hungry one, born hungry and dying hungry. But still he must climb to the pointless end. Sometimes he does not know why he climbs but he must. He craves to be on the top looking down.

Doers shape a world inside their hearts. A doer explores, produces and builds. He needs no recognition from the rest of the world and so does not feel the necessity to be on top. Some women are doers and indicate to their children that, 'Dad is the head of the household.' They understand that this feeling in no way detracts from their extremely important position of being mother. Is it possible that you are not satisfied with your own self-image?

You see, a person may have a problem or he might be one. I don't wish to minimize the hurt you suffer when your husband decides to go to a movie without you, or does a favor not too graciously for you. Something is wrong somewhere; of this I am certain. But I must point out that the person who is a problem does not feel he has a problem. He gets along taking from others who put up with him. The person who puts up with him is the real problem. In your case, it might just be *you.*

Many times, those who are problems have no incentive to improve their own behavior. They are quite content to continue with their way of life as long as it continues to pay them fair dividends. The one who needs the help is the one on whom they lean and the one they exploit. The victim must be taught to be more independent, more secure, and more adequate. He must also be able to examine his own behavior, his own reactions and responses to challenges of life. Why did your husband go from an attentive lover to a self-interested husband whose greatest desire is to do a 'solo'? Ask yourself this question and when you get the answer, act on it! This certainly does not imply jumping into the nearest taxi with your children and heading straight for the divorce court. That might only succeed in giving you many more uncalled for problems.

"Two persons who have chosen each other out of all the species, with the design to be each others' mutual comfort and entertainment," wrote Addison, "have, in that action, bound themselves to be good-humored, affable, discreet, forgiving, patient and joyful, with respect to each other's frailties and perfections, to the end of their lives."

You may not like what I am about to say but I'll say it nevertheless. When a man and woman marry, their romance ceases and their history commences. Motivate your husband toward greater achievements in his life. Make him feel how important he is to you and the children. The 'pie' of romance and history can be sliced in many directions.

What greater thing is there for two people than to feel that they are joined for life — to strenghten each other, to rest on each other, to minister to each other, to be united with each other, to find love, comfort and understanding by giving it.

Ask what you should do to make your husband realize that you are around? There are many answers, but nagging is not one of them. Greet him with a smile instead of a mop and a pail of soapy water. Greet him with a warm smile instead of complaints about the events of the day. Try to remember how he found you when he courted you during those wonderful earlier days, and try to look that way. Remember that your greatest asset is your femininity. No woman, nowadays, has the right to look plain and washed out, when she can look young and glamorous. Try some of these tonics and when you begin to see the light of love in his life, at that time discuss your need for family recognition. Whatever you do, don't run for a divorce; rather seek a marriage counselor and ask him for more detailed advice. You'll find it will pay off!

My husband lives like a king and demands that I be his maid in waiting.

– 27 –

My Marriage Is One-Sided!

THE PROBLEM

We've been married for nine years, and during most of that time I've kept my job in the office. I say most of the time because I did take time off to have our two children.

At the very start of our marriage, I was going to work for a few months to give us a head-start in furnishing our home. After nine years, it seems that the "Operation Head Start" is now a permanent routine in our home. I doubt that my husband can manage on his salary alone.

Neither of us are great spenders, but when you have to dress, feed and send two boys to a yeshivah, it is a great drain on the pocket. And so, each morning at 8:30 my husband and I leave for work. By then, our sons have gone off to school as well.

I have so arranged my hours that I am able to be at home by 4:30 in the afternoon. My husband arrives home just one hour later. When I get home, there are a million and one things I have to do. It isn't only the preparation of the dinner meal but greeting the children, doing some shopping, answering the telephone that consumes so much of the time. Many an afternoon, I grab out the ironing board and prepare clothing for my children for the next day. On weekends I am on hands and knees scrubbing floors and doing a very thorough cleanup. In other words, I do a full-time job after doing a full time office job, and this I do six days a week. Saturday may be a day of rest but to me it still means preparing meals, serving them, giving time to the children, and washing a mountain of dishes at the end of the day.

My husband lives like a king, a monarch with many maids and butlers around him. He comes home from work and makes a beeline for his favorite chair in front of the television screen, waiting for a call for dinner. I might add that he expects a full dinner, none of the last-minute scraps for him. It must be from "soup to nuts." He wants to be wined and dined and never lends a hand in any area of the home.

All I want is that he help with a few things in the house so that I don't feel like a maid, and also have a few minutes of time to relax. My husband tells me that he leaves the running of the house to me. Unfortunately, this means taking care of the budget and with it every extra and extraordinary expense.

I feel that I live in a beehive with my husband being the drone. I was always under the impression that men should be the heads of families, that they are the lions, the dragon slayers. If this is so, I've been fooled. If this is what the male world calls the equality of the sexes, I'm all for less equality. How do I get out of this situation? Remember, I'm not looking for divorce, just a change in status. I want my husband to wear the pants again. I'll be content with a dainty, feminine well-starched apron.

HELP!

THE REPLY

There are a few questions I'd like to ask before I get along in this letter. You are working and your husband is the type of man who does not get his hands wet or dirty. This would lead one to believe that you have successfully put yourself into a harness, and that you are getting quite sick of the traces. The double role of bread-winner and homemaker has become wearisome. Why not admit that you are not superhuman and hire a cleaning woman once or twice a week? It may mean that your children will have to do with a few less shirts, or even without a summer vacation in camp, but it will lead you to enjoy your life a great deal more.

Sounds simple, doesn't it?

In addition, I'd stand up and ask your husband to take a seat more to the front of activity. Make some very definite demands upon him. Ask him to help you set the table. Go into the living room, walk up to his front T. V. seat, hand him a towel and ask him to help with the dishes. Ask him to drive you to the store to do some grocery shopping. If he gets tired of waiting in the car next time, hand him the list and ask him to go alone.

It might just be that you work harder than your husband. This leads, as in your case, to deep resentment. It gives the wife the feeling that she is being used. In such an instance, the best thing to do is discuss the entire matter with the husband. "It's either I quit work and we tighten the belt," I'd say, "or dear hubby, you put your hand under the running faucet and wash a dish or two." Put it to him clearly, simply, and concisely, and give him the choice. Unless he is a complete egocentric, it ought to bring him around to the reality of the situation. Whatever your husband is, he knows how to add 2 and 2. He is quite capable of subtracting your weekly income from the gross and determining how things would look if you just remained at home, cooking at leisure, and ironing clothes during the rainy season. Sounds good, doesn't it?

"Togetherness In Marriage" has been a popular slogan for many years. Magazine articles preach this sure-fire recipe for marital happiness. Generally, writers talk about togetherness in interests, in activity, in thought, feeling, and attitude. Advertisers utilize it. Governments talk about it. Plays and movies utilize it as a theme.

Why not carry this idea a bit further into your own married

life? Inform your husband that togetherness is a two-way street with traffic moving in both directions. Sit down with him and serve up some of this togetherness pie, and don't fail to serve him a healthy, male slice. You can be democratic and offer him a choice of some household duties so that your own work can be made a bit easier. Togetherness includes watching television, going to the movies, bowling, visiting relatives, attending social functions, and taking turns at the kitchen sink.

Lest I'm hanged in effigy by angry male readers, let me add that I am speaking of togetherness where there are two working partners. Not for one minute am I suggesting that the apron be made part of the permanent apparel of the male. I certainly am not advocating a change in the male status, but what is right is right. Where the question of selfishness or fairness is a constantly intruding subject, the marital relationship must be painful. "When the idea of imposition comes in the door, love flies out the window" is the way one poet expressed it.

Your husband must understand and appreciate your needs. Such understanding presupposes a willingness to give as well as take; to love as well as be loved; to forget as well as remember.

Get out of the harness and kick over the traces, but do it tactfully, wisely, and intelligently.

He'd rather watch television than make love.

– 28 –

"I'm Married to a T.V. Set!"

THE PROBLEM

What is wrong with men today? They feel they are always overworked and must be permitted, upon reaching home, to rest, relax, snooze. They rebel at being asked to help around the house. Asking them to take the garbage out seems to be an infringement on their natural rights. They no longer help with the dishes, the family packing, and going to the store. "Marriage is a fifty-fifty proposition," they sing in chorus. "And our fifty percent is contributed with our daily stint at the office, factory, or salesroom." Too many marriages, mine included, operate on a strict union contract. "I go to work, you take care of the house. I don't ask you to work in the store, don't ask me to work in the house."

To make matters worse, husbands always seem to have one ear and one eye on the T.V. screen, one ear tuned in to the transistor radio, and one eye glued to the newspaper. Despite all this lack of communication, they feel they are fulfilling their marital vows.

Can so many wives possibly be such complete bores to their husbands? What are the rights and responsibilities of the marital partners? Do I have the right to expect my husband to help around the house? Do I have the right to expect him to spend his leisure time talking with me and catering to my needs? I always thought marriage was a partnership. It seems to me that in a partnership responsibilities as well as profits are distributed equally. I am positive many readers will be interested in what you have to say about this problem.

THE REPLY

Does it really matter who puts the baby to sleep the greater number of times each week, as long as the mutually loved baby gets the proper amount of rest? Does it matter if you take the garbage out when it isn't your turn? Does it really matter who did more to help get the family ready for the summer vacation? Not really!

What really counts is that the best result has been achieved through family effort. "In order to form a more perfect union," all records and ledgers must be discarded, minor infringements must be written off immediately, and more serious transgressions must be discounted and cancelled with the least possible delay. Due bills of patching things up must be cleared before too much interest accrues, and certainly before it becomes necessary to hand them over to a marital agency for collection.

Sometimes, people are sufficiently fortunate to make a match where each one compensates the other, where the sole aim of each seems to be the fulfillment of the other's happiness. This is the ideal way to be married and the way it should be . . . me for you and you for me. However, if you wish to be honest, you must admit that it is rare to hear such a duet of utter selflessness. The intentions are there and sincerely meant, but it seldom works that way. Indeed, such a marriage cannot be used as the example of an excellent marriage because it is perfection, and perfection is generally unattainable.

But there is a kind of excellent marriage which is accessible. Perhaps you have it and don't realize it. Perhaps you have it and would be happy with it were it not for the well-meant interference of friends and family. Your marriage may have inequalities, but the ideal marriage is not necessarily the one where each contributes exactly his 50%. As long as the sum of the two individual efforts is equal to 100%, the marriage equation works out.

You criticize your husband's television habits and his lack of cooperation in household chores. Wisely does the Midrash comemnt, "Love without criticism is not love." A wise man once counseled, "At times, a husband should be blind; a wife, somewhat deaf; both, a bit dumb." There are certain problems that arithmetic cannot solve. You cannot count the number of times your husband refuses to don the apron.

Far be it from me to belittle the woman's contribution to the management of the home. Her house must be in running order, her children must be sent to school, shopping must be done, meals must be prepared, to mention just a few. However, in no way, can you compare the stress and strain, the frustration and tension the husband experiences in his daily toil around the clock and the calendar. To expect him, after a difficult day at work, to pick up mop and pail, dish and dish-rag; to help feed the youngsters, to make the formula, to sterilize the bottles, to clean the basement, repair Moishe's bicycle, and tell the neighbor's off because they used the ashcan, is asking and expecting too much.

To-day's wife, surrounded by her labor saving devices, the telephone at her elbow to place orders, electric oven ready to bake the cake from the contents of a ready-mix package, her pressure cooker on the alert to boil the chicken in about eight minutes, asks too much of the male who just entered the home from his ordeal in a jammed-packed IRT subway train.

Marriage, rather than a 50/50 partnership, is built on a merit system. Your conscience is the proctor; your heart, the machinery; love is the reward. If the proctor is good, it will know how to manage the machinery. If your heart is a good worker, it will heed the wishes of the proctor. If both work together, the merit system insures success.

The word marriage should be synonymous with words like Love, Understanding, Communication, Blessedness, Consideration, Devotion, to mention a few. You were not pushed into marriage. On the contrary, from the time you learned to spell the word, you dreamed of entering into marriage and building your own little nest feathered with love and cemented with devotion.

If you use the right tools, you can improve your marriage. You must be willing to work things out. If you try hard enough, have patience, give love, the marriage will improve. Take a little, and give a lot more, and throw away the double-entry set of books you use to record your efforts on behalf of the family.

Don't sell the T.V. set, it won't work. But greet him at the door wearing something fresh and clean. Remember, your husband fell in love with the "feminine" in you and not your I.Q. or the cleanliness of your waxed floors. Say hello to him with a smile instead of a groan. Watch the T.V. shows with him. During mealtime, engage him in conversation. Show an interest in his job and his work.

To quote novelist Kathleen Norris, "Marriage is a job. Happiness or unhappiness has nothing to do with it. There was never a marriage that could not be made a success, nor a marriage that could not have ended in bitterness and failure."

*After being married for
32 years she learns that
her husband has strayed.*

– 29 –

Can I Remain Married to a Liar?

THE PROBLEM

I am 50 years of age, my husband is 53. We have been married for 32 years, most of them happy years, with our ups and downs. We have two lovely children who are married. I am looking forward to becoming a grandmother soon.

Three years ago, I began to notice a vast change in my husband. He began staying out late, and coming home from work later each day. When I questioned him about it, he always had some kind of excuse ready. His salary was never too big and I always had to struggle a little, but I never complained. I knew he was a hard worker and did the best he could. Suddenly, I got a cut in my house money. He said that business was very bad. I loved my husband very much and accepted all that he told me. "There is no fool like an old fool." Then he began to stay out until 2 and 3 in the morning. I asked him several times if there was some other woman. I could sense the change in his attitude toward me, even though he was still kind and considerate. Every time I spoke to him, he told me not to be foolish, that he still loved me. My children also told me not to be so silly.

However, things got worse. He lost his desire for me and our home. When I asked him to go with me, he said he was tired and that I should go alone. In the past, he had always gone with me. My friends and family thought he was the ideal husband.

Several months ago, on a Saturday evening, he came home late as usual. About an hour later, this woman (if she can be called a woman) came up to my house. One look at my husband's face and all my fears materialized. She told me that she had been my husband's mistress for 3 years and that there were others before her. This, he had told her. She is not of our religion and has three grown sons, the eldest 26, the youngest 20. None of them work, one has a prison record.

My husband supports the family, does their shopping, buys her clothes, pays her bills. My own telephone was disconnected because my husband said he could not afford one. She told me that he had promised to marry her and indicated that I was ill and would be given the news when I recovered. Some time ago, I did have a slight operation. I remember that when I came out of the hospital he left on a weekend vacation, despite my pleas for him to remain with me. He left with her and remained away five days.

She showed me love letters he had written her, and talked about the many gifts he had given her. I don't even have a winter coat. Unfortunately, one of my children was present when this woman told this terrible story. During the entire conversation, my husband did not utter one word in defense or protest.

When she was ready to leave, she asked him to go with her and he refused. After she left, I told him he could leave if he really wanted to. He said he loved me and always did. I can't believe it. He has always taken me for granted and still does.

Dr. Mandel, how can I still love him, knowing what I do? I love him very much but there are times I hate him. I don't believe any thing he tells me because I know what a liar he is. He tells me that he has learned his lesson, and will behave from now on. I want to believe him so much, but I can't. If he loved me how could he have done what he did to me? He's in debt for the thousands of dollars he spent for this woman and her family. It will take him years to pay. I still have to do without the things I want, and I never wanted much. Now I feel I've had enough and want the same that she had. Is that wrong? I've lost 45 pounds since then, can't eat or sleep. I forgave him but how can I forget? How can I have faith and trust in him?

THE REPLY

Many times, the medication prescribed by a doctor must fit the condition of the patient. Doctors, sometimes, are prevented from prescribing much needed medicines because the patient's condition makes it almost impossible for it to be taken regularly.

I find myself in the same situation now. The fact that you have written me is clear-cut indication that you want a "tonic" rather than an "operation." You lived a theme of love and trust all through the 32 years of your married life. You loved your husband, and even when you found him to be a deceiver and a fraud, you continued to love him. Confronted by his "other woman," and hearing a story of duplicity, the most you could do was to give him the choice of staying or leaving with "that woman." Doesn't that indicate the course of action you wanted to take? You want to hate him, but you say, "I love him very much!"

Because you say you still love him, I cannot prescribe the amputation that other women would have desired. You indicate that you forgave your husband. You still live with him, despite the additional fact that you were deprived of necessities while luxuries were bestowed upon an immoral woman and her indulgent, indifferent delinquent sons. What you are really saying by your action is "Please tell me that he will be good from now on because I don't want to lose him. I can't live alone."

You are a fine, loving, devoted wife, one who has lived a moral life. At the same time you are a weak individual. Perhaps it was this weakness on your part that helped your husband wander, which he did several times. You didn't demand what was rightfully yours. You accepted the handouts he gave you. You permitted yourself to be blinded even when your heart told you things were not the same. You just didn't want to believe the truth.

Another woman might have demanded that this type of man leave immediately with his "other woman." Another woman would not have given such a man a home, a wife, and a family again. With strength and determination, she would have insisted that he chose his life with an immoral woman and her immoral children, and that a decent home could never be his again. She would not have given him the choice of staying or remaining. She would have made the choice and made him live with the filth he had picked. She would have done this even if it meant going back to work and living without a husband for the rest of her life.

You are not that type of woman. You want your united family once again. You want to believe, trust and love your husband, You'd like to believe that none of this happened, that it was all a dream, but it isn't!

Live with him, if you wish. Forgive him as you have done. But from now on, demand what is rightfully yours. Don't expect to have faith in him for quite a while. Don't believe in him. He has shamed both you and his children. Stand up and be strong. Perhaps, had you done this years ago, this might never have happened.

I am not minimizing the wrong he committed when I ask you to re-examine your own past behavior. Where are you to blame for your husband's erring ways? You indicate that most of the 32 years have been happy ones. You are soon to become a grandmother and he a grandfather. Your letter almost pleads for a magic formula to help you forget what he has done. You want to forget, you want to keep the family together, you want to stay married to your husband. Forgive and demand your rights. Forgive and adopt a "believe-in-myself" attitude. With time, and with the joy you will receive from your grandchildren, with your husband's complete attention to you, your needs and your wants, you may yet once again recapture some peace of mind. Don't expect to forget, though you forgive, nor must you go out of your way to remember. Throw yourself into other activities. Don't be your husband's maid. Nor should you be so dependent upon him.

If he has any feeling in him, he too must be suffering, knowing that his children now know his past actions. A traffic ticket causes one to watch his driving. A heart attack causes someone to be careful in the amount of activity in which he engages. A prison sentence has some effect on some people, and causes them never again to err.

Your husband's selfish duplicity has now been uncovered. Perhaps, this will cause him never again to stray.

Marriage is a "do it yourself" proposition. It can be made to work.

-30-

Make Marriage Work

Ask a freshman in high school, "Son, do you understand love?" He will write you an essay. Ask an old bachelor. He will write you a book. Ask a married man. He just grins and shakes his head. He has learned that while love and marriage go together, it isn't the love that he has seen portrayed on his 21" color television screen. He knows that it takes two to be in love, and it takes both mates to make marriage work.

A marriage can yield lasting satisfactions. It can be rich in warmth and understanding, but it never can be the universal solution to all problems. Marriage does not basically change people. It can make a happy person happier, but it can never be a unilateral solution to one's problems.

If you have a piece of wire too short to reach a desired point you splice it. This is a simple procedure and one almost any amateur can do. But if you wish to make the splice firm and reasonably neat so the wire doesn't look as though it were wearing a fracture splint, you must take care and exercise good workmanship. Marriage works pretty much the same way. Almost any two normal humans can be successful in marriage if they are reasonable. Your marriage can be successful if both of you never cease working for its success. It is like a garden. It requires attention every day to keep the weeds from ruining it. The happiest marriages are generally those where husband and wife are eager to make the other happy. Marital happiness does not came packaged or ready made. It seems that people are willing to prepare diligently to become lawyers, plumbers, secretaries, but evidently not as candidates for a decent and lasting marriage. Marriage must be thought of as more than an adventure, more than a career. It is a school for developing virtues. It is the establishment of a home.

What does your wife want out of married life?

She wants to be accepted socially. She wants to feel she belongs to the group and is not an outsider. She wants to feel she means something to her husband. She needs to feel adequacy and worth as a person in her own right. Rightfully, we are taught "If your wife is short, bend down and whisper to her," i.e. the man should not think of himself as too superior to consult with his wife on his affairs. The best way to care for a wife is to encourage her to function to her fullest. Life is meant to be lived. The miser who hoards it cheats only himself. Marriage can be likened to a basket. It is woven by interlacing husband and wife with many ties. The shape, size, and beauty of this basket vary, for its construction is a "do it yourself" project. The durability and quality of the product will depend largely upon the combination of ties involved and their skillful use.

What does your husband want out of life? He wants a home, a bit of his own personal life. He wants some private areas of his own. He wants his own individuality. While he recognizes the fact that he is now a member of a new group, he does not wish to submerge his own ego. He wants to share his interests. He wants to earn praise and to hear it. He strives for warmth, for understanding, for love.

How this is to be done is another matter. A couple should try to eliminate needless antagonisms. Get rid of the chip on the shoulder. Stop listening to the relatives coaching from the side-lines. Be just and fair. Sincerity and frankness are to marriage what honesty and integrity are to business. Their presence insures success; their absence leads to bankruptcy. Discuss your marital problems but don't make this a daily diet of conversation. Develop areas of agreement. Be a good sport. Smile more often. Develop a sense of humor. Surrender your positions especially on non-essentials. It isn't really important to have the last word. Permit your spouse to develop ego satisfactions. Each of you must have an opportunity to feel important, wise, and intelligent. Develop and maintain outside interests. Keep improving yourself. Your looks may fade, but your interests must always increase.

Husbands, if you adore her, adorn her. This is the essence of a happy marriage. Show pleasure and satisfaction with her gifts. Compliment her home-making ability. Make her relatives welcome in your home. Do not air your grievances in public. Be punctual with meals and appointments. Call up during the day and chat for a few minutes without giving specific instructions as to some chore you wish carried out. Say some of the things to her you used to say in your counting days. Date her! Court her! Woo her! Don't take her for granted. Remember she may have come from one of your ribs, but not from your backbone. And bear in mind the advice a Quaker once gave to his son on his wedding day: "When thee went a-courting I told thee to keep thy eyes open; now that thou art married, I tell thee to keep them half shut."

Wives, don't make a big issue of your husband's shortcomings. Don't criticize him in front of friends or relatives. When he starts telling a story, let him finish it even though you feel you could do a better job. Don't gripe about entertaining his friends and relatives. Don't belittle his abilities as a husband or a provider.

Christopher Morley's definition is right: "The plural of spouse is spice." Spice is seasoning, adds taste to foods. Your married life needs spice. Don't spare it, spend it.

A man once took his fine Swiss watch to a jeweler for adjustment. The jeweler asked, "When do you wind your watch?" "Why, at night before I retire," replied the customer.

"Oh," said the jeweler, "a watch as fine as this should be wound in the morning, so that it can start the day on a strong spring. It would then be prepared against the bumps and shocks of the day."

What is good for the watch is good for the marital partners. They should start their marital careers on a strong spring. An important ingredient for a really successful marriage is high fidelity . . . in thinking and in actions.

BOOK FOUR

PARENTS AND
CHILDREN

PARENTS AND CHILDREN

Introduction

What is the greatest national emergency facing the United States? Is it poverty, crime, communism? A specially created federal committee, after making a study, decided it was none of these. They felt that the greatest concern to our country at this time was the breakdown of the home.

There seems to be no planning in the home, at least not in the spiritual, moral, and ethical areas. There are homes which move along without goals and without direction. It is this lack of direction that leads to the eventual bankruptcy of the home.

It is in the home alone that all the virtues can be practiced, starting from personal cleanliness to spiritual devotion and from earning one's own bread to the service of humanity. We must understand that the home is the cradle into which the future is born. There is no synthetic replacement for a decent home. Religion can preach, the school can teach, but the home must convert sermons and lessons into a way of life.

A child who has a good home, who can grow and mature in an atmosphere of love, understanding, confidence and harmony, who is surrounded by people who have a sound sense of values in life, who sees religion lived as well as studied, such a child has a better opportunity of developing a stable personality and a good character.

A home is a good home if children are taught respect and if they are given limits. Without limits, without knowing responsibilities they grow into irresponsible, selfish, and conscienceless adults. And this should be done without "thunder and lightning." It is better to teach with patience than with the stick.

"What are limits?" parents keep on asking. "May I permit my teen-age daughter to attend Saturday evening coed socials?" "What time may she come home at the end of the evening social?" "Can she accept dates?"

Dr. Alonzo G. Grace, former dean of the University of Illinois College of Education, commented that "too many parents try to advance their children socially too quickly. The junior prom, corsage and all the accompanying social activity at the seventh-grade level is stupid. Freedom without restriction at the adolescent stage—that is, no restriction and understanding on the hours out, the use of the car, the amount of allowance—spells trouble."

It is far too early for the 14-year-old girl to be given a pair of high heels. She finds both the physical and emotional balance too difficult. A parent asks for trouble when he sends his daughter to hotel week-end conventions. Many times, the teen-ager is completely unprepared for the social whirl into which he or she has been thrown. It is rather foolish for a young teen-ager, with her mountainous hair-do, with paint, powder, eye-shadow, to be going steady with an unsteady, immature young man, who, often must be reminded by his parents to do his homework, brush his teeth, and take a shower.

Children must learn that maturity cannot be rushed. They need limits and parents should again assume complete responsibility for teaching discipline to their children. They should not delegate this important job to teachers and schools. It is important to realize that each parent, in building the character of his child, also builds his nation and its future. The successful parent is truly the architect of tomorrow.

Parents must not permit their homes to become "child-centered." Rights of parents must never be ignored. When parents respect themselves and demand proper attention, the children benefit. It is obvious that children who are not controlled, and who know no limits when they are young, do not learn self-control as adults. To have too much too soon dulls the appetite and robs the child, rather than benefits him.

Parents ought to establish a curfew, and, odd as it may

seem to children, ten o'clock for 13 year olds is generous, and eleven o'clock for sixteen year olds is equally generous. After all, strength of character consists of two things—power of will and power of self-restraint.

When there is group dating the parent should be informed just where the group will be, and regular week-end coed socials in that age bracket should be discouraged no matter who sponsors them.

As long as the child lives under the parental roof, the parents retain the right to give and to withdraw privileges. Children demand freedom but they must be made to understand that freedom is a precious possession and they must learn how to use it. They must know that freedom is not the right to do whatever they please. Freedom should follow responsibility. As children gain in responsibility they can be permitted more freedom. Parents must set up restrictions and prohibitions until they are certain that a child has enough self-control and has assumed responsibility for his own discipline.

The important thing to remember is that children should not be forced into adulthood too quickly, and by this is meant, symbols of adulthood. Dating should be discouraged. Heels, cosmetics, new hair-dos, and hair colors should be prohibited. Emphasis should not be on the opposite sex but rather, are my assignments complete? Am I getting enough of an average to be admitted into college? Have I done my required reading? Is my project finished? And after these responsibilities have been taken care of, why not? Is my room clean? How can I make my mother's work a bit easier? Should I polish the furniture, take out the garbage, dust the venetian blinds?

Let us emphasize character instead of coeds. Let us build stability instead of socials. Let us motivate our teen-agers to study regularly instead of going steady. In a nut-shell, our children deserve their childhood years. Let them enjoy them.

Parents feel their life is over because they discovered their only child is a homosexual.

–1–

My Son Is a Homosexual

THE PROBLEM

You cannot imagine the tremendous shock my husband and I experienced when we learned that my 21-year-old son is a homosexual. He had returned from a trip abroad some weeks ago and was welcomed with open arms. Soon afterward mysterious calls came to the house, and his conversations on the telephone were always guarded.

One morning I entered his room and found a letter. When I started to read it, I thought I was reading a love letter from a girl he had met on the other side. When I came to the signature I was ready to faint. It was signed with a man's name.

That evening I confronted my son who answered, "Now you know that I am a queer." He told us the entire story, and how it had begun years ago when he was being used by a few older boys on our street for their own pleasure. Somehow he enjoyed the experiences and homosexuality became his way of life.

We should have realized this before. He never did date but we marked that down to his shyness, and we rather liked his attention to school and not to the opposite sex. We misunderstood his inactivity and felt he was just not a run-around, and when the time would come he would be ready for marriage and would settle down.

Now our world is all but shattered. How can we really face life, enjoy ourselves when our only child is a homosexual? We invested our total lives in our son and now we stand ashamed before our relatives and friends. Since we discovered this terrible thing, we just sit at home, look at one another, and keep asking what did we do wrong?

Now what do we do? Where do we go for help? I'm not so certain that he even wants help or feels he needs it. He keeps telling us that this is a new era, that homosexuality is a way of life and that we ought to grow up.

Where did we fail him? How did this happen under our very eyes? Again, what shall we do?

THE REPLY

There are so many psychological and environmental influences that could have caused your son to change in the direction of homosexual activity, that to attempt to explain all in the confines of a column would be much too difficult. Suffice it to say that a combination of situations plus the fact that he fell into the company of homosexuals caused him to sway from heterosexual interests and activities to homosexuality.

I might also add that whenever parents of young men and women discover that their offspring are homosexuals, tragedy sets in because most of these parents accuse themselves of being responsible in one way or another. This feeling of guilt is of no help to anyone—not to the parents and not to the young man or woman.

It is foolish to feel shame because of your son's sexuality. What he is doing is not because he is sinful but rather because he is a disturbed individual, compulsive, neurotic, and with a poor sex-role identification. I would like to believe that homosexuality is an acquired condition and thus can be unlearned Homosexuality is curable, and any number of psychiatrists and psychoanalysts will attest to this opinion. Dr. Albert Ellis, Dr. Edmund Bergler and many others have written about their successful treatment of homosexuals.

Of course none indicate that the process is easy, or that it is usually successful. As in every illness there are successes and failures. It takes the cooperation of parents, colleagues, friends, neighbors and the community, not to mention the homosexual himself to effect a cure. To begin with certain assumptions ought to be made:

1. The homosexual is no more antisocial than the person who suffers from claustrophobia and should be no more of a reason for ridicule, punishment, and embarrassment, than the fear of heights.

2. That like other fears, phobias, compulsions, and emotional difficulties and disorders, homosexuality can sometimes be alleviated, and where this is possible it is desirable for the individual that he be encouraged to do so.

The fact that fixed homosexuals are exceptionally difficult to treat is not phenomenal, since all seriously disturbed individuals resist getting better. In addition to which millions of human beings, for example, know very precisely that they smoke, eat, or drink too much. They always accept the fact that this is self-sabotaging behavior, and they often know exactly what they must do to cut down. Yet, in spite of their insights to cut down or stop, they fail to do either for any length of time.

Homosexuals are even more difficult to treat than most other psychotherapy patients for several reasons. They frequently do not admit that they are basically disturbed, but insist that only society is disturbed for persecuting them. They often enjoy their homosexual acts immensely and therefore cannot look upon these acts as disabling symptoms. Isn't this the case of your son? He keeps telling you that you are behind the times.

My advice to you is to motivate your son to go for help. This is no easy task, but it has been done before and you can do it now. A competent therapist will be able to fight the patient's symptomatology without fighting him, and in this way be able to show your son the error of his ways without demonstrating that he is a queer for displaying these erroneous ways.

There is nothing to be gained in discussing your son with friends, family, and neighbors. They cannot really help and it will afford them the juiciest piece of neighborly gossip.

Seek professional advice. Life isn't over. Things can be done for your son, and the more willing he will be, the greater the opportunity for change to heterosexuality. You can still be a grandmother, believe me, you can.

A teenager feels that he should be left alone to make his own mistakes.

-2-
A Teenager Speaks Up

THE PROBLEM

I think that teenagers are the happiest people on earth. Unlike a young child who may seem happier, teenagers appreciate and understand their happiness. Unlike adults, teenagers have few worries, and those they have they handle with apparent ease.

"Nonsense" would be the typical adult response to this thought. An adult is more capable of handling his troubles and worries than the teenager can handle his. An adult has knowledge, understanding, and experience.

The one word "experience," in reality, contradicts the complete idea of an adult's superiority in all matters. It seems to me an adult uses experience as a crutch which he feeds to his own doubtful feeling of superiority.

A teenager knows that experience is not what it is cracked up to be. Experience restricts you to one line of thought and often deters you from acquiring new ideas. Experience gives you maximum certainty and minimum research. It is the doubt that motivates a thirst for knowledge. So-called experience makes one lose ingenuity. Experience brings prejudice and makes it difficult for one to adjust to new environments and new ways of thinking.

How terrible it is that with this experience that parents rear their children, with this experience parents claim they know what is good or bad, right or wrong. It is their experience that makes parents claim that anything new and anything they don't completely understand is wrong and "bad for you."

Teenagers, like many adults, may think they know everything but their minds are at least open to question. I honestly think the teenagers should consider themselves fortunate they lack the most cherished adult possession: Experience.

THE REPLY

New ideas are like new shoes—it is difficult to discard the old which have been broken in, and to adjust ourselves to the new to which we are unaccustomed. I certainly agree with you that new ideas should be adopted into our way of life. But I believe the adoption of these new ideas should be considered in the light of our experience. Only after we study the new ideas and are convinced that the change will result in great and genuine benefits should they be adopted. Change in itself does not always spell out progress. I would not like new medications to be sold across a drug counter until they have been thoroughly tested, until experience has proven that they are both safe and beneficial.

I firmly believe that adults should not press their experience on children. Not that it is incorrect, but rather because I feel that teenagers are entitled to make their bundle of mistakes. A person can learn from his defeats as well as from his successes. If the child is always protected, if he is cushioned against failure, if he is told "learn from my experience," he will never really benefit. Early childhood and adolescence is basic training for life and might easily be rugged and difficult.

However, there is a duty that is incumbent on parents. They should act as directional signals to their children. They owe it to their sons and daughters to offer guidance. They should offer direction without directing. They should be the coach of the team, but not play the game. They should permit the boy and girl to mature and learn.

Experience is an extract of suffering, and as such, if properly used, can minimize the suffering of another. Yet, it has been said that no man will learn from the suffering of another; he must suffer himself.

"When I was young I was sure of everything," advised a middle-age man, "but in a few years, having been mistaken a thousand times, I was not half so sure of most things as I was before."

There must be a happy medium. A parent should reveal his own experiences with certain situations but he must also bear in mind that regardless of circumstances, each man lives in a world of his own making.

A teenager defends smoking pot and claims that the cigarette smoking of adults is more harmful.

-3-

I Smoke Pot, So What?

THE PROBLEM

Like tens of thousands of other youngsters throughout the country, I smoke pot. I smoke it and I like it. I do it because it's around, because I like it, and because it's one way to tell the establishment what a terrible mess they made out of life. Believe me, when parents say marijuana is bad for youngsters, it's just another example of the older generation not knowing the facts.

Now, in every magazine that wants to increase its circulation, an article appears warning the citizens of the menace of Pot Smoking. I must admit it is a subject of much controversy. It's much talked about, but little understood. Many questions have come up. Does it dull the senses? Injure the mind? Can it be habit-forming? Will it lead to stronger drugs? Or is it only a mild stimulus, no different from a double Scotch? Everyone and his grandmother seems to have an opinion.

To parents, the word "pot" brings fear. But they keep on smoking cigarettes despite all the studies made about cancer and heart trouble. My father lights one cigarette with the stub of another. Believe me, our television room seems like a smoke screen with my parents lighting up cigarette after cigarette. They smoke cigarettes and I smoke pot. Cigarettes cause cancer —pot doesn't. So why shouldn't we smoke it, especially when it makes us feel so good?

When I smoke pot and really get stoned, I feel different, better, much more observant. A feeling of peace and tranquility flows all over me. I don't cough, don't gasp for breath. In fact I feel like a man. By the way, have you ever tried pot? Try it and you will be able to listen more attentively and understandingly to all the tales of woe, related by all the non-pot smokers.

So, tell me what is wrong with pot smoking? Where is it dangerous? Why should I stop?

THE REPLY

Let's do this right. To begin with, I don't agree that your parents should smoke cigarettes. It does cause cancer. But by no means, do I feel that this fact should cause you to use marijuana. It makes no sense to me if you only smoke because your parents are bent on harming their own bodies, and shortening their own lives.

Marijuana is a drug which affects the mind. The active ingredient in marijuana is an oil prepared from the female hemp plant—whose scientific name is Cannabis Sativa. Marijuana is also referred to as "The Weed," "Pot," "Stuff," "Grass," "Indian Hay," "Tea," "Mary Jane," and on and on.

No doubt it is widespread. A 5-year campus survey in California showed that 57% of the students had smoked marijuana at least once. At Boston University, researchers indicated that it was difficult to find students who had never smoked pot.

In 1969, *Newsweek* reported that 32% of students on U.S. campuses smoked pot. At Berkeley, about 75% of the student body has used drugs at one time or another. No doubt these percentages are much higher today than they were in 1969.

Let me quote from the Pharmacological Basis of Therapeutics as to what happens to the physical body under the influence of marijuana. "On smoking the drug, there is usually an increase in pulse rate, a slight rise in blood pressure, and conjunctival vascular congestion; blood sugar is slightly elevated; there is urinary frequency without diuresis; and dryness of the mouth and throat as well as nausea, vomiting, and occasional diarrhea have also been noted." Other investigators report a sluggish pupillary response to light, slight tremors and a partial deterioration of bodily coordination.

Now read this report from experienced researchers: "The most common reaction is the development of a dreamy state of altered consciousness in which ideas seem disconnected, uncontrollable, and freely flowing. Ideas come in disrupted sequences, things long forgotten are remembered, and others well known cannot be recalled. Perception is disturbed, minutes seem to be hours, and seconds seem to be minutes; space may be broadened, and near objects may appear far distant. When larger doses are used, extremely vivid hallucinations may be experienced; there are often pleasant, but their coloring, sexual or otherwise, is more related to the user's personality than to specific drug effects.

In smoking pot, the user generally has no intention to go on to hard narcotics, such as heroin, but unfortunately, many seek even higher "highs." Said one heroin addict: "If I hadn't taken pot, I wouldn't have known how to get heroin or how to use it."

You talk about an evil world. Tell me, is marijuana really good medicine for these times? I don't think so. You know all the supposed reasons for smoking marijuana: Pressures of society, peer pressure, hypocrisy of the older generation, example of pill-popping parents, curiosity, enjoyment, thrills, easy availability of the drug. And on and on. But is it worth it to vent your frustrations and dislike for the Establishment by blowing your mind on pot? By dulling your ability to think?

Sure you have reasons to be upset! Who doesn't? Sure you are living in the shadow of the Bomb! You see man's inhumanity to man—nation against nation—race against race, and hypocritical action in the halls of the United Nations. It isn't a pretty picture. But why stick your head in the sand? Why hurt yourself? Why become a moral and mental coward?

There is a better way, one that works!

You are a physical human being, a unique creation of the Almighty. You don't like what you see! Change it and yourself. Don't blame your parents for a bad example. Become a better one. By all means, dissent—but not with drugs, not with losing your mind and body. That price of dissent is too high.

Close the generation gap. Begin to understand and improve your relations with your parents and society. Be willing to help society solve its problems. Learn concern for others. Respect your fellow human beings.

Don't be a pothead.

Be a man.

A mother is alarmed at discovering that her son smokes pot.

–4–

My Son Smokes Pot

THE PROBLEM

I just don't know how to begin this letter, nor do I know how to end it. I do know that both my husband and I are miserable and unhappy. Our world seems to have come to an end. We read about this in the papers, but never for a single moment thought it could happen to us.

Last week, we learned that our son smokes pot, and that he has been doing this for some time. Now we understand why his school work has not been up to par. Now we understand why he didn't converse with us too often. Now we understand why he is so anxious to get out of the house and be with his friends.

Where were our eyes? Why did we not see that he was having a problem? Why didn't we question him about what he was doing, where he was going. How could all this happen right under our noses?

Believe me, we both work hard. My husband has a business that keeps him busy 6 days a week. I, too, have gone back to work so that I could give my son luxuries. Believe me he lacks nothing. He has his own car, his own room, a generous allowance. We can afford it.

Yet, with exerything we have given him he has turned to others and to pot smoking for entertainment and release. Where did we fail him? Surely, we deprived him of absolutely nothing. When I was his age, I didn't have it so good.

I need help and I need it now. What should we do? How do we act with him? We both want to save our boy from going from bad to worse and he is headed in that direction.

THE REPLY

You ask why your son turned to pot. You relate how you have been so dedicated to his having every luxury in life. You describe how both you and your husband go to work to provide him with a car, a room, an allowance. You feel you have done your best to make life interesting and attractive. Now, you realize that you have failed. Frankly you have failed because you have not made life challenging and interesting.

Escapism is a primary reason millions are turning to drugs. The pressures of the modern world, war, the fear of the bomb, and the desire to get one's kicks before the hammer falls, influences many boys and girls to try drugs.

Boredom is another major reason young people try drugs. They have no real purpose in life which motivates them, inspires them, makes them feel useful and adequate. They feel dull, bored when everything is handed to them on a silver platter. Because of this they turn to drugs for excitement, fun, and glamour. Only too late do they realize that drugs do not give purpose to life. On the contrary, they confuse it, distort it, scramble up life's real goals.

The way to have turned your child away from smoking pot is to have made your home a happy one. It could not have been so with both parents working, with a father away 6 days a week and a mother who spent the greater part of each day in an office. It is true that the boy had an allowance and a car, but he lacked an interested mother and father. What he had was part-time parents attempting to do a full-time job, and failing.

Your boy needed the right kind of challenge and the right kind of interest at home, and he was not getting it. He was not living in a happy home where there was family love, unity, and understanding. There was a great deal of material wealth, but little if any spiritual wealth, a great deal of luxuries but not enough challenge and effort. Unfortunately for him, you were not there.

What should you do now that you have learned that he does smoke pot? The thing not to do is become angry. There is no point in blowing up in anger and rage, no point in giving your boy a list of all the sacrifices you have made for him. All this will do you absolutely no good. In fact, it will probably make him even more rebellious.

The thing to do now is to examine your own home life and the example you have set for him. See where you can improve both yourself and the home. You should sit down and have a sincere, frank parent-son talk. Try to understand his problem.

Give him an opportunity to talk himself out. If you feel you need professional help as well, by all means obtain it.

Get across to your son the idea that you will not permit him to continue what he is doing and that you are both ready and eager to help him and stand by him, but that he, too, must help the situation. At this time he needs your love, compassion, concern. He needs to know that though you are very disappointed in what he has done with his life, you love him dearly and want to help him get back on the right road.

Believe me, lecturing to him will not do the entire job. You can talk just so much and then all interest lapses. He turns you off by not hearing what you say. You see, he needs more than a lecture. He must find himself. He must be made to see the richness of life, the beauty of life, the goals of living. Yes, he must be made to see the depth of an adequate life.

Children today are not dull, not stupid, not backward, not bashful, not withdrawn. They want a full life and when it is explained to them, will not settle for an imitation. They want the real thing, make no mistake about it. Sometimes, they confuse the real with the imitation because they see their parents embracing a type of life and follow it, imitate it—to their great disappointment.

You did not indicate in your letter how old your son is, but I guess he is young enough for you to reach him. See if your husband can cut his working week down to 5 days. See if your husband can spend some time with his son. See if there can be a family conference, a family conversation, a family talk-in. It makes sense, doesn't it?

Your son needs your time; give it to him. Your son needs a challenge; make it available to him. Your son needs a purpose in life, try to motivate him. Stop making things too easy for him. Stop trying to buy his love and devotion with a car, a television set, and a generous allowance. Easy come, easy go. Give him opportunities to earn the money you want to give him. What he will earn by dint of his own labor will give him a sense of adequacy no allowance can ever accomplish.

Why don't you, worried mother, quit your job and take an interest in your home and family? Why have you sought to run to business to find purpose and adequacy? Why have you made your own home boring and uninteresting to you?

Become a mother again. Be at home when your son returns from school. Not only should you be at home, but you should be fresh, untired, ready to listen to your son's recital of the day's events. It can't be too interesting for him to return to an empty apartment. That might be a reason he turned to others for interest and excitement.

Stop worrying and begin to do things. Talk it over with your husband and both of you decide what is more important— family or fortune?

If you go all out to help your son, you will be successful. By all means do not permit the situation to deteriorate by not doing anything at all. Once again, if you need professional help, get it—for yourself and for him. The time to act is now!

*What does a parent do
when she discovers that
her young son steals?*

–5–

My Son Steals

THE PROBLEM

To get to the point very quickly I must tell you that my 7-year-old son steals. He returns daily from school with things that do not belong to him. His excuses for this are many and varied, and sound like this: "I found it," "Jakie didn't want it," "Larry gave it to me," or "He left it on the desk."

So far, nothing has helped. We've threatened, pleaded, deprived him of things he likes but to no avail. Both my husband and myself are aggravated at this terrible trait of character. Believe me, we are respectable people. We never had this problem with our other two children. What is the matter and how can the situation be changed?

THE REPLY

A young child has a natural desire to the things he wants. If he sees a toy in the home of his friend and he would like to have it, he does just that. This cannot be considered stealing because he sees no real distinction between that which is his, and that which is not. Nor does he understand that things which are not his do belong to other persons. The concept of ownership is still rather strange to him.

What should a parent do if he comes upon stealing in his pre-school child? To begin with, he must make every effort to determine whether the child intentionally or innocently walked off with the possessions of another child. If it were done intentionally, it implies a knowledge of wrong doing. If his behavior is innocent, correction and direction are purely intellectual. In other words, our treatment must be directed to the reasons he takes things that are not his.

If the child is unaware of personal property, it would be wise for the parent to develop a sense of property and respect for it. Only after that can a parent teach his child to control the impulse to take things. "I have bought you a toy," says the mother to her youngster, "it is all yours. Take good care of it." The child now understands that it is "his." He can make the distinction between "mine," and "his." This idea will help him build up restrictions against stealing. He has learned what the meaning of personal property is, and in due time he will respect this idea.

Unfortunately, a child sometimes learns in his own home that there is no such thing as personal property, that he has the right to examine and remove other people's property. When a child asks for money, he is wrongfully told to go to his mother's purse and remove it. His own pockets may be searched at night by a parent who confiscates anything she disapproves of. And this, she often does, without explanation.

A child cannot be blamed for his confusion about personal property when he sees his mother going through his father's pockets, or a parent opening mail addressed to the mate. To the child it seems as though there is nothing to this idea of personal property.

A child may steal because he is dissatisfied with his lot. He may steal because in this way he shows his rebellion and hostility toward authority. Stealing may be an outlet for his childish vengeful feelings against his parents. He may feel neglected, or unjustly punished, or discriminated against. He steals to get back at his parents.

The child who feels he has not been treated fairly, that his parents are not giving him as much as they can, steals to give himself as much as possible. In this way he feels he is making up for their meanness.

How to treat children who steal depends upon the reasons for their actions. The child who steals because he feels his parents are too demanding and too dictatorial should be given a sense of freedom to make his own choices. It might be well for parents to sit down with this youngster at a family council and discuss with him the type of freedom he desires. If the stealing has been going on for a long time, a calm, quiet, kindly discussion between parents and child can be of tremendous benefit.

The most important possession a child has is his own parents. A child requires a great deal of attention from his parents if he is to feel loved and wanted. A parent who gives more of himself can do more than anything else to improve the lot of his child. It must be noted that this does not mean offering him an over-protective, nagging attentiveness. Rather, it means a rich, warm, close relationship that will help him feel his parents are with him. With this type of attention and love, he no longer has to be rebellious and hostile.

It might be added that when a child feels loved, he wishes to please those who love him and be like them. It is for this reason that a parent's behavior must be above reproach. By word and action, the parent must indicate his honesty and respect for another's property.

Punishing a child who steals has little value at the outset. To begin with, what has been stolen must be returned. Parents must then sit down and determine what the reasons for stealing can possibly be. Why try to determine what the reasons for stealing can possibly be? We try to determine what it is that the child is failing to get in his own home. When we are convinced we understand what the child lacks, we should make every effort to give it to him. A sage once taught, "When you lead your sons and daughters in the good way, let your words be tender and caressing"; in terms of discipline that wins the heart's assent.

The habit of stealing can be changed. Stealing disappears as the real or imaginary defect from which the child is suffering is eliminated. It is important for parents to understand that beatings, nagging, threats have little effect on youngsters. In fact, these may be the very causes for stealing.

*What should be done
when a child is not doing
well at school?*

-6-

His Marks Were a Blow to Us

THE PROBLEM

Both my husband and I got the shock of our lives when we received the final report card this past June. My son is bright; there's no mistake about that. When he was given his I. Q. test prior to his acceptance at school, the psychologist predicted great success for him. Now he is barely passing.

I have visited with his teacher during open school week and we discussed the situation. "He has great potential," she said again and again. On every report card she indicated that he was not putting enough effort into his work. "He is an under-achiever," was the remark placed on his report card.

During the term he barely did any homework. When I asked him about his assignments he told me that he did them in school. Many times during the term he did not even bother to bring his books home.

Whatever long-term assignment he has, such as a book report, he leaves the work for the night before. Even then I have to prod him again and again. Often it ends with both of us doing the report.

It isn't as if he has chores around the house. His room is constantly in a mess and I just can't get him to give me any help at all. If there is anything he does right, it's his stamp collection. I must admit the collection is well kept and is always in excellent condition.

I just don't know if it is laziness on his part or unconcern. I don't know if I should keep after him, or just ignore his faults and let the school authorities punish him when he deserves punishment. Who is at fault here—my son, his parents, or the school?

THE REPLY

There is nothing to be gained in establishing who is at fault. The truth is, everyone is. Your son is an under-achiever and it might be wise to point out that under-achievers are made not born. Sometimes, it is the result of a child wanting to make himself into a unique separate individual. Generally, it is a good sign when children attempt to mature and grow away from their parents. But in the under-achiever something goes wrong. Instead of trying to see himself as a separate individual through accomplishing, he does it by not accomplishing.

It is believed that underachievement seems to occur in children whose parents expect a great deal of them, or where the mother has a strong need to control the behavior of her child, even though she may not be aware of it.

The under-achiever is usually rebelling against his parents. However, instead of rebelling with the words "I won't," he cries, "I can't." Underachievers don't usually say I don't want to do my homework. Generally they cry, "I can't do my homework." Why he resorts to this negative way can be answered by indicating that he loves his parents and does not want to recognize that he is angry with them.

You must get across to your son that he will reap the rewards of his successes, that he will have the pleasure of achievement, or that he will suffer from failure. This does not mean that you are to threaten him with "You'll be sorry." In other words he must be made aware of his own independent life.

Your son must be made to feel adequate and not helpless and lazy. Self-confidence must be established. He must be made to understand that underachievement is self-defeating, that above all, he is hurting himself the most.

He achieves with his stamp album because that hobby is his own. With it he feels independent. The same situation must be established with his school work. Try it, and you will see how it will finally work out.

*How can a mother win
back the love of her mar-
ried daughter who feels
she was neglected as a
child?*

-7-

My Daughter Hates Me

THE PROBLEM

My husband deserted me when my daughter was eight months old. My old-fashioned mother said, "Good for you, I told you not to marry him." She refused to help me in any way. I struggled all alone in this world as if I had no family at all. When my daughter reached 2½ years of age, I placed her in a nursery and I worked in a factory at a sewing machine.

My daughter had a difficult time; she rebelled at eight years. At that time she already hit me back. Nobody wanted her, not even a paid camp. When she reached 20, I had to lock her out of the house because I was afraid of her; she was so spiteful. During all these years she did go for help. She always lied. When I told my story, she found another psychiatrist.

She did get married and had terrible fights with her husband. Once she knocked his front teeth out. He wanted a divorce; she wanted to return home. I couldn't undertake taking her back. I could neither live with her nor without her. I worried about her.

At the time of my divorce I was 24. I had to have some recreation. As a result, I left her alone some of the time. I did the best under the circumstances though I admit she did have a horrible childhood.

She is now married ten years, has two children. She beats them with a strap. They are very nervous and fear her and love *me* very much.

Now she has an unlisted phone number so I can't even call her. She doesn't allow me to see the children. Her husband decided that he would go along with her ideas as long as it keeps her quiet.

I know that they go to a marriage counselor who indicated to my daughter that she hasn't grown up yet (she is 35 years old now).

There are no relatives around and the grandchildren have only me. Twice a year my daughter and her husband go away for two weeks and leave the children with an old sick woman or with an Italian family. I feel that the children should see me when the parents are away. I surely am willing to take off from work and show them a wonderful time. I must tell you that my daughter never calls me even once when she is away. I don't even know where to get in touch with her.

At home, she sleeps late and the children get breakfast about noon or later. Her husband takes the children to school. They dress themselves. The children suffer hunger and eat dinner at 5:00 p.m. She wants them out of the way early. She doesn't bathe the babies; she just uses magic.

About six years ago, she located her father. Now she invites him and his wife over and teaches the children to call HER Grandma.

The last time I spoke to the children on the telephone (my daughter dialed my number but she didn't speak) they told me how much they miss me, but that mother wouldn't allow them to see me. All I could do is cry. I am helpless in this matter. I now seek your advice. Should I still try to see the children, or should I stay away? I want to do what is best for them.

THE REPLY

You surely don't have anything good to say about your daughter. You depict her as a nervous, selfish, argumentative, careless, hostile, unconcerned person. She beats her husband, neglects her children, refuses to face reality, and is totally unconcerned about you. For someone who doesn't even know her phone number, you certainly are aware or think you are aware of what is going on in her home. Is her house bugged? Do you have detectives there? Who gives you the information about her sleeping late, not feeding her children, never bathing them?

There is no doubt that your daughter resents you and has not forgiven you for your own neglect of her and her needs. By your own admission she had a terrible childhood. At 2½ she was in a nursery. At 20 you locked her out of the house, and during her marital strife, when she came to you, you refused to accept her back. Surely, your actions are not those which would bring love in return.

In marriage, she is more successful than you were. For ten years she has somehow kept her marriage together, going away for vacations with her husband twice a year. Not only that, somehow she managed to locate her father (she was 2½ when he left) and establish a relationship with him and his wife. All this to your even greater unhappiness.

Did you ever ask yourself, why? Why no visits, no phone calls, no relationships? Is it because she feels you are not her friend; that you can only find fault, that you think she is a liar? Can it be that she feels your interference will break up her marriage as yours was broken?

By the way, if the grandchildren see you so seldom, how come they love you so much? You indicated that they love you, but fear their mother. Your daughter cannot be as horrible as you describe. She does dial the number and have the children talk with you, even if she refuses to take part in the conversation. Surely, you must have hurt her terribly.

Make no mistake about it. I have great compassion for you. You live alone and would love to have a relationship with your daughter and with your grandchildren. Every mother looks forward to the day she can play and romp with her grandchildren. This pleasure is being denied you, and for this I am sorry.

I don't believe that your question should be: "should I try to see the grandchildren or leave them alone?" I think the question should be: "How do I get my daughter to understand and forgive my own failure as a parent?" If that question is answered, you will not have to raise the second question.

Set your own house in order first. Make peace with yourself, something which I sense you haven't done. Bring a bit of sunshine into your own home. Get out and find some values to which you can cling. You have no right to impose your present loneliness upon your daughter. Not having enough sunshine is what ails you. Make others happy and there will not be half the quarreling, or a tenth part of the anger there exists at the present time.

Under no circumstances are you to attempt to see your grandchildren against your daughter's wishes. If you cannot phone her, then write to her. If she doesn't answer your letter write again and again and again; write until you can convince her that you are not the same mother you were years ago. And believe me, you were not great. Get her to understand that you are now aware of where you failed her, and that you would like to make things up to her.

Stop finding fault with her and with the way she raises her children. Stop calling her a liar. Stop all your criticism of her. On the contrary try to correct the faults in yourself before you even begin to correct the people around you. Daughters generally identify with their mothers, especially after they are married. If your daughter shies away from you, the fault lies with you—not her. Her fears of you might be unjustified but they are her fears nevertheless.

You have a job cut out for you, one that requires time, tact, and tolerance. You will not create a mother-daughter relationship overnight when one has not existed for 30 years—but you can try.

Her child has every nervous tick ever discovered—he bites his nails, pulls his ears, sucks his fingers. What should she do?

-8-

My Child Is a Nervous Wreck

THE PROBLEM

I have heard of nervous children but my child wins first prize. He seems to have all the nervous habits of all his friends. He bites his nails, pulls on his ears, and if I am not mistaken, has a slight tic. His fingers are constantly in his mouth. He acts as if he hasn't eaten in days. I have tried putting bandages on his fingers but he bites right through them. He is an unhappy child who walks around with the weight of the world on his shoulders. His teachers at the yeshivah keep telling me that he is not too responsive in class. His younger brother is not that way at all. He is the type of child who cuddles up to you and permits you to love him. I am at my wit's end. I have told him a thousand times I don't want to see him with his hands in his mouth. I've pleaded, promised, and threatened with zero results. My child is a nervous wreck and I am headed in the same direction.

THE REPLY

Stop pleading, begging, promising, and threatening. Why not try to understand your child?

A youngster bites his nails so that he can get relief from some pressure or anxiety too strong for him to handle. It might be the pressure of an all-day-school education. It might be the competition of his younger brother. It might be the demands made of him by his parents and teachers. There is one thing you can be certain of and that is he won't stop biting his nails merely because you dislike the habit. Telling him, "You make me sick," or "Don't let me catch you with your fingers in your mouth," will accomplish very little. This you have already discovered.

He won't stop biting his nails because he can't. He has a gnawing desire to do something about the tenseness inside him and when he bites his nails he gains some relief. An adult in the same situation might kick his tire, take a drink, or push some other adult around.

The expression "a nervous wreck" has different meanings for different people. Some think of the thumb sucker; others will picture the overactive, easily excited child or the whinning youngster who tires easily. To many, including yourself, it means the nail biter, or the child with a tic.

The tendency in a growing child to bite his nails is usually a signal of inner tensions. He has fears and worries. They may seem foolish to a grownup but they are terribly real to him. He may be afraid of not being loved by his parents. He may fear the competition of a younger brother. Nails are tough, insensitive and painless to bite. Of course, once the habit has begun, the rough edges of the nail and the exposed nail bed cause irritation and this provokes more biting. Direct restraint, such as bandages, or splints only intensifies and worsens the anxiety and strain that are the real basis of the trouble.

What has caused your son to become a nail-biter may be difficult for you to discover because the habit may have started months before. It will take patience and understanding on your part to help him overcome his habit.

There are certain things you can do now. Check on his general physical condition. See to it that he gets nourishing food and enough sleep. Ask yourself if he tires readily and if he is getting enough activity.

Now, check his emotional well-being. It is probably in this area that your boy has difficulty. If he regains emotional balance, he will have no need to bite his nails.

Try to build up his self-confidence. Make him feel that he can do things for himself and that when he will really need help, you will be ready and willing to offer it. Show him, again and again, that you are proud of the things he is learning to do for himself. Try to make him more independent. If you keep him too dependent on you, he may reveal his need for more freedom by nail biting. Do not expect perfection from him. If you expect too much from him and give him reason to fear that he won't be able to measure up to your standards he may show his anxieties and fears by resorting to biting his nails. Check with his teachers. It may be something in his school situation (work too difficult) or a teacher who is very severe that is causing him anxiety.

Try to have a relaxed atmosphere at home. Set an example of happy behavior. Do not boss him, nag him, or scold him too often. Check the television shows he watches. Remember that too much excitement is bad. Overstimulation causes strain. In any case, easing up on your discipline and not expecting too much from him will often help greatly. Put a pebble in your shoe for an hour and it will make you irritable, cross, and nervous. You will be easily upset and will react in accordance with the television commercials you have seen. The pill or powder you swallow may or may not give you any relief. But the pebble is still in your shoe. Taking the pebble out is certainly a surer way of getting rid of the irritation.

Similarly, if you get rid of whatever is troubling your youngster, you can change his emotional behavior.

And by the way, stop feeling sorry for yourself. Wringing your hand and wailing, "I'm on the way to a nervous breakdown," will accomplish nothing.

Her child lies about school, friends, marks, and constantly fights with his siblings.

–9–

What Makes My Child Lie?

THE PROBLEM

I am frantic with worry. My child lies—lies about his school work, his homework, his marks, his disputes with his brother. He is nine years of age and is in the fourth grade. Recently, I learned that he lies to his teachers as well. Right now, I don't know when he tells the truth and when he is fabricating another story. I am disappointed in him and in myself. My husband blames me and tells me that I have not brought up our son properly. I just don't know where I failed. I've always taken care of my son's wants and needs. I help him whenever necessary. I lecture to him about the evils of lying. Where did I make my mistakes, and tell me how I can break him of this disagreeable habit?

THE REPLY

There is a tone of genuine concern in your letter. You know what kind of person you hoped your son would become. You know the traits of character you prayed he would value. Like an artist, you saw the finished picture in your mind years ago. You were going to lead him along a path that would mold him into the human being you wanted him to become. Now, you feel you have failed. Your son lies and you feel that lying is absolutely unpardonable and that to permit it would cause your son the greatest possible harm. Your husband, blaming you for your son's mistakes, only increases your own frustration and sense of failure.

No child is born a liar, nor is anyone born bound to tell the truth. Character is not endowed by someone but has to be built little by little. It is the parents' responsibility to promote truthfulness in children and this must be done by both precept and practice, by both words and actions. Children develop honesty from the example set by parents.

The fact of the matter is that perhaps you too have lied and perhaps you occasionally still do. It may be that your husband, in the presence of your son, talks about taking a day off and calling in sick, so that he can take in an important ball game. Or perhaps your child listens to both of you discuss an insurance claim that you hope to increase.

A child's conscience is made, not born. During his early years, his conscience is molded chiefly by his parents. He may be confused when his parents conveniently knock a year off his age when the time comes to pay movie or bus fares. It must have been this confusion that caused a child to answer a question about his age with these words, "For the school, I'm seven years old, for the train I'm only five, but I'm really six years old." Your son could be confused by the use of what you might term the "white lie." Bear this in mind the next time you ask your child to answer the telephone and when you caution him that if Mrs. Cohen is on the wire to tell her that "My mother is not home." If Mom lies, why not the offspring? A youngster once asked his mother, "Mom, how old must I be before I can lie, too?"

Generally, children lie to conceal their guilt, to avoid punishment, to obtain praise and affection, and to let off their own hostility. At the very outset you ought to reassure your child about your feelings for him. This will demonstrate to him that there is no need to lie.

The way to raise a child is to love him. Make your son feel certain of your love and affection. Remind him constantly that you are on his side and show him that he need never fear telling the truth. "I'd like to know what happened," is a far better question than, "Did you break that lamp?" The second question implies severe criticism and quick punishment; the first indicates a desire to know all the facts, which may or may not be followed by punishment.

Your son may be lying to build up his self-esteem. Adults do the same and for the same reason. When an adult exaggerates his work on a committee, when an adult claims to be an executive in a firm when he is only a clerk, he, too, is trying to build up his ego. You might make it easier for your son to tell the truth by building up his self-confidence. Make him feel that he can do things himself. Show him you're proud of the things he is learning to do for himself. Ask him to help you with some of your own problems. Discuss a bit of news with him and ask for his opinion. Don't persist in belittling, correcting, and criticizing.

These days we seem to be preparing our children for the life that lies ahead. We give them singing lessons, dancing lessons, art lessons, skating lessons. We check on their schooling, help them with their homework, and worry about their grades. All this is valuable, of course, but we must not omit the one important lesson children can learn at home. Let's teach them by example to be honest. Let's set before them real goals—not making a fortune, but rather building a reputation. Boys and girls are not delivered as raw materials at the school door. They are already products—products of six years of processing in their homes. More and more, we realize that what the school can do is to develop a child's potential, is limited by what the home has already done, and is doing to him and for him.

It is unfortunate that your husband blames you for this problem. Perhaps, he should be reminded that "Fathers, too, are Parents." By commission or omission he, too, is responsible. In any event, blaming each other does little good. Get together and work toward a common goal. Eradicate lies from the home. Make lying unprofitable. Help your son toward better self-esteem. Believe me, it will all work.

BOOK FIVE

THE QUESTION OF
IN-LAWS

Book Five

THE QUESTION OF IN-LAWS

Introduction

Parents, in due time, become in-law parents. In this role they often exert a powerful influence on their children, so much so that they can make or break a marriage. The wise parent, who in the past helped his child grow up, will now step aside and permit the married child to make his own decisions. Yet, there are those who even after marriage, find it difficult to maintain a "hands off" attitude. And so many young married men and women find it difficult to cope with the problem of loyalty to their new partner, and obligation to their parents.

Even at best, problems arise: How can we divide our holidays between our two families? What should be done if one of the mothers insists in taking over the responsibility of raising the children?

Of course the first essential in handling one's relationship with either parental family is for the young couple to sit down and talk things over. They must come to some understanding as to what kind of family life they want for themselves. It then becomes the responsibility of the husband to talk things over with his parents, and of the wife to talk things over with her parents. The issues should not be evaded. Parents of both husband and wife must be informed about the true feelings of the young couple.

No doubt parents love their children and do not wish them to fail, nor do they wish to fail them. When possible their advice should be offered. But newlyweds must be permitted to fulfill their own mission in life, to make their own decisions, to be independent.

Do problems arise? They certainly do. Read the sampling of letters received.

What makes a daughter-in-law resent the presence of her husband's parents?

–1–

Do Grandparents Have Rights?

THE PROBLEM

I guess it takes the average mother some twenty to twenty-four years before she become a grandmother. During many of these years she sits and dreams of the coming of grandchildren. Again and again she hears that children are the profits of a marriage, but grandchildren are special dividends. I was not any different.

For many years I daydreamed about the grandchildren that would be born, with the help of God, to my two daughters and my son. God was good to me and my daughters were married. My eldest fell in love with a young man who resided in California. They were marired and now live at the opposite side of the United States. I get to see them once a year, and their children feel almost like strangers. We visit, bring them presents, stay for about a week or two, and leave until the next year.

My second daughter is now married for almost three years and so far has been unable to conceive. Two years ago my son was married. Both my husband and I were overjoyed. Now the family name would be preserved and we would have a real opportunity to watch them grow up.

When a son was born to him, we showered the little boy with gifts. We opened an account in his name, began a college-insurance program, initiated a mutual fund account, bought him his carriage, his high-chair, his play-pen, and other items, too numerous to mention.

Both my husband and I visited often to watch the baby—being given a bath, watch him being fed, watch him as he began to notice life around him. And when he began to recognize people, we played with him. We gladly became baby-sitters so that we could have the privacy to play with our grandson.

We now have run into a difficulty. It seems that our daughter-in-law resents our presence. She has never said so but it seems that she is curt with us. When we invite her to our home, she finds excuses for not coming. She's too busy, or, the weather is too cold, or, the baby is sleepy. However, the rules she applies to us, she seldom applies to her own parents. To us, this seems unfair.

Could our daughter-in-law be jealous of the affection we have for the grandson? Does she feel we are spoiling him with attention? Is she a mean person who hates for someone else to have pleasure. Whatever her reasons are, we are hurt. We could speak to our son about this but we don't want to cause a family feud. Just what do we do?

THE REPLY

I read your letter to a large group of middle-age men and women, and the groans that could be heard gave testimony to the fact that your problem is one that is shared by many. Grandparents just don't seem to get enough time with their grandchildren, and daughters-in-law seem to feel that children will have perverted personalities because of the excess attention given by grandparents. At the same time, grandparents always seem to feel that the other side enjoys privileges denied to them.

You are no different. You want to spend every available moment with your grandson for whom you waited so many years. You want to watch him being fed, being nursed, being bathed, being diapered. Not only do you want to watch, you also want to do. "Let me feed him," you urge. "I'll help you bathe him," you offer. Once again, you wish to play "mama" but this time to a grandchild. When you don't get your way, you become angry and feel that the "other side" is favored. Wisely, you refrained from informing your son of your feelings.

I have a feeling that your in-laws feel the same way. They,

too, probably would enjoy having more to say about their grandson. However, this is not the way of the world.

It is my feeling that grandparents should be a sort of holiday situation for grandchildren. Two generations are company; three's a crowd. Grandparents must remain something special in the lives of their grandchildren. Once they become an integral part of the work involved in bringing up a child, they complicate the picture and in many cases confuse the child.

Do you want to be a successful grandmother? Don't give too many presents and don't spend too much time with your grandchildren. Restraint, in short, is one of the more admirable virtues of grandparenthood. Don't give advice! Don't offer help when none is asked! Wait until you're asked for advice before you offer it. Your daughter-in-law may interpret the most innocent suggestion concerning the child's well-being as a critical attempt to make her appear inadequate.

The result of all this is to accuse you of usurping her authority, spoiling her son, trying to get all his love. If she is jealous of your son's attention to you, she is doubly jealous of your attention to the grandson. I have the feeling that your daughter-in-law doesn't get along with you in the first place, therefore, nothing that you can do with the grandchild is right from her point of view.

Some day, grandparents will be taken at their full value, and that is, that a child will grow in security if he knows he has a couple of indulgent and generous grandparents around. In reality, grandparents, at most, have a highly remote influence upon the children. If parents realize this, they would not be so alarmed and would fully enjoy the warmth and security grandparents have to offer.

You now have three married children. This is genuine *naches*. Permit them to grow up and raise their children in privacy. Visit them from time to time and make each visit a special event. Be like a steak dinner, not chopped meat. You understand, steak is served once or twice a month. Chopped meat is an everyday menu item.

Don't invest all your time and all your love in your grandchildren. If you do you will be making deposits in a bank from which withdrawals are difficult to conclude. Now is the time for you and your husband to enjoy each other's company. Visit friends, attend lectures, see shows, see the country. Have you been to Israel? If you haven't, take a few weeks or months and see the country. Instead of showering your grandson with presents, spend most of this money to bring you and your husband luxuries you have been so long denied.

Don't postpone living. Live now. Need I remind you that it is later than you think?

A mother-in-law attempts to clarify the relationship of mothers-in-law to daughters-in-law.

–2–

What Is a Mother-in-Law?

THE PROBLEM

What is this word, "mother-in-law" we heard so much about? Why is this group of dedicated women made the butt of comedian's jokes? Why are they so much more talked about than thought about?

Unfortunately, for years, the word mother-in-law always brought a groan from the lips of a bride or groom. Both husband and wife were always cautioned to be wary of "in-law" trouble, as if it implied catching a contagious disease. The word mother-in-law was never defined as the mother of one's husband or wife, but rather as a meddlesome, sour busy-body who didn't know when to keep quiet or leave well enough alone.

I rise to the defense of mothers-in-law. Why not try looking at them in a different light and see how much happier family life can be! Who is she? What is her aim in life? What has she done to deserve the barbs aimed at her?

Who is she? Just a woman like others, a mother and a daughter-in-law, the mother of your spouse.

I speak to daughters-in-law everywhere. Stop and analyze

for a minute. Your mother-in-law cared for your husband long before he knew you. At one time, not too long ago, he was dependent on his mother for his every need. The bed-time lullaby, the encouraging word, the warm smile, and the understanding heart were all part of his upbringing. It was she, as a matter of fact, who reared him into becoming the kind of man with whom you fell in love and married.

What it all boils down to is this. You love your husband as a whole human being—do you not? Well, as a whole person his mother is very much a part of him. To love the whole man is to love his mother. To have hostile feelings toward her is to have them toward him as well. To do her an injustice is to be unjust to the man you love.

Keep this in mind. I'm certain she will soon be a very dear person in your life. And remember, more energy goes into hate than into love!

THE REPLY

You sign your letter, "A daughter-in-law of the future." This can imply that you will be married in the immediate future.

If the date has already been set and you will soon be married, then I wish to congratulate your mother-in-law upon acquiring such an understanding new member in her family. If you hope to be married some day, though not immediately, then I urge you to reread your own letter from time to time. Do this especially after you are married. Do this when your husband wants to visit his mother or wants his mother invited to your home. Do this when he gently reminds you to shop for a mother's day present for his mother.

A careful reading of your letter from time to time will be of great help to you, and a service to your spouse, to say nothing of the benefit to your mother-in-law.

Sandra, years later, when your husband suggests taking his mother along for a ride to the country, for a Sunday dinner at a restaurant, for a treat to the movies, and you complain, take your letter and read:

Who is she?

What is her aim in life?

And then say to yourself, some day, God willing, I, too, will be a mother-in-law whose great desire is to spend some time with her dear ones.

Isn't it strange that soon after marriage, principles and resolutions change on the part of both daughter-in-law and mother-in-law? The daughter-in-law, who resolved against jealousy of her husband's affection and respect for his mother, should remember that his love for his mother does not lessen his love for his wife, his consideration for his mother does not minimize his consideration for his wife. On the contrary, the man who is considerate of his mother, who respects her feelings, who remembers her birthday is very often the husband who acts the same way toward his wife. Why should there be jealousy of the lady who will or has become the children's grandma?

On the other hand, a mother-in-law must bear in mind as well that the love her son has for his wife in no way decreases his filial love. She should remember that the new couple is entitled to make its own decisions and mistakes since the couple has many challenges to meet and much learning and experience to accumulate.

A story is told about a mother who asked if she had visited her married son living in a different state. "No," she responded, "I'm waiting until they have their first baby."

"You mean you don't want to spend the money for the trip until then?" she was asked.

"No," replied the wise mother-in-law, "It's just that I have a theory that grandmas are more welcome than mothers-in-law."

There is a great deal of learning that must be done by in-laws, daughters as well as mothers.

A mother-in-law must tread softly and quietly. She must understand that her son is no longer her little boy who must have his hurts kissed. He is now a husband, has established a home of his own, will be a father some day, and therefore needs independence of thought and action. Why should it be said of some mothers-in-law that they are like sandwiches: Cold shoulder and sharp tongue!

A mother-in-law has no right to be a permanent too-frequent visitor. A young couple was very happily married, but for the fact that the husband's mother insisted that they spend every holiday with her. Both husband and wife wanted to have their own home celebrations occasionally. They craved the privacy of a home holiday. The wife demanded that her husband inform his mother that this cannot go on. The husband felt he could not hurt his mother. The result was always the same—a forced visit, a frustrated wife, a timid husband—and a very poor dinner.

Mothers-in-law and daughters-in-law are real people, both at first a bit worried about their relationship. If at very outset, neither is jealous, if they are open, frank and honest, if they continue to live their own private lives, in-laws can be a source of tremendous joy and satisfaction.

The parents of the wife and the parents of the husband cannot agree. What makes a daughter-in-law who has been treated generously suddenly become distant and abusive?

-3-

An Ungrateful Daughter-in-Law

THE PROBLEM

My only son, now 37, was married exactly fifteen years ago, and is now the father of two lovely boys, ages twelve and nine.

My husband and I have had to struggle all our lives to make a living, but, we always managed to help our son and daughter-in-law. We always wanted to see them happy. With our help they now have a lovely home in the suburbs. We are very delighted to see him and his family happy. At the present time, my son is doing quite well and no longer needs our financial help.

Something happened during the last six months. My daughter-in-law, for no reason, has become very distant and even abusive. Her actions puzzle me greatly since we have always enjoyed a very close relationship, more like mother and daughter. Suddenly, she has turned against me. When I attempted to find out the reason for her actions, she as much as hung up the receiver.

All this has upset my son and it breaks my heart to see him so troubled. I do not go to them although they live close to us. Needless to say, all this is very detrimental to my husband's poor physical condition. He refuses to visit them without me. me. My daughter-in-law did tell my husband that she has some beef against me from the time she was first married. When my husband asked her what it was, she stated that she could not remember.

This does not make sense at all. I know in my heart and soul that I never knowingly interfered in their lives. My son is a devoted son—always calls us—and I might add that he is a very good son-in-law as well. We certainly gave him a fine upbringing and we are proud of him.

Her parents are permitted to interfere in their home. I must say that I thought that perhaps it was jealousy, but I know we showed her more love than we showed our own son, always making a fuss about her. I feel I have been overly nice and so just can't understand the reasons for her actions. Never, for a single moment, did I ever make her feel obligated for the help we gave.

Now, my 12-year-old grandson will be Bar Mitzvah next July. What should I do about the situation? She has found many faults with all our family—aunts, uncles, cousins. None are invited to visit them and my son is deprived of many occasions with the family because she refuses to go along.

I will not go to their home even should you suggest it. The humiliation is too much for me to bear. I am older and was insulted in several ways when I did try to approach her for my son's sake.

All our friends and family are shocked beyond words since they know that there has never been any cross words between us. But suddenly this—W H Y? Needless to say our grandchildren love us and want to be with us, but under these circumstances, it is difficult.

THE REPLY

Evidently, for fourteen and a half years, your relationship with your daughter-in-law was an excellent one. In fact, it was more the relationship between a mother and her daughter. There was an exchange of love, friendship, understanding, and courtesies. Then, suddenly, a coolness developed between the two of you. You feel absolutely innocent about the entire situation and can't understand your daughter-in-law's feelings. To you it seems that she is returning darts and arrows for all the good you have done for her. You are quick to point out that you helped them financially, and even aided them in the purchase of a home in the suburbs.

Your feelings are hurt and this is affecting the lives of your husband, son, and grandchildren. You don't enjoy this situation and want it changed once again. However, since you feel completely blameless you want your daughter-in-law to make the next move. "Why doesn't she appreciate what I have done for her?" you ask yourself. "I've done more for her than her own mother," you repeat again and again.

Don't you realize that wounded vanity is fatal to love? It causes one to hate the person who inflicted the wound. Anger has ten thousand eyes, but none with 20/20 vision. Anger blinds and prevents one from seeing things as they really are. You can only see yourself completely white and your daughter-in-law entirely black.

I don't doubt that you have done much for your two children, done it because it made you happy. The greater the sacrifice you made for them, the happier you became. You did it because the two of them were the most important assets you possessed. The truth is that for 15½ years what you did was appreciated.

It could be though, that the entire relationship was building up. It could be that you made them both feel too obligated to you, gave them guilt feelings because of the sacrifices you made. In any event, I just can't believe that it was an unexplainable situation, a sudden icing of what has been a wonderful relationship. This doesn't indicate that you are guilty of some intentional slight. It does mean, though, that somewhere along the line the relationship began to cool. Feelings were hurt and the war of nerves was on.

Sometimes, a mother-in-law can display great wisdom by being both blind and dumb—blind to the unexplained coolness which could have been the result of a husband-wife squabble. However, you must remember that affection can withstand storms but cannot live through prolonged frosts of indifference.

Love covers a multitude of sins. When a scar cannot be taken away, it should be hidden. There are realms in which book-keeping does not work. Certainly, it has no place in the kingdom of love. For instance, we are not to count and record the number of times we have helped; we are not to find what balances are due us from the people we love.

I wonder if you can ever change a human being with arguments alone: either by stabbing them with sharp facts or by blowing them up with great guns of truth. No! You can't! You cannot change them without understanding them. When you argue with a person, you tend to pull him down; but when you try to understand him, you make him more than he was before; and at the same time, you, too, become more. Your problem now is that you see the past better than it was, and find the present worse than it is.

You worry about whether or not you can attend your grandchild's Bar Mitzvah in July. Do you really believe that you will not make any move to probe, ask, examine what the reasons might have been? You have a mature, adult son, a father of children. Certainly, he can discuss the entire situation with his wife. After all, he is devoted and courteous to her parents and has great affection for you. It is up to him to try to repave the road to friendship and understanding.

If you are asked to visit them, by all means go! Call your son at his home from time to time and send your regards to your daughter-in-law. Exchange greetings with her parents at regular intervals. Send birthday cards, anniversary cards when they are called for. Encourage your husband to visit their home. Don't make the situation any worse than it is. For your sake, don't review in your mind and heart the great number of benefits you did bestow upon her in the past. That time of recollection only hurts.

Your son and your husband can ease the situation and can clarify the misunderstanding. I cannot believe that your daughter-in-law has just suddenly become neurotic. She has been hurt and is nursing wounds at the present time. Remember, I am not saying that you hurt her.

See to it that peace is made and that once again you can have a meaningful relationship with your children. If I can help in any way, please call upon me.

*A mother-in-law feels
her son-in-law is not
acting properly.*

– 4 –

My Problem Is My Son-in-Law

THE PROBLEM

My problem is my son-in-law, or would it be my daughter? They have been married for three years and I have a darling grandson who is a year old. I will come straight to the point and say it breaks my heart to have my son-in-law refuse me admission into his home and also will not come into my home.

He domineers my daughter and insists that she treat me like dirt, the way he does. I have spoken to my daughter many times concerning his attitude. However, her constant reply is that she loves him very much and must obey his commands, if she is to keep this marriage going.

I certainly have no intention of breaking up their marriage, but I would like to have some happiness in my remaining years of life. I am a widow and live alone, and I am not an interfering mother-in-law, therefore, I am at a loss to understand why my son-in-law feels so bitter towards me.

I am in desperate need of help and any advice you can give me would be greatly appreciated.

THE REPLY

Countless are the problems which we have to meet in living together. When we marry off our children, we face the problem of being able to accept a new member into the family. It becomes a test of ability to live closely together with a new comer, but nonetheless, an important addition to the family unit. No doubt, there is a bit of uneasiness during the early days of this new relationship—uneasiness that sometimes borders on jealousy.

You seem to stress in your letter that you are completely innocent of any wrong doing. You are not an interfering mother-in-law, yet both your son-in-law and your daughter treat you like dirt. You claim that your daughter is only doing this to keep her marriage together because of her deep love for her husband.

It is hardly possible that your son-in-law refuses to have you in his home and does not care to visit you in your home merely because of some whim. Your first problem is to really sit down and determine where the relationship went off base, as it most certainly has.

Unfortunately, as long as life goes on, interests will clash, demands will conflict. You, as a widow had a daughter who loved you, and stayed with you. Then, a man appeared on the scene and your daughter found interest, affection, and love in this relationship. It could be that you resented this loss, or at least this decrease in her love for you. You might have interpreted her actions as a rejection of you. Perhaps, this spilled over when she was married and set up a home of her own, and your feelings and reactions somehow reached her husband.

Interestingly enough, facts in themselves do not indicate the entire situation. At the present time, you are not welcome in the home of your son-in-law. It will be your attitude that will determine the nature of the facts. What you will do with the present situation will in the long run determine what the future will hold in store.

However, you just cannot decide to see only what you want to see. You cannot permit your "biased apperception" to turn into fictionalized reality. Learn by this experience. Contradictory points of view are responsible for many misunderstandings in personal relationships. But, relationships just don't sour because of themselves. It takes human action to mar the happiness and joy that could be the result of people getting together.

This I can say with some degree of certainty: One of the dangerous threats to marital harmony is provided by in-laws. This must be apparent in both your son-in-law and your daughter. Evidently, they feel that you are a source of friction. It is so unfortunate that you are so totally blind to this situation, and feel that your son-in-law has no reason for the way he treats you. No persons are more frequently wrong, than those who will not admit they are wrong. It is only an error in judgment to make a mistake, but it certainly indicates poor character to adhere to it when discovered.

This I'd like to make clear. I certainly do not condone your daughter's treatment of you. If she treats you like dirt, she is committing a grave offense.

Mothers do not come in pairs. Each of us receives just one from the Almighty.

I certainly understand your pain in not being able to play with your only grandson. How well I know the years of hope and expectation that one has to live through before the dividends begin to arrive. That you should be permitted to reap this joy is certainly in order.

There is a bit of wisdom that I would like to share with you. An ancient sage once counseled: "When the most insignificant person tells us we are in error, we should listen, and examine ourselves, and see if it is so. To believe it possible that we are in the wrong, is the first step toward getting out of difficulty." To this I might add that whenever anything is spoken against you that is not true, do not pass by or hate it because it is false; but forthwith examine yourself, and consider what you have said or done that may have initiated such reaction.

Certainly, the present situation brings you nothing but unhappiness. You are being deprived of joys which all of us look forward to in our later years. These joys you crave, especially when you are alone and live alone. You must do your best to change the situation—change it by changing the mind of your son-in-law; change his mind by proving to him that you yourself have changed.

The shortest route to this goal requires complete honesty. Discuss your relationship with your daughter. Ask her to tell you where you were wrong, where you angered your son-in-law. Admit to her that above everything else, you want peace in the family; that once you know and understand where you failed them you will make certain that it doesn't happen again. Tell her to intercede for you with her husband. If he has parents, discuss this with them. Don't permit personal pride to rob you of joys which can be yours.

A writer once stated: "No cord or cable can draw so forcibly, or bind so fast, as love can do with a single thread." This is your job now. You must be able to convince your family, not by words but rather by actions, that uppermost in your mind is to see their happiness. Love is the master key that opens all doors.

It has been said that the world is a gigantic mirror and reflects what we are. If you are loving, if you are friendly, if you are helpful, the world will prove loving and friendly and helpful to you. What you are is important.

Go out and make the first step toward peace. In fact, make the first dozen steps. Try to clear up the matter by speaking frankly about your own inadequacies and shortcomings. If your daughter loves her husband so dearly, he cannot be the demon you want me to believe he is. After all, you raised your daughter and are responsible for her actions.

Remember:

> An apology
> Is a friendship preserver
> Is never a sign of weakness,
> Is an antidote for hatred,
> Costs nothing but one's pride
> Always saves more than it costs,
> Mends feelings quickly.

She feels her mother-in-law talks too much, and is a constant trouble maker.

–5–

My Mother-in-Law Spells Trouble

THE PROBLEM

I never thought I would be writing to you, but that's exactly what I'm doing. In fact I am doing it at my husband's suggestion. He feels that my attitude is all wrong and that most of what I complain about I've dreamed up myself. Like most husbands, he sides with his mother.

We've been married just two years and have an infant child. I'm not going to write to you about the burdens involved in taking care of an infant especially with a husband who really doesn't pitch in. But I must write to you about my mother-in-law who talks too much, always has the answers, and is a genuine trouble maker. In addition to which she nags, criticizes, and complains. In fact, she measures up to what I've been told about mothers-in-law. Prior to my marriage, my friends warned me that a mother-in-law is not a mother and should be kept at a distance.

It's rather difficult to give definite instances of her annoying personality but everything I do seems to be wrong when she's around. She really doesn't say anything but I sense her own dissatisfaction with me and with the way I run my house. I never enjoy her visits, and I do not appreciate her telephone calls. It is my feeling that she would like me to tell her that I can't cope with things and that I'd like her to come up and help me. You can rest assured that I've turned down her every offer of help. Who needs a critic around. It's enough I have her son!

I've discussed this with my mother who has advised me to stay out of my mother-in-law's way, and not to visit too often. This advice I've followed. I seldom, if ever, call her on the telephone, and visit only when my husband demands it. Yet, despite my precautions, I have mother-in-law trouble.

I'd like my marriage to be successful, but tell me how do I cope with mother-in-law trouble?

THE REPLY

I don't believe you have mother-in-law trouble at all, but I am quite certain that your mother-in-law has trouble with you. What you need, young lady, is the services of a good psychiatrist who would help you understand your role in married life, the challenges you have to face and perhaps even try to develop in you a sense of security.

You entered this marriage with a pre-conceived notion of what a mother-in-law is, and no matter what your mother-in-law said or did, you interpreted it to fit the mold you made. You were taught (and your own mother helped out) that a husband's mother is a witch with horns and that it was best to keep her at a distance. I don't believe she could have done anything right for you because you weren't going to change your mind.

There isn't an iota of anything factual in your letter. You think she disagrees; you think she is finding fault; you can sense it. You must either be endowed with E.S.P. or you are an opinionated, insecure woman who strikes out before she is even attacked.

To begin with, I think a law should be passed making it illegal to use the term mother-in-law. It smacks too much of legalism; sounds too much like a long-term mortgage that has a high interest rate. It possesses no warmth or feeling. In fact, it is a name that suggests a relative that has been thrust upon you by law. If his mother is to be called mother-in-law, then he should be called mate-in-law or lover-in-law. It sounds pretty silly to you, doesn't it, to call the father of your children an in-law. It sounds just as silly to me to call their grandmother an in-law. Perhaps if she were Mom, her horns would disappear and her suggestions would be termed help instead of meddling. You might be able to call her mom if you, as a daughter-in-law would remember that some day, God willing, you will be a mother-in-law.

You have been conditioned against a mother-in-law; you anticipated trouble with her, and so you found what you were looking for. One writer explained it this way: "Prophecy is a source of its own fulfillment."

I understand that a newly-married couple must find themselves and must set up their own home. In marriage adjustments must be made by both husband and wife, and sometimes the unwillingness of one to make these adjustments causes a sense of insecurity. In that case, there is a feeling of being threatened. However, when good adjustments have been made, a sound relationship with both sets of parents can be expected.

If you were in my office I would ask several questions. Among them would be: How old are you? How much financial aid is being given by his parents? Today, too many people marry who are immature, and are really not ready for marriage. These people marry to run away from their own parental homes, and from what they believe is parental domination, and they run right into what they feel is in-law trouble. They enter marriage with the idea that no one will tell them what to do. The result is that any suggestion made to them is considered interference.

Generally, men and women who marry when they are young need financial assistance from parents if they are to survive. They both resent the help offered and given. Since they have to rely on parents to help them with their financial day-to-day living, they do not feel as independent as they would like to. Woe, then, to the in-law who is the source of help. "Just because she gives me money, she doesn't own me," shouts the husband. "That's better than your folks do; they keep their hands in their pockets," countered the wife. And so in seconds, both sets of parents are slandered—slandered though innocent of any wrong. In-laws make excellent scapegoats in every case. They are damned if they do, and damned if they don't. Frustrations, disappointments, and guilt feelings can always be attributed to in-law trouble.

I will admit that there are in-laws who give too much advice, give too much criticism, and make too many visits. They are in the wrong and should be advised to let the young married couple work out their own problems, make their own mistakes, and learn from their own experience. There are in-laws who hope to buy love, affection, and loyalty with money. They, too, are in the wrong. There just isn't enough money in the world to buy love and affection that isn't there, or even to buy loyalty that hasn't yet been developed. If money and gifts are given by any set of parents there should be no strings attached.

But you really have not drawn up a case against your mother-in-law, at least not in the letter you wrote to me. Why not therefore try to drain off your negative feelings, stamp out your preconceived notions of her, and give her a chance to prove herself? It really isn't necessary for you to join the neurotic frustrated women and trade your tales of marital woe with them. Try calling your mother-in-law "mom." It might be difficult at the start because you will be filled with what you will believe to be divided loyalties.

In-laws bring culture to a family. There is a sense of family heritage when they are around. They strengthen family unity, are mighty convenient in times of stress, and make the lives of grandchildren so full of joy. They have the patience and the time with the little ones that parents just do not have.

Early in this answer I suggested the services of a psychiatrist. I did this because sometimes an in-law problem is symptomatic of other feelings: inadequacy, lack of faith between husband and wife, lack of genuine marital compatibility. Examine your own self and see where you are contributing to this distressing situation. Take the horns off your mother-in-law, and at the same time remove the halo from your own head. Neither of you merits that type of head covering.

A husband feels his wife sides with her mother against him.

-6-

After All, She Is My Mother

THE PROBLEM

There are many families in which a husband begins to have less and less respect for his mother-in-law because of her interference in problems concerning the wife, himself, and his children. Often, when he tells his wife to kindly tell her mother not to interfere, the wife claims, "After all, she is my mother."

Why is the wife's mother more protected than the husband's mother? Many a time a wife informs her husband that she does not like his mother's interference and the husband will so tell his mother. But, when the "glove is on the other hand," the wife's defense is "after all, she is my mother."

What I would like to know is: "Has the husband the same right to demand non-interference from his in-laws as the wife?"

THE REPLY

After marriage, both husband and wife, feel love for, and obligation to their parents. They find it difficult to maintain the dual role of dependence upon their old home and independence in the new one. Too often, the result is a feeling of both guilt and revolt.

Any number of times I've heard marital partners complain, "But Dr. Mandel, how can holidays be divided between our two families in a satisfactory manner when his mother wants us there 75 per cent of the time." Or the husband will complain, "My wife isn't raising the children, it's her mother that's doing it."

Parents, who assume the role of in-laws, can make or break a marriage. They exert a powerful influence on the lives of the marital partners, and in some cases, try to "hold on" to their children after marriage. They do this by nagging, by demanding first loyalty, by reminding the children of how they sacrificed their own lives, by gifts of money, by depreciating the child's mate, and by attempting to dominate every detail of the home. Of course, it is the wise parent who helps the child to grow up, to mature and become self-sufficient so that he is not handicapped by fear and guilt when he or she makes independent decisions.

If parents were unselfishly aware of the needs of their married children, if parents themselves were sure of one another; if they devoted some of their love and energy to their own mates instead of their children, there might be fewer unhappy marriages and fewer divorces.

I believe that young couples be permitted to make their own mistakes, build their own homes, raise their own children, make their own friends, do their own planning. Of course, if they seek parental guidance and counsel it should be given, but like salt or pepper, it should be given in small quantities so that it can be received and digested.

It is quite normal for a wife to turn to her mother for advice about home-making. Certainly, it is easier for the young married woman to confess her inability to bake a cheese pie to her mother than to her mother-in-law. Reaching for a phone to ask a mother to help with the baby is not as difficult as making the same confession to a mother-in-law. In other words, it is quite natural for a young wife to turn to her mother rather than to her mother-in-law for advice and counsel. She doesn't mind exhibiting the "work in progress" to her mother; yet, she only wishes to show the finished product to her in-laws. Certainly, this is not to be viewed as parental interference or parental dominance.

Of course, there is danger in being tied too closely to one's parents. Young adults who are immature tend to remain dependent upon their folks. It could be that often they have parents who encourage dependency—otherwise the child would be more grown-up and independent by the time he married.

In-laws need not be the menace they are made out to be. Many mothers' interests in their grown children are normal and wholesome and might be quite helpful. There are many wise, experienced mothers of forty or fifty or sixty who could, if they were allowed, contribute a great deal to the new marriage and the young family.

During the second world war this was done when service wives returned to their parents' homes for the duration. Then, they went to work as grandma took care of the baby and as grandpa paid the rent and gave other subsidies. It was a war situation and the entire family pitched in and saw the young bride through until her husband returned and took over.

Truthfully, war or peace, parents are handy, especially, in a crisis. When the baby-sitter doesn't show up, the in-law comes in handy. When a nurse cannot be found, grandma becomes a necessity. When the second baby is about to arrive, husband and first born move in to mother who caters to both of them. Often, she leaves her own family and moves into her daughter's house to clean, cook, and cater.

I do want to point out to you that respect should be shown to both sets of parents. Both have rights, both are parents, both love their children and grandchildren. Husband and wife should be hospitable to parents and in-laws. Husband and wife should visit parents and in-laws. Both sets of parents should be remembered on mother's day and father's day.

However, husbands need not be jealous, if their mate goes for advice to her mother and not to his. Here, the wife can "rightfully" say, "but she's my mother." This does not mean that she should interfere, that she should hold a counsel of war. But it certainly does mean that if her advice is sought she should give it.

There is no doubt in my mind that both husband and wife seek advice and counsel from their own parents. This is not a bad procedure. Parents have seen more in life. However, neither the young bride nor the groom should permit parents to sow seeds of discontent, jealousy, or hatred. This poison should not be permitted to spread—not by her parents nor by his.

Marriage can be wonderful. It is a glorious experience of creating and building. However, like all experiences, there are traps around. In-laws are one of them. I suggest that young marrieds consult a marriage counselor so that this difficulty can be discussed. There is no need for them to wait until they land in the sandtrap when a map of the course can be carefully laid out and explained to them.

Getting married is not too difficult. Millions of people are doing it every year. Staying married is a bit more difficult. Marrying has been compared to building an edifice. Good, the married couple are the contractors. If they do their job properly the marriage will stand.

*What should a grand-
mother do who has been
deprived of her right to
see her own grand-
daughter?*

-7-

I Don't Know My Granddaughter

THE PROBLEM

I am turning to you for the help and advice I so desperately need, and hope that I shall find the answer with you. I tried, and so did my sisters at various times in our own way, to resolve this rift which is in existence for so many years, without any positive results.

Although I'm on speaking terms with my son whenever we meet by chance, and it is rare, I do not speak with my daughter-in-law, not because I wish it, but because she prefers it this way. With my granddaughter, there is no communication at all, not because I want it, but because her mother wishes it this way.

In order to keep peace at home, my son doesn't visit or call me on the phone—he never brought his daughter, their one and only child, to see me after the rift. When I asked him why he doesn't bring the child to see me, and why he doesn't call, his answer was always the same, "Mother must you ask?" Now this granddaughter will be 17 years old next February—I wonder how she looks and if I would recognize her at all. Eight years have already passed.

Shortly after the rift, my granddaughter had a birthday, so I sent a bond. It was returned with a note saying, "I do not accept gifts from strangers" written—to appear as though the child herself wrote it. I have kept the note.

Despite all this, each year I send New Year greeting cards, without ever receiving one in return, nor do I expect one. My daughter-in-law has not seen her parents for 18 years, nor does she ever wish to see them. The relationship between them was never good, even while living at home. Her parents never visited her home, nor ever saw their granddaughter. I have no idea what caused this deep hatred for her parents, but I do know what caused our rift.

It all started because I refused to baby-sit. My feelings about baby-sitting at that time by grandmothers, which was something of a new trend, was very strong against it—and knowing my feelings, my son and daughter-in-law never asked me to baby-sit. Then one day they did, when their daughter was 8 years old, and I refused. I see now how wrong it was, but that wrong cannot be undone and she won't forget it, nor let me forget it.

I was called a false and deceitful mother and grandmother by her and that I didn't know the meaning of mother love. Several years before this, I was prohibited from visiting them by her, and didn't see them for 5 years, all because I showed some baby pictures of my granddaughter to my daughter-in-law's mother and friends on returning from her grand-mother's funeral. My daughter-in-law didn't attend her own grandmother's funeral, because she didn't want to meet her mother.

At the time the pictures were given to me, I had to promise not ever to show them to her parents and I did. When I was asked by our friends if I had any pictures of my granddaughter, I immediately took them out and showed them, in the presence of her mother, without thinking of my promise. That same afternoon my daughter-in-law was called by one of the friends who attended the funeral to congratulate her on having such a lovely baby, and how they all saw the picture—and her mother too—that caused our first rift which lasted 5 years.

When my granddaughter's birthday came along, she called to ask me to come to the birthday, which I did; but was warned then, should we ever stop talking again to each other, she wouldn't care to renew our relationship.

They refuse all invitations to family affairs and it has now reached the point where they are not asked anymore, and I cannot accept it. My granddaughter has no idea who her close relatives are. She never met them. What your answer to my problem will be, I shall wonder and anxiously be waiting for.

THE REPLY

Hatred is one of the most dangerous of human qualities, and is responsible for much of the unhappiness of human beings.

It is a form of illness, as well as self-punishment. An ancient rabbi stated that hatred of people drives a person out of this world, especially the type of hatred that breeds in the heart. Your daughter-in-law is full of hatred—hatred of her own parents, hatred of her in-laws, and possibly hatred of herself.

It takes a great deal of inner poison to keep a child from seeing parents for over 18 years. How much hatred does your daughter-in-law possess when she does not attend the funeral of her grandmother because she did not wish to see her own mother? How much resentment does she have in her heart for you when she prohibits you from seeing your grandchild for 13 out of the 17 years of your granddaughter's life?

There is little doubt of the fact that this woman's inner self harbors hostility, malice, dissension, vindictiveness, and even cruelty. Her emotion is of one who hates with animosity, who is possessed by a sort of malignant ill-will. To return a bond by indicating that gifts from strangers are not accepted is an act of ruthlessness, hard-heartedness, and maliciousness. The lady in question is sick and evidently her sickness is contagious, else why doesn't your son call you, or even visit you, with or without her daughter? Have you offended him? Have you been cold to him? Have you been one who does not and did not communicate properly?

Whatever your reason, if your son asked you to be a baby-sitter just once in the first 8 years of your granddaughter's life, you should have dropped any plans for the evening and baby-sat. After all, they knew your objections and refrained from calling on you for 8 full years. How could you have refused them, no matter what your logical reasons? At the time, you surely were aware of your daughter-in-law's possible reaction; you had already been severely punished for showing pictures you had promised not to show. You knew your daughter-in-law's feelings about not showing them to her parents; how could your memory fail you at so critical a time? This, especially when you were aware that she had failed to go to her grandmother's funeral.

However, what I don't understand is your son's action, or, lack of it. Why doesn't he call you on the telephone? Does he feel that his wife is justified in not speaking or visiting with you? Why do you wait for accidental meetings with him? Surely, if he doesn't call you, you can call him—a mother who wants her son can do just that. You surely can call him at his place of business, or even meet him there. Your daughter-in-law doesn't wish to speak to you, but you can make it easier for your son to be in contact with you.

This is the first step. Open up the lines of communication with your son. Let him know how anxious you are to have a complete family unit once again. Tell him you made two mistakes, but that the punishment being inflicted on you is far greater than the unintentional wrong committed. See him again, and again, and again. Meet him for lunch. Force your way in again. Before you can hope to once again have a relationship with your daughter-in-law, you must have one with your son. This is obvious.

There must be someone somewhere who has a direct line to your son and daughter-in-law; not a member of your family, unless it is one who is accepted by them. If you know of such a person—rabbi, friend, attorney, teacher—get him to understand your feelings at this time, and see if he will communicate this to your daughter-in-law. I don't know if you attempted to write to them, explaining yourself.

In any event, I don't believe this situation should be permitted to last too much longer, or it will become a way of life, a set pattern. Sending a New Year's card once a year is not enough; that you don't receive one in return is an omission I lay directly at your son's door-step. Surely, he can do this much if he desired. So once again, I urge you to try to reach your son.

I wish I could communicate this poem to your daughter-in-law:

> The simple cunning of the wasp, the bee,
> Is how to sting, and sting, and still be free.
> The poisons human beings generate
> Fix them forever to the things they hate.

Yes, you can be a successful grandmother and enjoy the experience.

– 8 –

How to Be a Successful Grandmother

The life of a grandmother can be a glorious one, that is, if you live up to the constitution and the by-laws of grandmother-hood. First of all, ask yourself: Are you achieving great satisfaction and happiness in your position of grandma? Or are you one of those unhappy women who moan: "I just can't seem to get close to my grandchildren. I love them as my very life; try to do a great deal for them, but though I hate to admit it, they seem to like their other grandma better. What annoys me is that the other side doesn't see the grandchildren half as often as I do."

Now, catch yourself! Listen to what you are saying! That last remark contains both the fault and the cure. Being a grand-mother should be a richly rewarding relationship. Many times, when it isn't, it is because grandmas don't realize their true function, nor do they fully understand the young child and the world he lives in.

I know that children love older people who are uncompli-cated and who establish a warm relationship, rather than a pos-sessive, smothering friendship. If this is so, then the grandmother can serve best by keeping as objective as possible. To begin with, she should do no more than is asked of her. The function of a grandmother is to have her experiences and advice on tap, ready to give when and if it is requested. Gratuitous information, even at its best, is unappreciated. When your advice is asked for, give it casually. Don't assume the air of a professional expert. Offer advice in such a manner so as not to build up tension or re-sentment.

It is natural and human for you, the grandma, to consider yourself an authority on children. After all, you are a grandma and raised children of your own. As a grandma, you hope to save your grandchildren from unnecessary suffering. With this in mind you want to give the next generation the benefit of your experience. But, alas, the next generation may not be in a listening mood. Though nature has decreed my never being a grandma, I have spoken to hundreds of them and to hundreds and hundreds of grandchildren, daughters, and daughters-in-law. They have all offered advice on how to be a successful grandmother, and I would like to share these ideas with you.

To begin with, keep your distance. A grandmother should be hard to get, so don't make yourself available every day. Love your grandchild by all means, but maintain a "hands off" policy. Let him grow up and permit his mother to do her job without any emotional upset due to your constant giving. You can build a good relationship between you and your grandchild by loving interest tempered with a certain aloofness and by extreme tact in choosing words. Always remember that you are not the mother, or father. If you will always bear this important point in mind, you will create a loving climate in which your grandchild can mature.

A good axiom for grandmas to remember is: "Always remember there is a next time." If your grandchild just doesn't feel like playing "this little pig went to market," don't force him to. If he wants his freedom just when you want to play, he wins. Give him his freedom. You will discover that if you do not try to envelop him, he will soon rush to you with a hug and a kiss. He will realize that there is a wealth of love waiting for him when he is ready to stake his claim. A grandma should be remembered as a warm, strong, quiet, loving person. These are the qualities your grandchild wants of you—strength, poise, love, and, oh yes, silence.

As a grandma, you should realize that you have an advantage over parents. You have more time to relax and play, while parents represent the voice of authority. Parents are the ones who order children to wash, bathe, brush their teeth, do their homework, tidy up their rooms. But, you, the grandma, can be free to be a real friend. You can listen, share, and play. You can make him feel that your companionship is the real thing, something to be valued. You can play his games, fall in with his make-believe, talk about his magic, listen to his stories. At this point, I should emphasize the mistake grandmas make in giving presents every time they see their grandchildren. After a while, the grandchildren look for the gift and not for you.

Do you want to be a successful grandmother? Good, then stop preaching. There is a better way to teach, and that is by demonstration. Do the thing you want your grandchildren to do. The grandmother who will follow this rule will be sought for her presence rather than for her presents. It takes skill, love, patience, and imagination to get close to your grandchildren, together with a keen knowledge of the law of supply and demand.

A successful grandma once listed her ideas on how to become a happy and successful grandmother. She wrote out her own by-laws and I pass them on to you—the grandmas of America.

Satisfy the needs of your grandchildren, but not always with material things. Give him something to grow on—food for the mind as well as the body. And, of course, give him surprises, fun and magic. Cherish silence. He doesn't want to hear from you all the time so don't think you must make conversation. Try saying nothing so that he can take the initiative. This will help him feel important, give him a boost, inflate his ego, and strengthen his feelings of adequacy.

If you want to teach him or her, do it by action and not with words. Let the young child watch you bake a cake. Better yet, get her to help you with the baking. As you go about your business, talk out loud, as if you are reviewing these things for yourself. For example, "Now I must add the eggs and beat them well." Believe me, your grandchild prefers actions to words, for action is the real language of childhood.

Never, but never punish him. This job is reserved for parents. You can praise, can be proud, can treat him with more respect but don't punish. Make your grandchild feel he is maturing by acting your appreciation of his actions. Finally, under all circumstances be his unfailing friend. Be always ready to listen to his confidence, always ready to share your knowledge, to give him confidence and courage to grow up. If he wants to read his composition to you, listen! If he wants you to attend an honor assembly, then attend. If he is in a play and says, "Grandma I'd like you to be there," by all means, try to be there.

What is a grandma? She is a combination of a loving heart and willing hands, who can always be depended upon to give support to her grandchildren. She is endowed with wisdom and has an endless collection of stories of the days when her family was young. She has the ability to soothe hurts of the body and mind. It is said that God has a special place for them in heaven and when grandmas eventually go there, they can be seen looking down on earth smiling at their grandchildren.

It's just wonderful to be a grandma. If you doubt me, ask the lady who is one.

GROW ALONG WITH ME

BOOK SIX

GROW OLD ALONG WITH ME

Introduction

While crossing a street, a young man once found a dollar bill. From that time on, when walking, he never lifted his eyes from the ground. In the course of 40 years, he accumulated 29,516 buttons, 53,375 pins, 22 pennies, a counterfeit half-dollar, assorted keys, a drooping head, a bent back, and a miserable disposition. He missed the beauty of daylight, the smile of his friends, the song of birds, the beauty of nature, and varied opportunities to serve his fellowman. Not only did he waste his youth, he failed to prepare for his later years. It follows that full living during one age is the best preparation for abundant living in the next.

The span of life has increased over the past 50 years. Statistics tell us we will live longer. In fact, medical opinion has predicted that in the next few decades, the life span in this country will reach one hundred years with the retirement age being moved up to eighty-five or ninety years.

What is meant by age? There are many kinds of age, only one of which is easily measurable, and it happens to be the least significant—chronological age. This is useful as a basis for birthday parties, legal and voting qualifications, getting a visa, a driving license, and very little else.

Biological aging, however, goes on at different rates for different people. A man of fifty-five may have the body of a thirty year old, the emotions of a forty year old, the knowledge of a sixty year old, and the ability to learn of a sixteen year old.

Age is not measured by years. We don't grow old by merely adding years. Nature does not distribute energy equally. Some people are born old and tired, while others are going strong at seventy. This is what Oliver Wendell Holmes had in mind when he wrote, "To be seventy years young is sometimes far more cheerful and hopeful than to be forty years old." One man expressed it this way. "I'm not eighty years old at all. I am 4 times 20." In his case, age quadrupled the satisfaction of his youth.

Perhaps one cannot help being old, but one can resist being aged. A man was once advised by his friend, "In the central place of your heart there is a wireless station. So long as it receives messages of beauty, strength, courage, joy and understanding from fellow men, so long are you young." Having a purpose in life distinguishes those persons who grow old from those who get old.

The danger of the later years is that of "rusting" out rather than of "wearing" out. There are those of us who shudder at the thought of leaving middle age, who feel neglected, who start taking things too easy too quickly, who sit back and criticize the younger generation, who somewhere in every conversation say, "When I was your age." Any person who fits into the above description ought to stop and examine his ideas.

The most dangerous way to meet age is to let go. It may be that you have dreamt of retirement, wished for the day you would no longer have to punch a clock, longed for an age of complete leisure to do whatever you want to do. If all this is accompanied by sitting on a rocking chair thinking about the good old days, then you are not growing old, you are old.

You can dye your hair. You can stop counting your birthdays. You can answer questions as to your age with a cheerful "over twenty-one." The number of candles on your birthday cake needn't make you lonely and starved for affection. You must continue to live a purposeful life. Perhaps you can retire from a job, but you must never retire from a life.

Age need not be a period of life in which you lose your hair, teeth, initiative, illusions, and what little patience you once had. To avoid age you must keep taking on new thoughts and throwing off old habits. You are young if you are hopeful and eager; if you feel there are many wonders still to be seen, many books still to be read, many friends still to be made, many organizations still to be helped, many goals still to be achieved. Real happiness in the golden years can come only if you have created within yourself the proper attitudes; if you possess an inner philosophy of life; if your philosophy has provided you with inner resources needed to meet changing life situations. The truth is you really don't grow old. When you cease to grow, *you are old.*

It is the active, busy, aging person who retains his vigor. Do you want to retain your pep? Do you want to remain alert? Get yourself started at something truly meaningful. It may be a paying job, or with a paint-brush, a typewriter, or in some community project. However, it must be a big enough job to give you broader horizons. It should make you study and learn. It should give you a sense of being needed. A doctor once pointed out that there were few preventable diseases of old age that could not be cured by a brisk walk, a good book, or a dish of cooked prunes.

A person should think of himself as growing, rather than aging. He should look for additional interests. When a man comes to the point at which he can no longer believe that there is anything worth seeing or doing, he is old. This is true whether the man is nineteen or ninety.

Aging is like applying a magnifying glass to the personality. The older we get, the more we become like ourselves. The inactive person becomes more inactive; the unsociable, more unsociable; and the cynical person becomes more cynical. The things we failed to do at twelve, we cannot successfully accomplish at fifty. The joys we failed to experience during our teens, we can hardly expect to fully enjoy during our later years. Whatever joys we did not achieve when we were young cannot be achieved with the same degree of intensity during our later years. Yet, we must not face our aging with pessimism or fear, because it is not a time of waiting for some celestial messenger to tap us on the shoulder and say, "Brother, you're next, your lease is up. Follow me."

Do you want to remain active and alive, then heed the advice of poet Robert Browning:

> Grow old along with me
> The best is yet to be.

To begin with, do some manual work daily. Read some good books. Cultivate community activities. Take pen and ink, or a typewriter and do some writing daily. Take a humorous view of situations. Enjoy your meals and make them sociable. By all means, pay attention to your dress. Modify your ambitions in accordance with your ability. Walk buoyantly and sit erect. When you have something to say, come to the point quickly. Give others a chance to air their ideas and opinions. Share your conversation with others if you want to be interesting and stimulating.

There is no fountain of youth from which you can drink deeply. You can, however, reap great security from friendship, faith, love, and religion. If there is a fountain of youth, it exists in an inquiring open active mind.

How old is "old?" When William Gladstone, Primate of England, at 83, was asked that question, he replied, "We are always as young as our impulses to discover new experiences." Old age is a way of life and not a matter of duration. Each one of us can discover for ourselves Ponce de Leon's Fountain of Youth.

"How to grow old," counseled Amiel, "is one of the most difficult chapters in the great art of living." A person is as old as his view of life—no more and no less. What a person sees in the world corresponds to what the world sees in him. The man who views the world as an exciting place is alive and vibrant.

*Are you, too, frightened
when you look in a mir-
ror? Is the fear of aging
tomorrow making you
lose today? How can you
enjoy the golden years?*

-1-

I'm Getting Old Too Quickly

THE PROBLEM

I'm really frightened. I get up each morning, look in the mirror and see that age is very definitely showing its tell-tale marks in me. I am in my late fifties, married, have five grandchildren. My husband goes to business and is most generous. My children are devoted and visit me quite regularly. I have friends and we go out from time to time. All this is good, but I am frightened because I feel I have lost my zip in living.

It's getting so I dread birthdays and anniversaries. Frankly, I run from shop to show attempting to buy beauty in tubes and jars. Sometimes I think I succeed. I look for a new dress, a new hair-comb, a fancy piece of lace; a regular slave of the fashion experts, I am. Then, as I sit at my window and see a young girl of twenty go by, I get a sinking feeling in the pit of my stomach. I certainly do not look like her any more. No use! I'm old. I look old and I feel old and the thought just spoils my day for me.

It's a pity that we say "a person grows old." It would be so much better if we could say, "a person grows young." There should be a sort of plateau at the time a person reaches forty. It would be glorious if we could remain at forty for about thirty or forty years. That would be real living. Too often I indulge in this type of wishful living.

My husband is no help. He keeps himself busy with his business and his community interests. Where he gets his strength and enthusiasm to do both, I'll never know. He laughs at my fears, and then I am furious with him and his lack of understanding.

I need help and I am sure tens of thousands of women in my situation need the same type of help.

THE REPLY

You remind me of an ancient Greek story. It seems that a child was born to a devoted mother, one who had longed for a son of her own. The mother loved the child and prayed to the gods for her child. The story relates that the gods answered her call: "Ask any gift that you want for your child," they said, "and we shall grant it."

The mother thought for a moment and then replied: "O great and high gods, grant my child eternal life." The wish was immediately granted.

Years passed and the mother was called to her ancestors. One day, after many decades, the mother returned to earth to see how her child had fared. True enough, the child still lived, but to the mother's horror, it presented a hideous repulsive sight. The eyes were sunken, the flesh was flabby; creases and folds were everywhere.

The mother was angry and cried out in her anguish: "See what has happened to my son, he who you promised to bless with eternal life."

The reply came back quickly, "You asked for eternal life, not eternal youth."

How true this is of your letter! You want not only long life but lasting youth. And you ask me if this is possible.

It is! Don't get me wrong. I am not suggesting any secret waters from the fountain of youth. I have no pills or powders for diminishing physical powers, no magic lotions for the skin and hair. This is nonsense, a fraud perpetrated by a money-hungry business. The way to look young on the outside is to remain young on the inside. This is the trick: not waning physical powers, but decreasing inner enthusiasm and motivation. You see, you are growing old on the inside and it begins to show very quickly on the outside. So let's repair the damage where it began. Let's treat the cause, not the symptom.

What is youth? It is enthusiasm for daily events, eagerness to venture into new experiences, delight in the surprises to come. It is curiosity combined with a thirst for knowledge, a feeling that today is the best time of our life, an involvement with the present. You are young when you do everything to make yourself happy.

You are young if you love to work and create and are grateful that you can pull your own weight. You are young if you receive at least partial satisfaction from gratification of your desires. You are young if you are ready to forget the disappointments of yesterday and look forward to the delights of today. You are young if you keep the door to your life open wide.

Let me give you a few simple suggestions!

Make up your mind to exclude from your everyday vocabulary thoughts that begin: Why didn't I?; I should have; If only I had; Such regrets are worse than useless. They drain your energy, perpetuate your conflicts, poison your present, and cripple your possibilities for future pleasures. The moment you find yourself starting a reproachful thought, turn it off. In its place, say—I have done; I have had; I can do; I will have.

When lonely, stop subjecting yourself to oceans of self-pity else you will surely drown. Instead, say, "And this too shall pass." Loneliness will not last forever; others have felt the pang of this emotion as well and have licked it. Give birth to the hope that tomorrow will be interesting and exciting. This does not mean that you are to remain in bed until the coming of tomorrow. It means taking an active part in shaping the events of tomorrow. Don't play dead. Unfortunately, that, too, will some day meet up with you, so why anticipate it?

You want to grow old but look young. That's a good trick, but you can do it. Believe me it has been done before. Have faith in life itself and take an interest in living. And by the way, stop worrying about dying. The person who fears death is not really alive.

*He complains that time
runs too fast and wants
to know at 70 how he
can slow it down?*

-2-

Time, Time—Why So Fast?

THE PROBLEM

I'm one of the old codgers who keeps annoying you. It's not that I have ever written to you before, it's just the feeling I have that you have heard my story before from others.

I've just reached 70 and don't like it. Oh, I want to go on living, but 70 seems like an old age, and of course, the thought comes to me, where do I go from this 7th avenue in my life?

When I was 5 years of age, time moved at a snail's pace. Then, a week was a month, a month a year; and a year was just an entire life-time. When I was a teenager, time moved just a wee bit faster, but waiting for Saturday evening and my date still took a long time.

When I was 35 I wondered what had happened to all those early years of my life. School years had passed quickly. Graduation came with its millions of problems. I was married, cared for a family. Weekends then came faster, summer vacations began to speed up. We started making plans months in advance. Before we looked around, the family was gone, with each of our children setting up his own household.

At 60, my birthdays began to race by, or at least so it seemed to me. Each year became a fleeting bit of time. I began to think of life and how short it is. Now at 70 I am worried, a bit frightened, somewhat anxious about each day. I know that time cannot be made to stop, but, Dr. Mandel, couldn't it be slowed down, just a little at least?

What words of advice do you have for a brand-new 70-year-old widower? What would you do were you in my place?

THE REPLY

Throwing out the clocks will not prevent them from ticking away. Discarding every calendar will not do away with the passing of days, weeks, and months. Time keeps pressing on very much like an hour-glass, which once it is inverted keeps giving up its tiny grains of sand until the upper half is left absolutely bare. Time cannot be stopped, and the only way to feel it is slowing down is to do more and more during each day.

Of course you hope to grow older. What you don't like is growing old. The thought of being 70 is frightening to you because all you think about is your age. To the man of ideas, of actions, to the person with vision, age does not arrive. To that man may come silver hair, gray hair, or white hair; his feet and hands may not be able to carry the loads they formerly carried, but his heart is young. He grows in faith, lives with hope, plans for the future.

It is when your entire life is centered on yourself that you feel old, that your days are filled with fear, frustration, disappointment, and sometimes despair. But if you spend time thinking of what can be done for others, then age will not rob you of what is rightfully yours. If you think and act, you are in no danger of feeling aged and decrepit.

It is the belief in life, not the fear of it, that makes for youth. What a curse it is to dread old age! And dread it you do when you think that your life's work is ended, and that your long journey is nearing its close.

You ask what I would do were I in your place? I'd begin to plan for the next decade of my life. I'd think about the places I'd want to visit, the books I'd want to read. I would become more civic minded, more community minded. I'd work for certain charitable organizations. Over and over again I would think of how marvelous it is to be 70, and how much I still have to do before, with the help of God, I reach 80. I would think about every great leader who did so much after reaching 70; think about every writer who wrote so beautifully and meaningfully long after arriving at "7th avenue," bring to mind every poet, artist, musician who did so much creative work in the final 15 years of his life. Were I in your place, I would believe and strive for the coming of the Messiah the next hour, the next day, the next week. Yes, were I in your place, I'd keep on thinking, loving, doing, dreaming, creating—in short, I'd concentrate on living.

*The thought of retire-
ment frightens him and
he wants to know how
he should face the facts
of life.*

-3-

Retirement Frightens Me!

THE PROBLEM

I've been in business for the past 46 years. It's been a small business, one which has consumed much of my time. Yet, with this small business I married off my children, made parties and weddings, and supported my wife and myself with some degree of comfort.

At the present time, the business has sunk, and there is no immediate sign of its eventual recovery. My children all tell me to retire, that with my income and social security I can get along. I know they mean well, but the thought of retiring frightens the life out of me. What will I do with all the time I will suddenly have? How will I feel useful? Without a business, without a job, without a purpose, there seems to be no reason to go on living.

I must add that my wife is just a wonderful woman, who goes along with whatever I suggest. "If you will feel happy working," she told me the other day, "go out and find something to do. Certainly, with your experience some firm will be happy to engage you."

However, working for the next person is something I've never done in my life-time, and I don't know if I will be able to do it at this time. So you see, I am caught in one net or the other. If I retire, I might just bore myself into an early grave. My business is dying, that is, if it isn't dead already. Working for another person, punching a clock, are all foreign to me.

How do I face retirement, Dr. Mandel?

THE REPLY

One of the keys to a happy retirement is your attitude. Recently, Helen Hayes, beloved actress, made some wise remarks on what might be termed the "scars of age." Talking to the residents at a home for the aged, this talented actress said she would not swap one wrinkle for all the smooth skin of youth because every wrinkle represented a smile or pain and disappointment. All the lines and wrinkles stand for some part of being fully alive—and being fully alive is what we should always aim for.

She wanted all older men and women to realize that the wrinkles and other marks of age are nothing to be ashamed of or to be concealed. On the contrary she thought they are like a badge of merit—the evidence that one has met the struggles, the hurts, the disappointments of life—and has survived them.

This brings to my mind the many interesting letters I have received on how attitudes can affect us as we grow older. Most of these letters agree that one's mental outlook has an important influence on our health and happiness as the years go by.

One reader wrote: "Imagination plays such an important part in our entire life that it is surprising we have overlooked its importance on our health." He went on to say that he and his wife have for a number of years been practicing the philosophy that the pictures one holds in one's mind helps to determine the future—and that this philosophy has had very gratifying results.

These thoughts remind me of the way an expert in mental health described the difference between a helpful view of life and a harmful one. He said that the person who is able to say it has been a good day if only one thing during the day went right is in good mental health, while the person who says it has been a bad day if one thing has gone wrong is in poor mental health.

Retire and become active in some charitable endeavor or community project. This will give you purpose to go on living.

*He feels that the young
wrong the aged by not
taking the time to un-
derstand their needs.*

–4–

Old Wine, Old Violins

THE PROBLEM

At 73 years of age, I feel as though I should be moved into
a museum of relics of the past. It is not that I want to feel this
way, it is rather that I am made to feel like a museum piece.
My children give me little time. "Papa," they claim, "we have
lives of our own." My grandchildren see me about three times
a year. My friends are ill, have moved to senior citizen hotels,
or have departed this life. I live alone in a three-room apartment, and my life is one monotonous day followed by another.

What a useless feeling! How terrible it is to feel unneeded,
unwanted, unnecessary! My two children take turns at making
2-minute telephone calls which sound like recorded taped messages. Why do children forget so quickly? Why do they fail us
when we need them the most? Old wine is treasured. An old
violin is cherished, but old age is belittled. What's wrong?

I must point out that I don't need their financial support.
In fact, at my death, my children stand to inherit quite a large
sum of money. I never remarried because I did not want a second wife to lay claim to any part of my savings. Even in this
area, I thought of my children.

My children tell me to move into a Senior Citizen Hotel.
Too many of my friends have been placed in such places where
they await the Heavenly Call, wait to be reunited with their
departed loved ones. This is not for me. I don't want a rocking-
chair. I don't want to sit with glazed eyes, peering into emptiness. I want my children and my grandchildren to know that
I am alive. I'll trade in all their visits to my grave for a few
meaningful visits to my home.

Can't you wake up the young to the needs of the old! Perhaps somehow you can awaken them to their responsibilities, because if God will be good to them, they, too, will live to a ripe old age.

THE REPLY

The young wrong the aged! How much impatience lies with young people! The young, who have drained every ounce of patience from the old, now have no time for them. The old ask for attention and interest, but their requests go unheeded. Years ago, I often heard the remark, "One mother or father can care for 8 children, but 8 children cannot care for one parent." I resented that remark then, felt it was untrue. Now that I am older, I understand the deep truth.

Fortunate, indeed, are the aged who are blessed with good health, a sufficient income, and are able to be active in the things that occupy their time and give them pleasure. There is a well-known engraving of the sixteenth century which represents an old man sitting in a child's wheel-chair, with the inscription over it, *"Ancora Imparo—I Still Learn."* This phrase, deeply meaningful, was constantly on the lips of Michaelangelo as in his old age he hewed at the marbles and refused to rest. The lucky aged are those who have interests in life, who have open windows in the mind, who are not self-absorbed with pity for their lot in life.

Unfortunately for the majority, old age brings with it physical aches and pains. Too many spend their days looking back upon past pleasures: the memory of a child's baby-talk, a graduation, a wedding. These past dreams bring a smile to lips that are no longer red and full, but also bring a sharp pain of loneliness.

There are painful memories as well, the memory of a departed spouse. As the sequence of meeting, marrying, raising a family and then losing the greatest love of all is relived, the lights in the eyes are temporarily rekindled, only too soon to fade away again. As the vision is brought into focus of the mind's eye, the heart beats faster and momentarily a warmth fills the heart and a glow appears on the cheeks which have long turned pale. But how quickly the dream vanishes! And the glow and the warmth, and the smile and the love are soon turned into pain, longing, and emptiness.

Psychologists are busy filling up reams of paper, advising the aged to have a healthy outlook about life, as if it depended entirely upon them. Most of them have given the "best years of their lives" to raising a family. They saved, scrimped, labored to make their children professionals, educated, cultured, and successful. For the sacrifices they have made, for the love they have given and infused into their children, for the moral support they have given these children all through their formative years, for the pride they have shown in all their accomplishments; for these and many other innumerable reasons it is up to the younger people to support the cause of old age.

It is not their choice but their duty to see that their parents are made happy in their old age. A letter, a phone call, a visit are but small payments for the fortune of health, time and emotion they spent on them. Did I say spent? WRONG TENSE! As long as the eyes of parents are open, they will never cease worrying, planning, or caring about their children. In the eyes of a parent a child always grows. Where in the world can such devotion be purchased?

I say to your children and to all children that they ought to begin at once to declare dividends on the investment of parents, parents who have been the originators of the "take now, pay later" plan. Fill the emptiness in their hearts with a kind word, a ready ear, a willing heart. Too soon will parents be called to report to their heavenly abode where they will be asked about their stay on earth, questioned about the bitterness of old age. Make it possible for them to have something warm and comforting to say.

The truth is that children want to find time to spend with their parents. Time can never be found for such visits; time must be made. The same urgency that compels men and women to arrange home socials, to go to teas, luncheons, banquets and theater parties should also move them to visit parents, and to make them feel that they can still contribute a great deal. It isn't just years that make some people senile, it is a feeling of uselessness produced by children's lack of interest, lack of attention, lack of any communication.

Not all children neglect the needs of parents. There are those who are completely devoted and dedicated to their mothers and fathers. I remember meeting a man of 75 in a summer resort. He had come with his son and daughter-in-law. He was alert, interested in what was going on. He attended our daily discussions and didn't hesitate to voice his own opinions. At the table he made his own choices from the menu. Never was he made to feel that he was a relic from the past. One day, he gave me a slip of paper which he said he always kept in his prayer book. He indicated that when he prayed he wanted this prayer to be included. It was a sincere prayer and went like this:

"Dear God, when I was young, You did not forsake me. You gave me a wonderful mate, blessed me with delightful children and helped us all acquire the things necessary for life. And I thanked You over and over again, and taught my children to offer thanks to You for Your loving care. In my old age, dear God, my children did not forsake me either. They took time to listen to my problems, they helped me when I was ill, and at all times showed me great respect.

"Dear wonderful, beautiful, loving God, whom I hope to see soon—because they were so good to me, I beg You to be good to them. Because they visit me, visit Your love upon them. Give them joy and happiness from children and grandchildren. Make their own lives an improvement over my own. And dear God, as for those who haven't treated parents well, I pray that You will forgive them. They just don't understand how it is when you get old."

He just turned 50 and feels he has done little or nothing with his life.

–5–

Birthdays Make Me Sick!

THE PROBLEM

The other day I turned fifty. My wife, daughter, son-in-law and even the grandchildren were on hand to help me blow out the candles. I received the usual gifts and some very expensive birthday cards. Everyone remembered something I wanted to forget. In short, my good doctor, instead of being happy, I was a sad, dejected, disappointed old man. "When they all shouted, 'Make a wish, Dad,' I wanted to say, "Dear God, make me twenty years younger.'

As I think it over, I feel I had every right to be sad. I've done very little with my fifty years of living. I have some education and a more or less successful accounting practice. My daughter is happily married and my wife doesn't complain either. From time to time we see a show, take a vacation, visit the family. But I feel like a failure. Oddly enough, I didn't feel like a failure when I was twenty, nor when I was thirty or forty.

Then, I had grand ideas, impressive ideas. I would shape the world and make it realize that I was alive. I would write, work for national organizations, make a name for myself in the accounting field, teach in a business college. I would do big things that would make people sit up and take notice.

Now, I look around and find the years have slipped by—fifty of them—count them dear doctor. Put the fifty years on one side and my accomplishments on the other side of a balance sheet and I feel like a bankrupt. I regret the lost years, the lost opportunities, the failure to accomplish things of lasting value. I resent my fiftieth birthday, resent the term 'middle age,' resent thinking of challenges I can no longer meet.

Don't get me wrong, doctor. I still have my own hair, or at least some of it. I can still do a mean Polka, or a Cha, Cha, Cha. I still do setting-up exercises each morning and I feel that I can out-swim and out-play a much younger man. I'm not in a wheelchair yet. I've still got young ideas. But then I remember I am fifty and I get all sick on the inside. I do some mental arithmetic, subtracting fifty from the usual life-span, and the answer throws me into a panic. I look at my wedding picture and then look into a mirror, and my appetite leaves me.

I feel miserable. I am miserable, and I make the lives of people around me miserable. Do I need tranquilizers or a transformation? What is wrong with me, doctor?

THE REPLY

You are suffering from the "Middle Age" blues. You are fifty and you're much too good at mental arithmetic. All your shortcomings and frustrations are catching up with you. You feel neither young nor old, yet you suffer the discomforts of both. You go forward but keep looking backward. In short, you want to live long but not grow old. Good trick if you can do it!

You sit and take inventory of your past years. You feel you have passed your prime and it is too late to be a hero. Your back aches, your legs draw, your stomach rebels, and often, when nature forgets, you need the help of the local pharmacy to remember. And all the much advertised pills, powders, and tonics fail to make you feel or look younger.

> Vocational opportunities are not knocking at your door. TRUE!
> Some of your ambitions will not be realized. TRUE!
> The stairs are getting steeper. TRUE!
> You are no longer picked for hero's parts. TRUE!

So what! Admit to yourself that you are fifty! Accept the fact that you are fifty! Reconcile yourself to the fact that you as well as your friends are aging.

Face it, your life is half over. At forty you were an "old" young man. At fifty, you are a "young" old man. Close the window and get out of the draft. Remember you are fifty. Stop competing with the twenties and the thirties. Why the necessity of out-swimming and out-diving them?

Face the second half of your life honestly and without despondency. You were young once now you are middle aged. The movie reel of life cannot be played back. What you missed, you missed! What you didn't accomplish, you didn't accomplish. Stop worrying about your thinning hair line and bulging waist. Act your age. Stop trying to conquer the world. Teach your grandson. Don't go on three mile hikes to display your masculinity. Instead, go through the business section and solicit packages for the synagogue bazaar. You didn't fail—your wife is happy, your daughter is happy, your grandchildren are happy, and they all come to you to celebrate with you and to show you their affection. *"You must have done something that's right!"*

*Like Lot's wife he keeps
looking back and sees
only romance in those
good old days.*

-6-

Those Were the Good Old Days

THE PROBLEM

I wanted to write to you some weeks ago in regard to your column, called, "Happy Birthday." At that time you replied to a man who was obviously unhappy at being reminded that he had reached his 50th birthday.

Frankly, I feel exactly as he did. I am over seventy. To be a bit more accurate, I am approaching eighty, and every birthday of mine makes me realize all the more how much better off we all were some eighty years ago.

Yes, young man, those were the good old days when a person was a person, a dollar was a dollar, and life was beautiful. We had time to do so many things then, and in such a relaxed manner. We had time for friends and family. We had no need to compete for status symbols, for large material balance sheets. When you went into a grocery store, you needed help to carry home the packages you could buy for a dollar. You could get the best poultry for 15 cents a pound, fresh eggs for 28 cents a dozen, steaks for 28 cents a pound, excellent coffee for 31 cents per pound, a good sized loaf of corn bread for a dime, a tasty shmaltz herring for eight cents, and a dozen rolls, thirteen to the dozen, for twelve cents. A penny bought you the best newspaper; a nickel took you all over the city. Better yet, a nickel not only bought you a mug of beer, but permitted you to eat free of charge all the hard-boiled eggs, chopped liver, herring, hard cheese, pretzels found on the bar. And no one watched you!

What kind of happy birthday can it be? If I were a poet, I would plead—

Time, time, please stop in your flight,
Make it 1880 just for tonight!

THE REPLY

You're like the man who lost his glasses and insists that he can't look for them until he has found them! What are you pining for? a dozen rolls for 13 cents? a 28 cent steak? a 5 cent mug of beer? or your youth? To begin with, eighty years ago you didn't know the difference between a diaper and a dimple, so let me tell you just how you lived at that time.

Your bathroom was in the hallway of a tenement house, that is, if you were of the more fortunate. If not, most likely, it was in the yard. And on a cold day, you had to leave the black coal-burning stove in the kitchen and make your way to the refrigerated outhouse. If you had caught a cold, your mother would have to walk to the doctor's home to summon him, that is, if she could spare the fifty cents or dollar he asked as his fee. Alexander Bell, you see, had just invented the telephone, and Edison was full of joy because he had successfully made an electric light bulb. Reading a newspaper was quite difficult by the flickering gas-light in the kitchen, and if your mother neglected to put a quarter in the gas-meter, you had no light at all.

Some 80 years ago, the time for which you long, there was no workmen's compensation, no unemployment insurance, no old age pension, no social security. You worked six days a week, some 12 to 14 hours a day. And you could count your salary on your ten fingers, and this you didn't bring home regularly. If you were too old to work, you became a charge of some charitable organizations, or squeezed in with your children.

Typhoid, scarlet fever, malaria took a terrific yearly toll. There were no wonder drugs, though spiders were still spinning their webs on the dining room ceiling. Antiseptics were unheard of, and smallpox and diphtheria killed thousands. To ward off fatal illness, you wore small packages of camphor balls around your neck.

And let me tell you the relaxed life your mother led at the time you were cuddling in your iron crib. She worked like a slave at the washtub, the black stove, and hung clothes on an outside line. She had no refrigerator, no electric or gas range, no vacuum cleaner, no toaster, no mix-master, no freezer, no washing machine, no dryer. She made her own noodles, baked her own bread, washed her own clothes. She relaxed when she collapsed at the end of a 17-hour day. And then she could not listen to the radio, could not watch television, could not call her friends on the telephone, and could not go to the movies.

A trip to the country, if you could afford it, took 10 hours on bumpy dirt roads. If all this isn't enough to chase the blues out of you, I might add that thousands of towns in the United States had no sewers, and that cold water flats were the rule— not the exception. The truth is, that at the time you were so happily gurgling in your diapers, millionaires and noblemen could not procure, with all their wealth, half the enjoyment or ease that the average wage-earner has today.

What you are longing for is not lost bargains, but lost time! So hear this! Lost wealth may be replaced by industry, lost knowledge by study, lost health by medication, but lost time is gone forever. The only thing you might do is to stop losing time in the present.

> Live your life in the hours of today.
> Waste no time, permit no delay.
> The clock waits for no one from the day you were born,
> So reach your goal, ere the curtain is drawn.

You're living today by the grace of the Almighty God; others have been called away. You're alive today so make every moment of today be as productive as an eternity. Remember, it's not the number of years that a man puts in, but what he puts into the years that really counts.

You can't be longing for eighty years ago when running water was a rich man's luxury, when laborers received a dollar a day, and a white collar worker averaged ten dollars a week, when household work was a backbreaking toil and women drudged at the tubs; cooked, baked, darned, ironed and sewed from dawn to dark, without the boon of electric equipment.

God has been good to you, wants you here, feels that you haven't completely reached the goal of your life. He has endowed you with health, presented you with years, granted you an alert mind. Use this inheritance to your best advantage. Don't permit yourself to lead a sedentary existence. There are countless joys for you to experience, much warmth and happiness that you can bring to others, many miles of traveling left. Remember, the ticking of the clock marks the passage of time. It is a reminder that another hour, another day has gone. At eighty, time travels by jet, so don't waste days dreaming of the past!

I know you're eighty, but remember, just because there's snow on the roof is no reason there shouldn't be a fire in the hearth. Be like the old man, who, when he was asked how he retained the vivacity of youth, knew how to reply. He pointed to a blossoming apple tree, and said, "That apple tree is very old, but I never saw prettier blossoms upon it. The tree grows a little new wood each year, and I suppose that it is out of that new wood those blossoms come. Like the apple tree, I like to grow something new each year."

His wife seems to enjoy life even though she is growing older, but he gets sick at the thought of aging.

-7-

Use Time Wisely!

THE PROBLEM

So I am fifty-eight and the thought of soon reaching 60 frightens me. Don't get me wrong. I certainly want to live on and on; yet the thought of aging and not being able to do the many things I still have not done sends me into seas of depression. I worry about the future, worry about possible illness, worry about financial reverses. I worry so much about tomorrow that I am too tense to enjoy today.

It seems to me that I haven't been taught to enjoy life. I, and I presume thousands of others, have never learned the art of using time. When we are young, we squander it; when we get older, we hoard it. Never during our lifetime do we use it properly.

My wife does seem to be able to enjoy life. She visits the children, plays with the grandchildren, knits a sweater here and there, talks on the telephone, and her laughter sometimes irks me. How can she laugh when I am blue! How can she enjoy life when she realizes that we are now so much older and so many challenges are no longer present? She laughs; I get angry; yet I envy her lightheadedness.

It's interesting. I had no influence during my early years and now I am doubtful about the future. Who ever said we are the masters of our fate? I don't believe it. If I could shape my own future, I would give myself freedom of movement, freedom of choice and freedom from anxiety and concern. Is this possible?

I'm not going to re-read what I've just written because should I re-read it, I would probably tear it up. This I can tell you, this confused letter can be written by thousands of unhappy men and women. Can't you give us some guidelines, we who are reaching the sixties?

No doubt, I'm seeking an oral tranquilizer but that's no crime. How does one deal with time, dear doctor? Tell me, won't you?

THE REPLY

There is no doubt about it. The future is of your own making. You can fashion its clay as a sculptor, or stand aside and let it fill in the patterns of your own emptiness. The future is but the child of what you are today. It is the finished product of a raw material known as *time*.

There are two ways of dealing with time. Perhaps this concept can best be expressed with a verbal illustration. In some city parks, there are fountains with streams of water shooting out of the mouths of marble animals, or seem to gush out of the hands of water nymphs. The water sprays upward in the air and drops back to the base of the fountain. Some of it splashes on the concrete walk and is lost forever. Some of the supply of water evaporates during the hot summer months. The water here is decorative but has no other useful purpose.

However, men who are adrift in a boat on the ocean, or who are crossing the desert, measure out the water drop by drop. They are on rations because they realize its value for they understand that the water they possess is their very life. Do you understand what I'm getting at?

I overheard a wise golden-ager talking to his friends. They had met, as was their custom, in the local public library. One had remarked that he was a little frightened at the passage of time. "There is so much I should have done in the past," he said, "and so much more I want to do in the future that my birthdays have become frightening experiences."

"Nonsense," replied another of the group. "There are two days in the week about which I never worry. I have two complete carefree days; one of these days is yesterday. Yesterday with all its cares, pains, frustrations, disappointments, mistakes and faults has passed forever out of my reach. It was once mine; now it is God's. The other day I never worry about is tomorrow. Tomorrow is the unborn sister of yesterday. It, too, with all its possible advantages and adversities, perils and promises, belongs to God, not to me. This week—*today*. That's the day I live because it is completely mine."

Words of wisdom indeed. What a rule for you to follow! If you are to be productive, you must fashion the future by using the present. If you merely wait for tomorrow you are doomed because tomorrow is a "sleep" that paralyzes the efforts of man, a snare that traps man's ambitions, a deceiver of mankind. It is the epitaph upon the graves of those who failed and did not achieve life's true goal.

Today is here, and today's initiative spells tomorrow's standard of living. Today's energy spells tomorrow's security. Today's investment of time, effort, and skill is the grip we have on the future. It can be a big grip if we forcibly compound the interest.

Today is here. It offers you one thing in common with the rest of the world—twenty-four hours. You draw the same salary in seconds, minutes, and hours. You must exert yourself to help change the face of the world. You must work today even though you plan for tomorrow, with energy and foresight. Envision a better future if you will, but don't just wait for it to materialize. Do something about it.

At 80 he feels like a mu-
seum piece, like a relic
out of the past.

– 8 –

Dignity in Old Age

THE PROBLEM

My hearing isn't what it should be, neither is my eye-sight. I am almost 80 years of age and feel like a dated model of a human being. Every once in a while I am reminded of a statement my father used to utter: "An old man shouldn't be born." How true!

I don't seem to get any joy out of living. I eat, sleep, watch television and do very little else. Every cold or cough frightens me. I look for aches and pains which don't exist. Needless to add that I am frightened about the coming of each day. Sure, I've read about the glories of the golden years but believe me, I haven't found them.

You can be of immense help to me, and comfort to tens of thousands of men and women who feel they have outlived their usefulness. Guide me, please. I am desperate. I just don't want to go on living, if living is waiting to die.

THE REPLY

Statisticians state that, at this time in our country, only 4 out of every 100,000 people reach their one hundredth birthday. We hear, with some pleasure, an idealist declare that life begins at seventy, that only the aged are really alive in the complete sense. Long lists are made up of dignitaries in art, government, business, and community who have fully flowered only in the ripe eighties or the mellow nineties. We are reminded that Verdi produced *Othello* at 74; at 80 he composed *Falstaff*; at 85 his beloved Ava Maria, Te Deum and others.

Yet, the average person approaching sixty or seventy has both fears and doubts about the joys this period of his life can offer. He looks upon calendars and birthdays as terrifying threats to peace and happiness. He feels defunct, is afraid of aches and pains, and is terrified at the thought of "making room for a younger man." He derives scant comfort from Robert Browning's

> Grow old along with me!
> The best is yet to be,
> The last of life, for which the first was made;
> Our times are in His hand
> Who saith, "A whole I planned,
> Youth shows but half; trust God;
> See all, nor be afraid.

He doesn't believe that old age can possess a joy of its own; can contain a satisfaction all its own. It is refreshing therefore, to receive this note from an elderly lady: "The house I am living in is 82 years old. Considering its age, the house is in fairly good repair, though I don't think it looks quite as well as it did fifty years ago. I have neglected to keep it painted, as so many women of this modern generation do. To tell the truth, I have been spending my time on interior decorating. The windows are fairly clear and I am happy to say I have a most reliable tenant in the upper floor."

Old age certainly has compensations. It allows you time to reap something of what has been sown. It enables you to look back upon your ills with some pleasure, instead of looking forward to them with fear. It gives you a chance to change your mind and to command a certain charity in judgment. You can look at people and events in a new perspective and learn tolerance and patience. The world of heart and understanding grows larger as the years roll on. Perhaps, you can't cover as much ground, can't hear as many sounds, can't read the fine print, but your inner world can expand with new opportunities for wonderful awe, understanding, simplicity. As the other things fade, the stars can shine on and on, sometimes even brighter than before.

Two men can sit with identical glasses of water before them. One complains that his glass is half empty. The other rejoices that his is half full. Both are telling the truth; but one speaks out of despair while the other lives in a state of hope and optimism.

I overheard someone say to a kindly old man, "Why Samuel,

you're already 80, how much longer do you think you'll be here?" Quickly Samuel replied, "WELL, it should be a long time. Statistics indicate that few people die after eighty." Your age depends upon your philosophy of living. When living has been learning, old age does not bring with it a feeling of mental insolvency.

A wise man taught:

> How beautiful judgment is for hoary hair,
> And the knowledge of what to advise for the elderly!
> How beautiful is the wisdom of old men,
> And consideration and counsel in men of distinction
> Rich experience is the crown of old men,
> And their boast is the fear of the Lord.

Whether you are 70 or 80, you have a right to be useful, a right to a fair share of the community's recreational resources, a right to live independently and with dignity. Together with these rights are allied responsibilities. It is your obligation to seek and develop potential avenues of service, to make available the benefits of your experience and knowledge. It is your obligation to attempt to maintain such relationships with family, neighbors, and friends as will make you a respected and valued counselor throughout your later years.

Age is relative. In reality there is no age. You develop an age-consciousness when you keep looking at life through aged eyes —when you constantly find fault with youth, when tomorrow no longer interests you, when you become "age-centric." You can grow old beneficially like good wine, or your age can turn you into vinegar. Life is a sort of stock exchange—a market place where you trade years for precious morsels of living. The skill in bargaining is fun. You have a certain number of years to spend. During that period your heart will beat, blood will course through your veins, you will breathe and you will grow older. You cannot put this time in a safe-deposit box for some more convenient time to spend. You must spend it now or waste it forever. As long as tomorrow interests you, today will not be dreary. Find a new goal to look forward to and work toward it. Go on and live, and by the way, Happy Birthday.

*He feels that long life is
no bargain and dislikes
his doctor saying, "for
a man your age you are
in good health."*

-9-

Who Needs the 20 Years?

THE PROBLEM

I've just come from the doctor, a once-a-month routine for me. At 72, I'm told I ought to see the doctor regularly. What a bargain! I don't know how many times he has told me about the wonders of medicine and how it has added at least 20 years to my life. I repeat, *what a bargain!*

To me it is twenty additional years of worry, concern, anxiety, doctor visits. If I had had my way, I would have selected a short life and an active one. It's depressing to be an unwanted, helpless has-been.

I'm in "good health for my age." I say this because these are the words of my doctor. He keeps on saying, "for a man of your age, you are really in good health." What these words signify is his secret.

I lead a pretty aimless life. I am retired; my children saw to that. "Dad, why must you go into business day after day? You really have earned a rest," they kept saying until I did just that. What a mistake!

It's a misfortune to get up in the morning with nothing to do, especially since my need for sleep has decreased. There is a sort of aimlessness in my life, a void, an emptiness which leaves me waiting for illness and death. My children function very well without me. My grandchildren visit me at rare intervals, kissing me on the cheek as if I were some sort of frail antique. If this is the grandeur of old age, you can have it.

What advice can you give me? How can one enjoy the so-called Golden Years of one's life, or is this too, a dream of some Madison Avenue advertising agency. How can you change my feeling of being a healthy horse retired to the pasture to make room for some livelier, faster running animal?

Boy, do I wish I were young again!

THE REPLY

You make an error in underestimating the value of the gift of prolonged life. These twenty years tacked on to the life span of a person whose physical health is good, should be appreciated. After all, you do not indicate that your aches and pains outweigh your ability to do more than sit on a rocker waiting for your grandchildren to peck at your cheeks. You ought to think of your prime being prolonged, your uselessness postponed. You have been given twenty additional years of adventure, service, achievement and enjoyment.

The pity is that you are wasting them, accepting your age as a time for patient waiting for infirmity to set it. What are you rebelling at? Why do you beat your breast? Are you jealous of the younger ones? Are you looking back and taking inventory of the challenges you did not take? Forget it. You are 72; accept the fact.

You ask about the enjoyments of old age, the dividends that one receives when he has entered the seventies. There are many, and the rocking chair, the gray hairs, and the double chin are not any of them. You are free from routine. You can sit up late and finish the book you are reading. After all, there is no 8:00 A.M. appointment waiting for you. You no longer have to repeat and act out: "Early to bed and early to rise makes a man healthy, wealthy, and wise."

There are so many activities which are now open to you because you do have the time. You can join many philanthropic organizations where your time, talent, and wisdom will be appreciated. You can travel around the world seeing and living in places you used to read about. Don't make the mistake of staying at home playing with radio and television dials. Get out of the house, out of the chair, out of sitting and watching into thinking and doing.

Make peace with your age. Grow old gracefully, not rebelliously. As has been said again and again, "Years have been added to your life; now go ahead and add life to your years."

*We all want to live to a
ripe old age but we don't
want to get old.*

– 10 –

What's Wrong With Growing Old?

All of us change with age, whether we want to or not. Some of us make these changes eagerly. Others prefer to imitate the ostrich and pretend that everyone around us is growing older but that we remain the same. But, every once in a while, we come across an old portrait and a quick look shocks us back to reality. We, too, are aging!

The truth is we start aging at birth and the best time to prepare for it is in childhood or soon after. It is rather late to prepare for old age when sixty candles adorn our birthday cake. Yet, even at that age, though the work is more difficult, there remains a possibility for us to learn how to get the best out of the years of living that are still ahead.

We cannot treat the subject of "growing old" with the inspiration of a poet. It isn't faithful to the facts of life. Growing old is hard because living is hard, and the longer our tenancy on earth, the more difficult it becomes. No lines of poetry can eradicate illness, loneliness, frustrations, inadequacy, and infirmity. "Grow old along with me, the best is yet to be," is Browning's tranquilizer, but like a tranquilizer it wears off all too quickly. According to the "whistling in the dark" writer, life starts at forty, sixty, or eighty. If this is true and not merely a wishful dream, then many of us have wasted the earlier years of our lives.

Life begins the day we open our eyes to God's wonderful world. There are things to be done during every period of our life. The things we fail to do at twelve, we cannot successfully accomplish at fifty. The joys we failed to experience during our teens, we can hardly expect to fully enjoy during our so-called "Golden Years." Whatever joys we failed to achieve when we were young cannot be achieved with the same degree of intensity during our later years. Yet, we must not face our aging with pessimism or fear because it is not a period when we await some celestial being tapping us on the shoulder and saying, "You're next brother, your lease is up. Follow me."

To begin with, if we wish to live long, we must be willing to grow old. The secret of enjoying longevity is acceptance of giving up certain challenges in exchange for other values.

A friend of mine, who is in his fifties and wants to live until the Messiah puts in his earthly appearance, always asks every octogenarian he meets the following question: "To what do you attribute your long life?" My friend wants to make certain that he will follow the formula that will surely outwit nature. Unfortunately, the answers are confusing and therefore not reassuring. Here are a few:

1. I always drink 6 cups of coffee a day.
2. I eat three "squares" a day.
3. I start each meal with a Scotch.
4. I eat two meat meals a day.
5. I take things easy.

1. I never touch tea or coffee.
2. I eat sparingly. We dig our graves with our teeth.
3. Never take a drop of tap water. Distilled water for me.
4. I'm a vegetarian. Meat is poison.
5. Hard work is my formula for long life.

This is the list and we can have our pick as to the proper way to increase our own stay on earth. However, if I were questioned I would first seek to determine how long my grandparents, parents, uncles, aunts, brothers had lived. There is no crash program, no magic formula and no genuine money-back-guarantee for living long. In any event, not one that can't be found in our Holy Writings. We certainly can find counsel there that can help us extend life. We must realize how proper moral and spiritual living can extend our years. But more prohibitions such as: "Don't do this; avoid that; rest a great deal; give up tennis" don't necessarily prolong life. They do, however, succeed in making life seem longer and duller, I might add.

Perhaps a good philosophy to follow in approaching old age is, "Ah, lovely, wonderful, interesting world, I will enjoy every day in it." It certainly is more therapeutic than thinking, "Oh, dreadful, tearful old age, how can I escape it?" There is a way of escaping old age but the method might not be pleasant though it is final.

The truth is no one wants to classify himself with the aged. Yet, acknowledging oneself as being chronologically in that age group is the first hurdle we must overcome if we wish to enjoy the remaining years of our life. We can still remain emotionally, mentally, and socially young by paying scant attention to our wrinkles though we know they are there. We can refuse to blow out the birthday candles but nevertheless must face the facts that there are many more of them now. And we must stop saying, "You know, at my age I can't. . . ." If we find ourselves saying this, we might conclude that we must have said the same things many times in the past when we were younger.

Do you remember people advising, "You must learn to grow old gracefully." Well said! but why not add to it—"grow old creatively, adequately, social-mindedly." We can grow old with wisdom and usefulness. We can live and let live—and we can lift a little more than we share! We can attempt to live each day so that we enjoy living with ourselves. We can feed our curiosity and exude tolerance and good will by participating in community affairs and becoming workers for neighborhood charities. Whatever we do, we must not retire and withdraw from life. If we do—well, the dead are not always buried at once.

Research on aging conducted at the University of North Carolina has shown that the person who thinks of himself as young or middle-aged rather than "old" tends to have better reflexes, is able better to cope with stress, and is better adjusted emotionally. He tends very markedly to be mentally and physically more like a youthful person.

Age is a question partly of chronological age and partly of our ideas and ideals. Our body can be one age; our emotions can be another; our efficiency a third. We certainly do not decline evenly in all abilities.

INDEX TO PROBLEMS DISCUSSED